# THE KEY STAGE 3 DRAMA TOOLKIT

# THE KEY STAGE 3 DRAMA TOOLKIT

## A Teacher's Guide for Ages 11 to 14

DEBORAH GIBBS

BLOOMSBURY ACADEMIC
LONDON • NEW YORK • OXFORD • NEW DELHI • SYDNEY

BLOOMSBURY ACADEMIC
Bloomsbury Publishing Plc, 50 Bedford Square, London, WC1B 3DP, UK
Bloomsbury Publishing Inc, 1359 Broadway, New York, NY 10018, USA
Bloomsbury Publishing Ireland, 29 Earlsfort Terrace, Dublin 2, D02 AY28, Ireland



First published in Great Britain 2026



A catalogue record for this book is available from the British Library.

A catalog record for this book is available from the Library of Congress.

ISBN: HB: 978-1-350-56770-2
PB: 978-1-350-56769-6
ePDF: 978-1-350-56771-9
eBook: 978-1-350-56772-6

Typeset by Integra Software Services Pvt. Ltd.
Printed and bound in Great Britain

Many thanks to the wonderful students of Chancellor's School for their tremendous energy and courage during my workshops and to photographer Rebecca Harris for capturing their work. Thanks also to David Croston, Headteacher and Sophie Hoy, Head of Drama, for setting up my visits to this impressive school. Thanks to Anna Brewer, Senior Publisher, for her tireless advice, expertise and enthusiasm; to Issy Bowyer, Aanchal Vij and Claire Weatherhead at Bloomsbury for their guidance and support; and, of course, special thanks to the brilliant, creative students I have taught over the years.

**Deborah Gibbs** has led several highly successful drama departments in UK secondary schools over thirty-eight years, working across both the state and private sectors and collaborating with international schools. Throughout her career, she has staged numerous productions, often writing her own scripts and plays for students.

# CONTENTS

# PHOTOS AND TABLES

## Photos

# Tables

# PREFACE

As a primary school student, if I worked hard and made good progress during my morning lessons, I was allowed to choose what I wanted to study for the rest of the day. It probably comes as no surprise that I wanted to make theatre. With no teacher supervision, a group of us were given access to the costume store in the attic of the oldest part of the school. In this treasure trove, I started writing, directing and performing. From the perspective of a drama teacher with many years of experience, I often reflect on how fortunate I was to have been given the freedom and opportunity to discover my passion at such an early age. When I think about it, I became a drama teacher at the age of seven.

With thirty-eight years of experience teaching the subject, I understand how hard the drama teacher works. The challenges of delivering a successful drama curriculum and providing a rich and varied extra-curricular programme are exciting but huge. Departments can be small and often include colleagues who specialize in other subjects. Exam courses are complex and rigorous, and I can think of no other subject where students are assessed in so many ways.

As drama teachers, we balance multiple responsibilities, and the time-intensive demands of preparing students for exams and directing school productions can limit our opportunities to review and develop our work with the eleven-to fourteen-year-old age group. Throughout my career, I have found that resources for teaching these students are relatively sparse, and the challenges of dedicating sufficient time to building their curriculum can be considerable.

We must strive to deliver exciting and well-structured drama lessons for this age group. We want them to flourish, feel confident about choosing to study the subject further, and be ready to tackle the challenges ahead. (Incidentally, I have found that if we deliver a strong eleven-to-fourteen curriculum, the numbers who go on to choose it radically rise.) This book represents the culmination of many years of developing the best possible lesson plans and experiences for this age group, as well as working with drama teachers of varying levels of experience. It serves as a guide for both new drama teachers and experienced ones who are busy juggling many responsibilities and want everything consolidated into a single resource. For those teachers seeking to select material and activities to support and enhance their current practices, the book is carefully structured to facilitate this approach.

The material is designed to help you provide a creative, well-structured and progressive drama course over three years. In line with the requirements of exam courses, you will teach students how actors use elements of voice and movement to convey meaning to an audience. Throughout, there is an emphasis on using improvisation and both original and published scripted material to develop performance skills. There are also activities for exploring different types of stage spaces. In each part, links are made to theatre practitioners and relevant techniques and practical exercises are suggested. There is also a short focus on different directorial methods to introduce students to some of the ways they might rehearse and develop their practical work. A *Further Reading* list offers recommendations for materials that enable you to explore practitioners and ideas in more detail.

The primary focus of the material is on acting skills; however, throughout the book, there are also suggestions for design activities to develop students' understanding of lighting, sound, costume and set in preparation for exam courses. It also aims to foster an early awareness of the range of future career pathways that drama can offer. There are written activity suggestions linked to practical tasks to help students prepare for the types of questions they face at exam level, as well as offering some creative opportunities. At the end of the book, I have provided a list of pieces of music I use when I want to create a particular atmosphere for rehearsal and performance work.

Being a drama teacher should bring great rewards for you and your students. I hope that this book helps you deliver a rigorous, aspirational and progressive curriculum that harnesses the wonderful imaginations and creativity of eleven-to-fourteen-year-old students. It is a great privilege to share my experiences with you. I wish you every success.

**Photo P-1** Student improvising.

# STRUCTURE AND LINKS TO THE FUTURE

## Structure

The book offers a rigorous, skill-based drama course that can be delivered over three years, ensuring growth and progression, readying students for examination courses. It will clearly guide the drama teacher of little or no experience, as well as support the busy, more experienced teacher. It is also structured to make it easy to dip in and select relevant activities that support and enhance your own approaches.

The book is divided into three parts:

**Part One**: For students aged eleven to twelve years.
**Part Two**: For students aged twelve to thirteen years.
**Part Three**: For students aged thirteen to fourteen years.

There are four chapters in each part, where the focus is on distinct areas:

**Chapter One**: Voice.
**Chapter Two**: Movement.
**Chapter Three**: Stage space.
**Chapter Four**: Applying skills explored in Chapters One to Three.

Each chapter has been given a student-friendly title, a method I always used in my work to foster enthusiasm.

You can deliver Chapters One to Three in any sequence, working through the activities in the order they are presented. The chapters feature a combination of games explicitly tailored for that area of study, along with warm-ups, improvisation tasks and activities based on both original and published scripts, crafted to enable students to rehearse and refine their skills. In Chapter Four of each part, improvisation tasks and diverse, age-appropriate published script excerpts offer your students experience of combining and applying the skills developed in Chapters One to Three.

Given that the length of lessons and arrangements vary, the course is structured to give you flexibility and can be adapted accordingly. Generally speaking, for students who have forty to sixty-minute lessons each week, each chapter can be taught over a six to ten-week period. The activities have been designed to work in both single-sex and co-ed environments; the original texts have been created to be accessible to all students, and the published excerpts can be modified for use in all contexts.

# Links to the future

The book is designed to enable students to flourish and progress, building skills to transition smoothly to examination courses. It also fosters an understanding of how studying drama can open up doors to a variety of opportunities. The activities offer a clear pathway to the next stage of their studies through:

- Practical activities exploring how performers use voice and movement to convey meaning.
- Written activities examining how voice and movement are employed in performance and the impact on an audience.
- Creative writing opportunities.
- Practical activities exploring different types of stage space and how actors navigate the challenges.
- Examination of the role of performers, directors, designers and writers, and their relationship in theatre.
- Development of set, lighting, costume (including make-up), and sound design ideas.
- Devising an original piece of theatre in a group.
- Performing excerpts of published script.
- Designing for excerpts of original and published script.
- Writing evaluations of their own practical work and the work of others.

In the 'Preparing for the Future' section, within the introduction to Part Two, you will find creative suggestions for sharing with parents/guardians, students, and colleagues the benefits of studying drama, as well as ways to begin communicating the wide range of skills developed and the career opportunities it can support.

## Links to the future

# PART ONE

# AGES ELEVEN TO TWELVE

## Introduction to Part One

### Chapters One to Three can be delivered in any order. Chapter Four should be delivered last

At this age, students bring vast amounts of exuberance, creativity and courage to lessons. They require careful management, as they are likely to arrive in your class with very different experiences of the subject. These four chapters provide clear, structured activities to channel their natural enthusiasm for the subject and guide them on how to work practically in a drama space. The lessons are ambitious and will challenge your students to start building strong foundations for the next three years and beyond.

Voice, movement and stage space are explored separately in the first three chapters. The fourth chapter includes activities and excerpts from published scripts to provide students with additional experience in applying their learning from the first three chapters. Each chapter has been given a student-friendly title which you can choose to use. Chapters One to Three can be delivered in any sequence; however, the activities in each chapter should be taught in the order they are presented to ensure development and progression. Each chapter is designed to be taught over a six- to ten-week period, providing flexibility for you to adapt to your timetable and the needs of your students. There are suggestions for design and written activities throughout. The design tasks relate to the practical activities and enable your students to start learning about the work of set, lighting, costume and sound designers. The written activities include creative exercises and evaluative tasks to lay the groundwork for future exam challenges.

# Preparing your students for practical work

Practical work is an intrinsic part of the drama students' experience, so before starting the course, it is worth spending time instilling good working practices. It is helpful to explore the suggestions for organizing students into groups and creating the best environment for sharing practical work. When performing, students must be disciplined and focused, while also feeling confident that audience members will be supportive, constructive and respectful.

## Dividing students into groups

1. It is highly beneficial for students in the long term to start by becoming familiar and confident in your ability to organize them into groups. This allows you to ensure good balance, avoid certain combinations and give them access to different experiences.
2. Students walk around the space. When you call out a number, they should form a group consisting of that number of individuals. Eventually, they stop thinking about remaining with their friends, and once you are confident, you can fix groups to work on an activity.
3. Students form groups of people born in the same month or who have the same favourite colour.
4. Ask students to sit in a circle and allocate them all a number. If you have twenty-four students and want them to work in groups of four, label them with numbers from one to six. All the students labelled as number one form a group, followed by the number twos forming another group, and so on.
5. There may be times when you allow students to select their groups; however, it is best to avoid having leaders who take turns choosing group members, as this can result in individuals feeling excluded.

# Guidelines for performing

1. When students are ready to perform, consider both where audience members sit and, most importantly, how they are seated. Students should appear prepared, engaged and interested. Lying on the floor is never conducive to creating a purposeful atmosphere.
2. When others are performing, audience members must always be silent. Eyes should be on the performers.
3. It is helpful to establish a culture of applauding one another at the end of a performance. This may not always be appropriate, so establish a routine to confirm whether applause should be given. If students are to applaud, make sure that they all participate. For a drama lesson, applause always means clapping. Avoid cheering and stop students from calling out individuals' names. This type of favouritism detracts from an environment where all students feel valued.
4. It is essential to foster an atmosphere where students feel comfortable enjoying and sharing laughter when appropriate. However, individuals may easily find themselves giggling unexpectedly if they are surprised by another student's performance. This usually occurs when an individual has performed something particularly unusual, creative or brave. The response is usually not meant in an unkind way; however, students need to recognize that such reactions can be misinterpreted and can stifle creativity and confidence.

5. Performers must be encouraged to concentrate at all times and to continue performing, even if something goes wrong. Instil the belief that an audience won't usually recognize mistakes unless the performers give it away by giggling, looking flustered, or stopping to inform them. If a performance falls apart for any reason, it is helpful to stop it and resume it at a later stage.
6. As soon as you start working with your students, stress that a performance must never end with a 'that's it' or 'finished'. In the introduction to Part One, Chapter Four, you will find suggestions for teaching students how to open and close a performance.

## Ways of sharing practical work

Setting up opportunities for students to share their work can be challenging for the drama teacher. You may find that all students in some classes want to perform, while in other groups, they may be much more reticent. There are several approaches you can take to build students' confidence and keep audience members focused and engaged.

1. Generally, young students tend to feel more confident when they perform in the space where they have been rehearsing. In most teaching spaces, audience members can easily adjust their positioning to view the work. This technique will not be suitable when exploring different types of stages, but it can be very effective for many exercises.
2. For presenting monologues or solo activities (improvised or text-based), ask the students to form pairs or threes and share their work. Spend time organizing them so they have sufficient space to perform and concentrate. Once they have done this, ask them to recommend any work to be shared with the whole class. Students often gain confidence when they realize that a peer is endorsing them.
3. When presenting pair work, ask one pair to join with another. Organize them carefully in the space to share the work. Provide students with something to discuss after both have performed, so they have a focus if other pairs in the room are still presenting. Ask them to recommend work to be shared with the rest of the class.
4. If students are working in pairs or small groups on a piece of script, organize them to show small sections of their work. Arrange the groups in a large circle so that they are all able to perform and watch one another without having to move around the space. Stress that they need to keep their scripts close to hand. Choose one group to start performing from the start of the text. After a short section, stop them and instruct the next group to continue from where the first group finished. Continue around the circle, allowing all groups the chance to perform. When one group reaches the end of the script, the next group should return to the beginning. Ideally, each group should present three different short sections.
5. When working individually, in pairs or in groups, students can perform a snippet of their work. It is a particularly effective strategy for sharing work in progress, teaching students that performing for one another helps them develop and improve their work. They might share the beginning, the ending or a short section (you can stipulate the length) of work that they are most proud of.
6. As students develop, they start creating longer pieces of work which combine different skills. It is essential to allow them to share this work, providing time for subsequent discussion and

evaluation. To establish momentum, all groups can perform one after the other, with discussions only taking place after all have completed their pieces. If you choose this method, start by establishing the performance order and inform students that they should take their positions to start immediately after the preceding group has finished. It can be helpful to allocate each group the task of keeping detailed notes on another group's work to inform later discussions.

# 1
# VOICE – VOLUME AND TONE
## 'CHATTERBOX'

**Photo 1-1-1** Vocal exercise.

## Introduction

This chapter introduces you to a range of creative activities that teach students how they can use different volumes and tones of voice when performing. The exercises draw on their ability to be spontaneous and imaginative, while also recognizing the need to be ambitious and lay the foundations for future studies and exam courses by developing their understanding of how actors use voice to create meaning. It is helpful to work through the activities in the order presented in this chapter to ensure progression and development.

## Games

### 1. Taking the register

Using a register at the start of a lesson to link to the lesson's objectives is a powerful way to establish focus and concentration. In this case, if you take a formal register, ask the students to respond to their name using different volumes and/or tones of voice.

## 2. Count to ten

The aim of the exercise is for students to deliver a sequence of numbers in one breath with control and precise articulation. In unison, they take a deep breath and count the sequence below out loud with no gaps between any line:

One
one two
one two three
one two three four
one two three four five
one two three four five six
one two three four five six seven
one two three four five six seven eight
one two three four five six seven eight nine
one two three four five six seven eight nine ten.

Lead the whole class in delivering the sequence simultaneously. Some will find that they won't get to the end of it without needing to take another breath. Work on ensuring that diction is good and that students articulate the different numbers clearly.

Repeat the activity using different volumes: loud, medium and quiet. Explain that when using a quiet volume, clear articulation is vital and that the audience needs to hear what is being said.

You can also split the class into smaller groups and ask them to experiment with using different volumes to deliver the sequence.

## 3. Pick an emotion

The purpose of this game is to examine different tones of voice. You need two hats, bags or boxes. Instruct the students to pick a phrase of dialogue from one and a tone of voice from the other. Alternatively, you can project or write out the phrases of dialogue and tones on a screen or board and allow students to select. Individually, students rehearse their line of dialogue, applying the vocal tone assigned to them. Students can work in pairs or small groups to share their work and guess which tones of voice others have picked. You can also ask volunteers to share their work in front of the whole class, stimulating early discussions on how performers convey different moods through vocal tone.

### Dialogue examples

1. You should never have said that. Please don't do it again.
2. Please stand over there, be quiet and don't move a muscle.
3. I've bought you a present, but I left it at home. Sorry!
4. I didn't get an invitation to that event. I don't know why. Do you know?
5. That fairground ride was incredibly fast, and then we did this double loop. I didn't expect that.
6. I knocked on the door. It opened so suddenly. I didn't know what to do.
7. It was my first time on a plane. I sat by the window next to the engines.
8. I found this in the street. I have no idea what it is or what to do with it.

9. The night was dark. The bright stars were twinkling in the sky.
10. I didn't mean to do that. I wasn't thinking clearly. Please accept my apologies.

**Tones of voice examples**

1. Angry.
2. Sad.
3. Scared.
4. Excited.
5. Confused.
6. Amused.
7. Grumpy.
8. Threatening.
9. Bored.
10. Suspicious.

### *Written activity*

Creative task: Students choose one of the lines of dialogue and compose what the character might go on to say. They can then rehearse their speech, applying a tone of voice of their own choice.

## 4. Shopping with attitude

This is a version of a memory game which adds the extra challenge of applying a particular tone of voice. It can be played as a whole-class activity, but is often more engaging for students when they work in smaller groups of about five. Each group should sit in a small circle and be assigned the task of creating an alphabetical shopping list. The first person chooses an item beginning with the letter A, the second person chooses something beginning with B and so on. Explain that this shop stocks everything possible, so they should use their imaginations to think of unusual items. Once the activity starts, they are responsible for remembering all the items. They should go around their circle as many times as possible. For example:

> **Student one:** I went to the shop and I bought an antelope.
> **Student two:** I went to the shop and I bought an antelope and a boat.
> **Student three:** I went to the shop and I bought an antelope, a boat and a castle.
> And so on.

Once the students understand the basic rules, display a list of five different attitudes, such as happy, sad, grumpy, suspicious and angry, on the board/screen. Each student must choose one of the attitudes whenever it is their turn to list the items. When they take their next turn, they must choose a different attitude. For a group of five who complete five rounds, each student will have the chance to express the five attitudes, and the group will have created a list of twenty-five items in total.

# Warm-up

## 1. Breathing exercises

As you continue to work on voice, consider starting each session with some simple breathing exercises. Follow these instructions:

1. Students stand in their own space facing the front.
2. They breathe through their noses for a count of eight and out through their mouths for eight. Repeat three or four times.
3. They breathe through their noses for a count of eight, humming as loudly as possible to get rid of all the air during the eight-count exhalation. Repeat three or four times.
4. Repeat the exercise, instructing students to project the 'ahh' sound as loudly as possible during the eight-count exhalation. Repeat three or four times.

## 2. Stage whisper

Introduce the students to the principle of the stage whisper. Explain that although the audience must be able to hear the words clearly, they should also be able to imagine that other characters cannot hear. Explain that actors have to use good technique to project a stage whisper. Excellent breath control is required, and actors should project the sound using a slightly raspy voice with crystal-clear articulation.

Students start standing, facing in one direction. Instruct them to count in unison using the stage whisper. It is often helpful to demonstrate what this would sound like before they attempt it. Once students appear confident with the technique, they progress to discussing their current school day experience to an imaginary audience in front of them, using only a stage whisper. If individual students are confident, they can demonstrate their skills in front of others.

## 3. Let me tell you

Divide the students into pairs, with each pair facing one another across the centre of the room.

All pairs conduct a conversation about what they did over the holiday, weekend or evening before. Advise them that this could be real, imagined or a mix of both, stressing that it must be something that they are comfortable sharing with others. On a signal from you (a whistle, clap or physical gesture), all students take one step away from one another, continuing their conversation as they move. Repeat this process until all pairs are as far apart from one another as possible. Analyse what happened during this exercise and whether they used different volumes as they moved apart. Begin discussing when and why people use different vocal volumes in real-life situations.

Repeat this exercise, restricting the students to use only a stage whisper as they move further apart. This will help to improve their stage whisper technique.

## 4. Angry neighbour

Divide the students into pairs, labelling themselves as **A** and **B.** Explain that they will both have the opportunity to play an angry person complaining to their quieter neighbour about several annoying issues. Discuss examples of what a neighbour might be annoyed about. Ensure they have a range of ideas, such as noisy children, screaming babies, barking dogs, cars obstructing others, arguments, drones, ugly decorations and unruly parties.

In version one, character **A** complains to character **B**. **B** can speak but is quite monosyllabic and never apologises. **B** should aim to appear quite relaxed, which makes **A** grow increasingly angry. The conversation consists of three stages, and you will signal when **A** moves from one stage to the next. The three stages are:

1. **A** is complaining to **B**. **A** is angry, but it is a controlled anger. Demonstrate to the students that using a quieter volume and speaking through gritted teeth can still communicate annoyance.
2. **A** gets angrier and starts using a louder volume and a more angry tone.
3. **A** gets very angry and is now using their loudest volume and angriest tone of voice.

This is an excellent exercise for establishing some fundamental rules with younger students. Stress that there must be no physical contact between the characters. They can perform the scenes standing or using chairs. They must follow your signal for moving between the three sections, and must always be in total control. If at any point you feel that students are losing control as they build the emotion, revert to stage one.

Repeat the exercise, giving character **B** the chance to complain. Students can have time to polish sections of their work and perform in front of others.

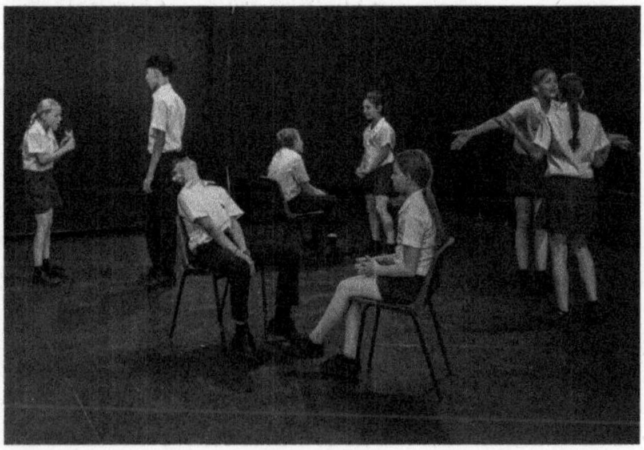

**Photo 1-1-2** Students improvising.

### *Written activity*

To develop your students' understanding of how to use different tones of voice and volume, give them all a copy of *The Last Parking Space in the World* script. They should read through the dialogue and complete the instructions in the blank spaces in the brackets as illustrated before the first three exchanges.

## The Last Parking Space in the World

**Joss** *and* **Tai** *are driving their cars. They have approached from different directions and have both turned to park in the last space in the supermarket car park at the same time.*

**Joss** *(frustrated tone of voice, quiet volume)* You need to move out of my way. I was here first.

**Tai** *(amused tone of voice, medium volume)* You have to be joking. You must have seen that I've been waiting for this space for ages.

**Joss** *(annoyed tone of voice, louder volume)* That's just not true. Anyhow, I have a baby in the back of my car, so I obviously have priority.

**Tai** *(                                        )* Go and park in one of the many special places reserved for drivers with babies, and get out of my way.

**Joss** *(                                        )* They are all full!

**Tai** *(                                        )* That's unfortunate. It doesn't mean that you are entitled to park here instead of me, especially as I was here first.

**Joss** *(                                        )* Please, I am going to be really quick. I only want a pint of milk.

**Tai** *(                                        )* Look, I'm sorry, but I have been driving around this car park for ages. I saw the spot, I waited. You will have to persevere.

**Joss** *(                                        )* Unbelievable! It's always the same! People who drive red cars are always particularly unpleasant.

**Tai** *(                                        )* So now you are insulting my car! Well, to be honest, I don't think much of blue cars.

**Joss** *(                                        )* Oh, now look at what you have done. The baby is awake!

**Tai** *(                                        )* I'm sorry, I really didn't mean to wake him. Or her?

**Joss** *(                                        )* Oh, forget it. She cries all the time. I never get to sleep anymore. Oh no, look in front of you. We're both too late! The shop is shut!

Once students have completed the written exercise, they can work in pairs to stage their two versions.

## Improvisation

This age group usually approach improvisation with huge enthusiasm and spontaneity. Without diluting this natural energy, it is also important to teach students ways to reflect on and improve their work. Establish a set routine which students regularly employ when working on improvisation tasks. With younger students, it is helpful to structure the amount of time they spend on each stage without curbing their natural enthusiasm.

Recommended stages and timings for this younger age group to employ:

1. Before improvising, they should spend time discussing their aims and a possible structure for the scene. (Two to three minutes.)
2. Improvise the scene. (Three to five minutes.)
3. Discuss the scene, considering ways of developing and improving. (Two to three minutes.)
4. Repeat the improvisation. (Three to five minutes.)
5. Repeat stages three and four as many times as necessary.

## 1. What mood are you in?

For this exercise, students continue to develop the skills introduced in the games and warm-up activities. In pairs, they will improvise three everyday situations, playing a gender-neutral role based on the *Mr Men* series. The characters are:

**Laz Lazy**
**Fudge Fib**
**Gee Grumpy**
**Paz Perfect**
**Chaz Cheerful**
**Adie Angry**
**Kit Kind**
**Ice indecisive**

Discuss the names of the characters with your students, focusing on how they might sound and how actors could employ volume and tone when playing them. Share the following snippets of dialogue:

1. Afternoon. I am Laz Lazy. I don't like the mornings. I try not to do or say too much until after midday. My motto is 'if someone can do it for you, let them get on with it'. I don't have anything else to say to you.
2. Fudge Fib here. Before we go any further, I need to tell you that I didn't do it. You can trust me; I had absolutely nothing to do with it. I must say, you are looking great today. I love your shoes.
3. What? What do you want? Yes, I'm Gee Grumpy. So what? I'm not feeling so good at the moment. It's raining again, and it makes me so fed up. So, please, leave me alone!
4. Good morning. Look at me! I'm Paz Perfect. I know everything, I can do anything. I don't make mistakes, and I get everything right. I'm just perfectly perfect.
5. What an absolutely beautiful day. It's so wonderful to meet you. I'm Chaz Cheerful, and I'm super positive and, remarkably, amazingly cheery. Have a fantastic day!
6. Look, I'm Adie Angry, and I have had enough of this. You really are annoying me, and I mean, really, really annoying me. Now, do go away. Go away!
7. Hello, I'm Kit Kind. And, if there is anything I can do to help you, please tell me. I'm here for you. I want to help. I want to support.
8. Um … well … er, I'm Ice indecisive. I'm actually not sure what to say … you see, I … no, that's wrong. Sorry … I can't make up my mind. Um … er.

Once you are confident that students have developed a sense of the characters, divide them into pairs. The improvisation scenes are:

1. A customer returns an item of clothing to a shop assistant and wants a refund.
2. A friend asks another for help with homework.
3. A manager is telling a player that they have been dropped from a team.

The activity must be carefully structured for this age group. Allow students about five minutes to work on each of three tasks. They are:

1. Select one of the three improvisations for all pairs to improvise. Ask the students to label themselves **A** and **B**. **A** plays **Chaz Cheerful** and **B** plays **Adie Angry.** Watch and discuss some of the work.
2. Select another one of the scenarios and allocate different roles to different pairs (this time drawing from the whole list). Watch and discuss.
3. For the final task, students work on the third scenario, selecting their own characters from the list. If they wish, they can choose to play the same role in the improvisation, allowing the audience to see what it is like when two similar characters interact.

Students select and polish their favourite improvisation. Watch and discuss the performances, highlighting effective use of tone of voice and volume.

## *Design activity*

In pairs or small groups, students plan costumes for two characters to help convey their personalities to an audience. They should choose the specific items and colours of the clothing and accessories for the chosen characters. Spend time discussing how colour can help convey different moods on stage. It is important to stress that it can mean many different things depending on context and other factors, but as a starting point for this age group, it is helpful to introduce that the following colours might **suggest** various moods:

1. **Red**: boldness, power, anger, love, and danger.
2. **Blue**: peace, calmness, coldness, sadness, and honesty.
3. **White**: coldness, purity, and innocence.
4. **Black**: boldness, strength, worry, fear, and mourning.
5. **Green**: jealousy, nature, and luck.
6. **Orange**: excitement, warmth, humour, and energy.
7. **Pink**: warmth, creativity, and fun.
8. **Yellow**: warmth, consideration, and care.
9. **Purple**: wealth, royalty, and power.

Students can pitch their ideas to you and the rest of the class, imagining they are competing for the role of costume designer for a new production. They should consider the most creative ways to present their proposals.

## 2. How on earth do we sort this out?

This exercise builds on the previous 'what mood are you in?' activity and encourages students to examine how a character's mood can change, prompting an actor to consider varying their tone of voice and volume.

Divide the students into pairs, labelling themselves **A** and **B**. **A** is the teacher, and **B** is the student. It is Monday morning in a history lesson, and the teacher **A** is collecting an important piece of homework from student **B**.

Speak to **A** and **B** separately. Send one group to one end of the class and ask them to sit in silence with their eyes closed and hands over their ears.

> Tell **A**s (teachers): You have been very worried about **B**'s progress this term. They have been daydreaming in class and have not participated in the lessons. They have not handed in any homework tasks this term, and you have already given them a detention and called home to discuss your concerns. You hope they have completed the homework this time. If not, you will need to report them to the Headteacher, and they will face serious consequences at school.
>
> Tell **B**s (students): You have not been doing well in history this term. You didn't complete any homework at the start of the term, and last week, you were given a detention; your family was also informed. You want to put things right. You spent a lot of time on the homework you were set and are very proud of your work. However, when you come to hand it in, you realize that you have forgotten it. It is back on your desk at home. You need to convince your teacher that you are telling the truth.

Once the students have been given the background, allow them to improvise the scenes spontaneously. You can choose to watch some examples of the work or discuss what happened. Draw out the various ways the two characters responded to the situation. Explain that characters on stage are more interesting if the audience sees different sides of their personalities, and they do not always behave in the same way. Allow them time to polish their scenes, ensuring that both characters display different emotions at different points, and remind them to use tone and volume in varying ways. It can be helpful to give the pairs large sheets of paper so they can work out and plot their characters' journeys through this scene and how they will use their voices. Watch and discuss the scenes which you can link to the next written activity.

### *Written activity*

This is a good point to gently start introducing students to evaluating their own performance work.

**Suggested title**: Give five examples of how you used tone of voice and volume to show the audience how your character felt. Explain what you did and what you hoped to show.

To guide them, share these two examples:

1. I wanted to show the audience that my character was trying to convince the teacher that they had completed the homework. I used a pleading tone of voice and a medium volume.
2. I wanted to show the audience that my character was annoyed with the student for not handing in the work again. I used an angry and frustrated tone of voice, speaking loudly.

The next part of the book for students aged twelve to thirteen focuses on assessing success and exploring ways to develop and improve practical work. You might want to start introducing these areas to your students at this earlier stage.

# Original script

## 1. My turn

This monologue explores how the use of varying volumes and tones of voice brings the character of **Kit** to life. Vocal directions are included, and students can work independently or in pairs, splitting the monologue into two parts and helping one another. After staging the monologue and following the written directions, students can be asked to experiment with different volumes and tones to perform the monologue in a new way.

### My Turn

**Kit** *has been persuaded by their teacher,* **Ms Brady**, *to audition for the school play.* **Ms Brady** *has indicated that she has always felt that* **Kit** *would be perfect for the leading role, saying that it is 'Kit's time to shine'.* **Kit** *has just found out that they have only been given a non-speaking role.*

*Imagine that you are performing this monologue to an audience sitting directly in front of you. Start by sitting on a chair. You can decide when you might stand and move around. Ensure that you follow the directions on how to use your voice.*

**Kit** (*loud volume, angry tone of voice*) A non-speaking part! I have been given a non-speaking part. I'm now expected to spend weeks and weeks attending rehearsals with absolutely nothing to say. It's unbelievable. I am so angry and upset. (*Takes some deep breaths to calm down.*)

(*Quieter volume, more controlled tone of voice.*) You are probably looking at me and thinking that I am behaving like a spoilt monster. Now you need to listen carefully. I didn't particularly want to be in this play. I'd rather have been in the football team. I'm good at football, and at least you get to do something worthwhile when you play a sport. (*Volume is increasing and tone of voice is becoming a little bit annoyed again.*) But, oh no, Ms Brady ruined all that for me. 'Who is Ms Brady?' you are probably asking. Well, Ms Brady is our long-standing drama teacher who is well-known for her brilliant plays. Now, let me tell you how Ms Brady played me!

(*Medium volume, friendly tone of voice, imagine you are sharing something important with a friend.*) About two weeks ago, Ms Brady pulled me aside and said that she wanted me to play the main part. She said I was by far the best person for the role and that she needed me. She said I would still have to audition, but she smiled and (*whisper these following words*) whispered in my ear, 'this is Kit's time to shine'.

(*Medium volume, enthusiastic, energetic tone of voice.*) Anyhow, I auditioned. I took it seriously. I worked hard, so hard. I wanted to live up to her expectations of me. I wanted to do my very best. She caught my eye after the audition and gave me a sweet smile.

(*Medium volume, which gets louder as you go on, grumpy tone of voice.*) The cast list went up on the notice board at lunchtime today. I had been practising my surprised face for the moment when it was confirmed that I had the main part. I didn't need to bother, because I was *really* surprised. I was *really,*

*really* surprised. Next to the main part, my part, was the name Jaz Jackman. I couldn't believe it. I hunted and hunted for my name, and near the bottom of the list was a heading, 'non-speaking parts', and that was where I found my name, next to the role of 'passenger two'.

*(Loud volume, angry tone of voice.)* I am so angry. I can't begin to tell you how angry I am. Who on earth would want to play passenger two? *(Medium volume, sad tone of voice.)* I had drama that afternoon with Ms Brady. She kept praising me for my work even though I couldn't be bothered to try. She kept me behind at the end of the lesson and said that she was sorry. Jaz Jackman had just been better on the day, and she hoped I would enjoy playing passenger two. She said it was a significant part and that the production wouldn't work without it.

*(Quiet volume, sulky tone of voice.)* I wish I had stuck to football.

## 2. The broken mirror

In this scene, two characters discuss who is responsible for breaking a precious mirror. Directions regarding the use of vocal volume and tone are included. Students can make their own decisions about the use of voice to stage the text. The activity can be developed into a written task, which is outlined after the extract.

### The Broken Mirror

*Character* **X** *is staying in Character* **Y***'s house.* **Y** *has just discovered that a valuable, precious, antique mirror has been broken.* **Y** *blames* **X. X** *claims to know nothing about it.*

*You can decide if* **X** *is guilty or not. Make sure to follow all the directions on how to use your voice. The scene is set in a bedroom at* **Y***'s house, where* **X** *has stayed overnight. It is early the next morning.*

**Y** *(happy tone of voice)* Morning, did you sleep well?

**X** *(a little quiet, slightly exhausted tone)* Not really. This house makes lots of strange noises at night.

**Y** *(loud voice, dramatic tone)* It's haunted!

**X** *(scared tone)* Truly?

**Y** *(increasingly dramatic tone)* Yes, lots of ghostly dogs roaming around, a lady in white …

**X** *(increasingly scared tone)* Don't terrify me, I hate that sort of thing.

**Y** *(amused tone)* No, I'm only joking. It's just an old house with old pipes and heating noises.

**X** *(slightly calmer tone)* Well, there were certainly lots of creaks and groans. I got up a couple of times and checked out of the window. I thought about pushing something against the door.

**Y** *(amused tone)* You are funny! *(Noticing the mirror. Surprised and anxious tone.)* Oh no, how did this happen?

**X** *(confused tone)* What?

**Y** *(loud volume, very anxious tone)* The mirror is broken!

**X** *(calm tone)* Really?

**Y** *(highly anxious tone)* Yes, really. I'm being serious now.

**X** *(calm tone)* It must have been like that.

**Y** *(loud volume, panicked tone)* No, it wasn't like that. I looked at it yesterday. It was perfect.

**X** *(louder volume)* Well, I haven't touched it. I haven't been near it.

**Y** *(suspicious tone)* You must have done something.

**X** *(slightly annoyed tone)* I haven't, I promise. I noticed it, but I didn't pick it up or anything.

**Y** *(quieter volume)* Look, it's best just to be honest.

**X** *(loud volume)* I am being honest.

**Y** *(panicked tone)* My mum is going to go absolutely crazy about this.

**X** *(calm tone)* It's only a mirror. I know people say it's bad luck and all that, but it is just a mirror.

**Y** *(angry tone)* It's not 'only a mirror'. It's special. It's been in the family for years. It's probably worth a fortune.

**X** *(quieter volume, convincing tone)* Look, I'm sorry, but I didn't break it. It's got nothing to do with me.

**Y** *(loud volume)* I don't believe you.

**X** *(upset tone)* Are you calling me a liar?

**Y** *(confused tone)* I suspect you don't want to admit to the truth. I think you're scared.

**X** *(loud volume, angry tone)* I've told you that I haven't touched it. I'm annoyed that you don't believe me.

**Y** *(angry tone)* I'm the one who should be annoyed.

**X** *(angry tone)* You think so? You are incredible!

**Y** *(angry tone)* What's that supposed to mean?

**X** *(quieter volume, upset tone)* I have been your best friend for so many years, and yet you want to blame me. This is unbelievably upsetting.

**Y** *(quiet volume, worried tone)* Look, I'm sorry, I'm just so concerned.

**X** *(quiet volume, sad tone)* Yeah, well, don't take it out on me. That mirror has nothing to do with me.

**Y** *(pleading tone)* I am sorry.

**X** *(very sad tone)* Perhaps I should go back home.

**Y** *(sad tone)* I don't want you to go, but if that's what you want.

**X** *(determined tone)* I think I do. It's for the best.

## *Written activity*

If you decide to ask your students to perform the text again, using different tones of voice and volumes, set them a task to justify their decisions.

**Suggested title**: Choose five of your character's lines, giving details of the tone of voice and volume you used. Provide clear reasons for your decisions and explain what you wanted to convey to the audience.

To guide them, share this example:

- On the line 'Perhaps I should go back home', I used a very frustrated tone of voice and a quiet volume. I wanted to show the audience that my character was upset with character Y and the situation. I wanted the audience to suspect that my character didn't want to go home.

Alternatively, you could ask students to continue writing a further exchange between **X** and **Y,** including directions for tone and volume at the start of each line and explaining what they hoped to convey to the audience about their character at the end of each line.

## 3. It's behind you!

Students should have completed the previous monologue and pair scene activities before proceeding with this exercise. This scene has been written for four performers. It focuses on the distribution of pantomime roles for a forthcoming production. Details about the personalities of the different characters are given; students make their own decisions about the appropriate volumes and tones of voice.

### It's Behind You!

*In this scene, four actors with very different personalities are given their pantomime roles for a forthcoming production. They then start reading through the first pantomime scene.*

***The Actors***

**CM:** *Very impatient, gets annoyed with others quickly.* **CM** *is given the pantomime role of* **Wick the Wicked One**. **Wick** *is the evil character who causes lots of trouble.*

**SG:** *Very kind and gentle, tries to be a peacemaker and look after others.* **SG** *is given the pantomime role of the* **Prince**. *The* **Prince** *is brave and strong.*

**MB:** *Wants to be in charge, very bossy***. MB** *is given the pantomime role of the* **Magician,** *whose tricks often go wrong.*

**BT:** *Always joking, doesn't take life too seriously.* **BT** *is given the pantomime role of* **Ceecee the Cat. Ceecee** *is a kind and good cat, but is always getting into trouble trying to find extra food.*

*The four actors have met to learn about their roles in the pantomime. In this scene, you need to think carefully about the personality of your character and their pantomime role. You need to make decisions about how you use your voice, thinking particularly about volume and tone.*

**SG** Right, I have been sent the cast list for our incredible new pantomime 'Ceecee the Cat Saves The Day'.

**MB** Why have you been given the cast list to read out? I have been here the longest, and I think that duty should fall to me.

**BT** MB, you are so funny. You do make me laugh. Does it matter?

**CM** Oh, do get on with it. All of this is monumentally dull.

**MB** We would be getting on with it if I were in charge.

**BT** Listen, have you heard this one? Why did the tomato blush?

**SG** I don't know why did the tomato blush?

**BT** Because it saw the salad dressing! *(BT laughs loudly.)*

**CM** I've never heard anything so stupid in my life.

**SG** There's no need to be rude, CM. Thank you, BT. That was a great joke.

**BT** Why didn't the teddy bear eat dessert?

**SG** I really don't know BT.

**BT** Because he was stuffed … he was stuffed. How funny is that?

**SG** Yes, it's very funny, completely hilarious.

**CM** It's not funny at all. Completely ridiculous!

**MB** SG, pass that list to me. You have lost control of this meeting, and as the most experienced and, perhaps I should also add, the most successful, it should fall to me to read out the cast list.

**CM** Pathetic!

**SG** I'm happy to pass over to you, MB. Whatever is best for the company.

**MB** Thank you, SG.

**BT** Have you heard the one …

**CM** *(cutting in)* Shut up BT! We are not interested!

**SG** Don't be unkind. I like BT's jokes.

**MB** *(taking charge)* Quiet, we must cease this bickering. We need to get on. Let's have a look at this cast list. CM, let's start with you first. You have been cast as Wick the Wicked One.

**CM** What? Why do I always get cast as the bad guy? Every year, it's the same. I'm always the baddie.

**BT** *(laughing)* I can't imagine why!

**CM** It's rubbish. I wanted to be the goodie for a change.

**MB** Ok CM, I am confident you will do an excellent job. Let's move on. SG, you are going to play the Prince.

**CM** I want to be the Prince.

**SG** Fabulous, I am very happy with that. But I don't mind playing any part. CM, I'll swap with you if you want.

**MB** No, no, we are not swapping roles around. I'm sure a great deal of thought has gone into this. Let's move on. BT, you are playing Ceecee the Cat.

**CM** Well, that's not right, that's the title role.

**BT** Is it?

**MB** Yes the production is called 'Ceecee the Cat Saves the Day'.

**CM** I want to play Ceecee.

**SG** I'm sure it doesn't matter. Pantomime roles are all significant. After all, it has to be titled something.

**MB** Yes, you are right, SG. Let's move on.

**BT** See, see, I'm Ceecee … do you get it?

**CM** We don't want to get it.

**MB** And, I'm playing the Magician!

**CM** I want to be the Magician.

**BT** *(laughing)* See, see, you are the Wicked One! Do you see see?

**SG** Oh isn't this just wonderful!

**CM** I am not happy with any of it.

**MB** We must remember that we are professional actors with a job to do. I suggest we have a read-through of the opening and review how we get on.

**SG** Lovely.

**MB** Ok, scene one – it's nighttime. There is a massive thunderbolt, and in a puff of smoke, Wick the Wicked One enters. Over to you CM.

**CM** *as* **Wick** Haha, I am Wick the Wicked One. I'm here to cause trouble and mayhem. The local townsfolk are planning a big party to celebrate being named the happiest town in the Kingdom. But no no no … I'm not having any of this nonsense. With my tricks and my wicked ways, the town will soon be demoted to the unhappiest in the kingdom. I'm Wick the Wicked One!!! Hahahaha.

**SG** That was marvellous CM.

**CM** I thought it was rubbish, but what can I do with such a terrible script?

**MB** Thank you CM. That was splendid. Right, let's move on. The Magician comes in next. That's me.

**SG** Oh wonderful! I do love a magician.

**MB** *as the* **Magician** Hello boys and girls. I am the Magician. I heard what that awful Wick just said, and I'm going to stop any wickedness and protect these lovely, happy people. I am going to cast a spell and create an invisible wall which Wick won't be able to get through. Here we go-

> Abracadabra, hear my spell
> So I can make sure that everything is well.
> With a sprinkle of glitter, some rays from the sun
> We will get rid of Wick the Wicked One.

*(Lots of flourishes of wand.)* Oh no, nothing has happened. I don't understand. Back to my magic revision book. I must have forgotten the spell. I must put a stop to the Wicked One's nasty plan.

**SG** Beautifully performed MB.

**MB** Thank you, SG. Now, to continue, BT and SG, over to you. You enter the stage together.

**SG** *as* **Prince** What a wonderful day, Ceecee. We have been named the happiest town in the kingdom. I need you to help me, the Prince, to organize the biggest party the townsfolk have ever seen.

**BT** *as* **Ceecee** Stop right there for a minute Prince, I can't organize anything on an empty stomach.

**SG** *as* **Prince** But I fed you about an hour ago.

**BT** *as* **Ceecee** A lot can happen in an hour, and if you want me to use my creative kitty thinking powers, I suggest you provide me with a special treat to bring out the best in me.

**SG** *as* **Prince** You are the greediest creature I have ever met in my life.

**BT** *as* **Ceecee** Are you talking about meeeeow? I'm just a poor pussy cat with a healthy appetite.

**SG** *as* **Prince** Ok ok, what do you want?

**BT** *as* **Ceecee** Some of those special fishy treats. The fish oil will be good for my brain, and then I can help you organize the best party the world has ever seen.

**CM** This is utter rubbish. I want to go home.

**MB** Maybe it is a good place to stop for a tea break.

**CM** I hate tea.

**MB** Let's come back in fifteen minutes to read scene two.

**CM** Do we have to?

### *Written activity*

Creative task: Students work in pairs to write a scene between two of the pantomime characters.

# Published script

## 1. *Pied Piper: A Hip-Hop Family Musical* – Conrad Murray

This excerpt is from the start of Conrad Murray's exciting hip-hop reimagining of the folk tale *The Pied Piper of Hamelin,* which premiered at the Battersea Arts Centre in 2023. It offers excellent opportunities for students to creatively apply volume and tone of voice to a piece of published text.

Start by reading the excerpt with students and then divide the class into small groups of three or four. Their goal is to create a lively and energetic performance. They must consider the different volumes they might use and how to apply varying tones of voice.

Before they start work, discuss some of the techniques they might use as a group to deliver the excerpt, including:

1. **Unison**: They can choose to deliver parts of the extract in unison, thinking carefully about how they use volume and tone of voice. Warn them that speaking in unison can sound monotonous and robotic; they all need to deliver the words as if they are the only ones performing to achieve the necessary energy and attack. It would be helpful to practise delivering some lines together as a class to perfect this technique.
2. **Solo**: They can take turns to deliver lines on their own, thinking carefully about individual use of volume and tone of voice.
3. **Variety**: They can choose to vary the number of people delivering lines, ensuring that the audience is unable to recognize a regular pattern, such as:

- Two performers deliver line one.
- Two different performers deliver line two.

- One performer delivers line three.
- The whole group deliver line four.

4. **Use of round**: Choose four volunteers to demonstrate reading the first six lines of the excerpt using this technique:

- Student one starts reading through the six lines clearly and expressively.
- As soon as student one delivers the word *time* at the end of the second line, student two joins in to read all six lines from the beginning.
- As soon as student two delivers the word *time* at the end of the second line, student three joins in to read all six lines from the beginning.
- And so on.

Students must keep reading until they have delivered the six lines. They all need to speak clearly as if they are the only person talking, and they must not rush their words to catch up to another performer. After the technique has been established, students experiment with applying different volumes and tones.

## Context for students

The following excerpt is from the 2013 hip-hop version of *The Pied Piper of Hamelin.* In this version, the young people are upset about the mayor's ban on music and are also dealing with the problem of rats in the town of Hamelin. This excerpt is from Scene One and establishes that things are not particularly good in Hamelin. You have the freedom to use as many voices and techniques as you want to deliver any of the lines. You should think carefully about your use of volume and tone of voice to create an exciting and original performance.



# WELCOME TO HAMELIN

## Pied Piper

Welcome to Hamelin
Where once upon a time
Anything could happen
A nation so great
But the vision has faded
The colours are jaded

Welcome to Hamelin
Where back in the day
Had feeling and passion
So misunderstood
It looks good from far

But far from good

It's a town that looks like yours
Streetlights
Stray cats
Front doors
But the kids here work every day
For next to no pay
All sweat no play
They work in a factory of pies
Some say factory of lies
And it's just as bad for mum and dad
But the mayor reassures them

**Mayor**

It's the best day they've ever had

**Piper**

In Hamelin
So proud they stand in old clothes
And seeing the town's anthem so loud

**Ensemble**

We pledge with pride to the pastry
Bake every day, make sure that they're tasty!
Even if we don't get no dough
We will go we will go we will go
Till we can't cook no more

**Piper**

They make so much waste from the pies
And the cakes
The streets are crust-filled
Plus kidney and steak
Rats have filled the floors
Because of the state of the place
The mayor must know
Make no mistakes

Welcome to Hamelin
Where once upon a time
Anything could happen
A nation so great
But the vision has faded

The colours are jaded

Welcome to Hamelin
Where back in the day
Had feeling and passion
So misunderstood
It looks good from far
But far from good

## 2. *Alice* by Laura Wade

This extract is from Act Two of Laura Wade's adaptation of Lewis Carroll's *Alice in Wonderland,* which was first performed in 2010 at the Crucible Theatre in Sheffield. It is a modern twist on the original story, providing a slightly more challenging experience for this age group. In Wade's version, Alice is a young Goth who is mourning the loss of her brother. This excerpt is ideal as the unpredictable Queen offers a wide range of possibilities for experimenting with volume and tone of voice. The gender of the performer does not matter when working on the piece.

Read the excerpt with students analysing the different sides of the Queen's personality and discussing examples of the various tones of voice and volumes that could be applied to depict the character. Students can work individually or in pairs, supporting one another. Alternatively, they could perform together, delivering lines in different ways to show the many sides of the Queen.

### Context for students

This excerpt is taken from a play adaptation of the famous story *Alice in Wonderland* by Lewis Carroll. In this speech, the **Queen** invites a crowd of people to tea and asks for volunteers to play a game of croquet. The **Queen** is a very changeable character. She has authority and can be charming, demanding and moody.



**QUEEN**: I simply cannot tell you how pleased you are to be here, in the presence of me. Me are happy to invite you all - or those of you still in possession of your heads by that point – to a croquet tea at which my home made tarts will be served to the most deserving among you.

But before that – to the match. What a happy coincidence that croquet, my favourite sport, is also the favourite sport of all Wonderlanders everywhere. And what an exciting game me will have today – a champion, undefeated for twenty-five matches, and an unknown challenger. Who among you is brave enough to take on this quest for glory?

*The QUEEN looks at the crowd. No-one volunteers.*

I SAID – who among you is brave enough to take on the challenge?

### *Written activity*

For this task, students evaluate the performance work of others. To help them focus and concentrate on being specific in their evaluations, identify which performance each individual is to write about before they watch any of the live work.

**Suggested title**: Evaluate one of the performances of the Queen's speech. Explain how the performer(s) used tone of voice and volume to deliver the text, and explain what impact this had on you.

Clarify that the word *impact* means any response and could include making the audience laugh, smile, feel happy, feel sad, or feel sorry for someone.

To guide them, share this example:

- **Name of performer** used a very excited tone of voice and a loud volume when delivering the line 'Who among you is brave enough to take on this quest for glory?' This exaggerated delivery was very amusing and made me laugh.

## 3. *Secret* from *Love and Information* by Caryl Churchill

Caryl Churchill's *Love and Information* premiered at the Royal Court Jerwood Theatre Downstairs in 2012. Consisting of over fifty separate short scenes, it is a useful play to access a range of interesting excerpts. In the original production, over one hundred roles were played by sixteen actors, making this an appropriate point to introduce your students to the technique of multi-roling. Churchill gives each excerpt a title but provides no further information about the context, number of characters or character names. Divide the class into pairs to read through the excerpt, taking turns to deliver the lines. Once they have done this, discuss how they might vary their voices to play the character who wants to know the secret and the one who hides the secret. You might want to select a few individual lines and start by exploring different ways these could be delivered.

### Context for students

In this short play, one character attempts to persuade another to reveal their secret. Think carefully about the various ways you can use voice to play the two roles.



### SECRET

Please please tell me
no
please because I'll never
don't ask don't ask
I'll never tell
no
no matter what
it's not
I'd die before I told

it's not you telling, even if you didn't
I wouldn't
it's you knowing it's too awful I can't
but tell me
no
because if you don't there's this secret between us
stop it
if there's this secret we're not
please
we're not close any more we can't ever
but nobody knows everything about
yes but a big secret like this
it's not such a big
then tell me
will you stop
it's big because you won't tell me
no I won't.
Is it something you've
don't start guessing
or something you want to
please
or you've seen or heard or know or
please
and if it's something you've done is it a crime or a sin or just embarrassing because whichever
no I don't want you to know.
All right.
All right I'll tell you
you don't have to
I'll tell you
yes tell me because I'll never
it's not that
tell me because I'll always
all right I'm telling you.

*Tells in a whisper.*

No
yes
no
I warned you
but that's
yes

oh no that's
yes
how could you
I did.
Now what? now what? now what?

## *Written activity*

Creative task: Devising original performance work is a key component of exam-level drama courses. Many scenes develop through improvisation, but some students also produce exciting original work by shaping their ideas through writing. As a follow-up to the practical exploration of *Secret*, ask students to continue writing the exchange between the two characters using Churchill's style.

# 2
# MOVEMENT – GESTURE
## 'STRIKE A POSE'

**Photo 1-2-1** Students exploring gesture.

## Introduction

In this section of the course, you use games, warm-ups, improvisation exercises and original scripts to introduce students to how actors employ movement on stage. Given that exam courses require students to develop a sophisticated understanding of how different elements of movement convey meaning in performance, this chapter emphasizes the use of gesture. Remember, it is up to you to decide on the sequence in which you deliver Chapters One, Two and Three. However, to ensure progression and development, it is most productive to work through the activities in this chapter in sequence.

## Games

### 1. Teacher says

This activity is based on the childhood game *Simon Says*. Replace 'Simon' with the word 'teacher', your name or a significant name from the school. Instruct the students to perform a variety of physical tasks, incorporating as many gestures as possible. Students only perform the instruction if preceded by the command 'teacher says'. Deliver these instructions as quickly as possible. The game is often set up as a competition where students are eliminated if they make a mistake until a winner is determined. In the drama classroom, your students develop more skills if they are allowed to continue playing the game even if they make an error. Examples of instructions:

1. Nod your head.
2. Shrug your shoulders.
3. Stroke your chin (as if thinking).
4. Cover your mouth (as if shocked).
5. Tap your foot (as if impatient).
6. Wave your hand.
7. Finger on lips (as if saying quiet).
8. Point your finger.
9. Thumbs up.
10. Thumbs down.
11. Salute.
12. Cross your arms.
13. Shake hands.
14. Tap your fingers.
15. Put your head in your hands.
16. Stand up straight.
17. Touch the floor.
18. Rub your hands together.
19. Fiddle with your hair.
20. Place your hand on your cheek.
21. Touch your nose.
22. Hands on hips.
23. Hands behind your back.
24. Shake your arms.
25. Jump up and down.
26. Click your fingers.

## 2. Musical statues

Most students enjoy playing the childhood party game, *Musical Statues*. Ask them to walk around the whole space. They should travel in different directions and avoid making contact with one another. As the music stops, call out an adjective; students must then freeze in a position using interesting gestures to convey the word appropriately. Stress that the position they take is the most important part of the game. Point out any particularly effective positions and gestures. Examples of adjectives:

1. Happy.
2. Sad.
3. Angry.
4. Frustrated.
5. Calm.
6. Brave.
7. Enthusiastic.
8. Cheerful.

## 3. Footsteps with attitude

This is an adaptation of the game *Grandma's Footsteps*. In this version, one student takes on the role of the **judge**. They stand at one end of the space with their back turned to the rest of the class, who spread out at the other end. The objective of the game is to be the first person to reach the **judge**. Instruct students to move slowly and carefully so they can immediately take a freeze position when the **judge** turns. If they are seen moving, they are sent back to the start. As an extra challenge, they need to ensure that their freeze position is engaging and incorporates gestures. Ask them to consider what kind of poses they might adopt and the facial expressions they might display. The person whom the **judge** deems to have taken the most exciting, creative position in each round is allowed to take one step forward. Once the winner has been determined, that student can take on the role of the **judge**, and the game can be repeated.

## 4. Movement Murder

This game is a development of the popular *Wink Murder* and builds on the previous activity. Students sit in a circle with their eyes closed and their hands over their eyes. Pick one student to take on the role of the **leader** by tapping them on the shoulder. The rest of the class should not be aware of who has been chosen as the **leader**. Select another student to take on the role of the **investigator** (all students should know who has been selected for this role). All students now stand in a large circle with the **investigator** positioned at a fixed point in the middle of the circle. The **investigator** can turn on the spot but is unable to leave that position. In the *Wink Murder* version of the game, the **leader** tries to eliminate others by winking at them without the **investigator** seeing. If winked at, a student counts to three, averts their gaze from the **leader,** and sits down to indicate that they are out of the game. In this new version, the **leader** begins with a simple, silent movement, such as clicking fingers, tapping a leg, scratching the head, nodding, or shrugging shoulders, all without the **investigator** noticing (and stopping if the **investigator** looks towards them). As soon as any other students become aware of the movement, they copy it accurately whenever the **investigator** is not looking in their direction. The **leader** can change the movement at any stage. The object of the game is to work together so that the **investigator** does not notice anyone moving and has difficulty identifying the **leader**. The **investigator** has three guesses to determine the **leader**. As this version is more challenging than the original, it is helpful to assume the role of **leader** yourself in round one to demonstrate a range of different gestures that can be used.

# Warm-up

## 1. Words or mime

Divide students into pairs, labelling themselves **A** and **B**. For the first part of this exercise, the students sit with their hands under their legs, facing one another. Describe three simple tension scenarios to be improvised using dialogue. Stress that they must remain seated and cannot move from their position. Suggested scenarios:

1. **A** wants to go swimming, and **B** wants to go to the cinema. Both characters must discuss their preferences and attempt to reach a decision.
2. **A** wants to play sports, and **B** wants to watch television. Both characters must discuss their preferences and attempt to reach a decision.
3. **A** wants to borrow money from **B,** who isn't comfortable about doing this. Both characters must discuss the situation and try to reach a decision.

After students have improvised the three scenes, discuss how they felt when performing with the physical restriction. Ask them to start thinking about the type of movement and gestures they would have liked to include. They should now repeat one of the scenes from a seated position, using both speech and gestures. Watch some of the work, drawing out examples of effective use of gesture. Ask them to repeat the scene from the seated position using only gestures. In this final version, emphasize that there should be no physical contact and that they must carefully consider the gestures they use to present their case.

## 2. Individual still images

Still images are a remarkably useful device for students to employ in their drama work at any level. Younger students need to learn how to create effective still images; these early skills will be developed in increasingly complex ways over the next two years. For this exercise, students work independently. Discuss what makes a strong individual still image. Cover these areas:

1. **Balance**: Still images must be absolutely fixed and still. It is not advisable to stand on one foot.
2. **Shape**: It is important to think about the shape of the position taken. Interesting frozen gestures help bring the still image to life.
3. **Facial expressions**: Characters come to life in still images if the performers think about the most appropriate facial expressions.
4. **Eyes**: Students need to fix their eye focus on a particular point. This could be on a part of their body or a certain point in their surroundings. They do not have to stop themselves from blinking, but must ensure that their eye focus is held, and they are not looking around.

Start by asking students to create individual still images that present several different characters. Explain that after you describe the character, you will count **one, two, three and freeze**. The students freeze on the final **freeze** command. They hold their position as you describe the next character and move once you restart counting. Students can stand or sit to depict the different characters. Encourage them to be creative and ignore what others are doing around them. Examples of characters:

1. You have won the lottery.
2. Oh no, you haven't, you forgot to buy a ticket this week.
3. You are playing a trumpet.
4. You are cleaning your teeth.
5. You are watching a scary movie.
6. It now turns into the funniest movie ever.
7. You are auditioning for a lead part in a show.
8. You are being told off for something you didn't do.
9. You are the person doing the telling-off.

**Photo 1-2-2** Still image work.

10. You are a clown in the circus.
11. You are studying a large map.
12. You are on a tightrope.

Once you are happy that students are developing good technique, they can create another set of still images, thinking even more carefully about the gestures they employ to bring these characters to life on stage:

1. A person giving instructions to another about how to get from point A to point B.
2. A cook on a television cooking competition.
3. A student explaining how a chemistry experiment went wrong.
4. A person wrapping up a huge birthday present.
5. A juggler performing a complicated routine.
6. A dancer demonstrating a dance move.
7. A dentist explaining some treatment they wish to perform.
8. A sailor hoisting up the sails in a boat.

## 3. Gesture dynamics

For this activity, students learn how to use different dynamics to flavour their gestures and present various attitudes and feelings. Introduce them to the actor and practitioner Jacques Lecoq, who was well known for his mime and movement performances and theories. Explain that he developed a technique called *Seven Levels of Tension* to help actors think about different ways of performing movement on stage. Examples of the seven different levels include being totally relaxed, feeling interested and alert, and feeling extremely tense and threatened. Although Lecoq drew on seven levels, for this exercise, students apply four different levels of tension:

1. Bored, disinterested and tired.
2. Curious and careful.
3. Excited and positive.
4. Angry and annoyed.

Working individually, students mime these three activities in turn:

1. Baking a cake.
2. Packing a bag.
3. Building sandcastles.

As they perform, instruct them to use different levels of tension, naturally prompting them to start employing varying dynamics. Divide the class into pairs. They should select one of the three activities to mime with their partner. They must both use all four levels of tension at some point during the activity. They can use a particular level at the same or different times.

## 4. Miming

In this warm-up activity, read out the three separate short scenarios, asking all students to mime the events, paying particular attention to their use of gesture. Alternatively, students can work in pairs with one student reading out a scenario whilst the other performs it.

### *Traffic controller*

I take up my position in the middle of the road. My feet are firmly planted. It's the morning rush hour, and I have to take charge of this busy junction where the traffic lights are not working. I hold my hand up high to stop the traffic moving from one direction. I beckon the traffic from the other direction to move. The drivers are very slow. I need to get them going, so I use strong, fast gestures to encourage them. I count the cars secretly on my fingers- one, two, three, four, five, six, seven, eight, nine, ten. Ok, that's enough, it's time to stop them. I hold up my hand powerfully until they are all stationary. I turn to the other line of traffic and start beckoning so they know they can move. Again, I have to gesture very vigorously to hurry them up. Somebody hoots a horn at me, and I glare at them, raising my arms in annoyance and despair.

### *Music conductor*

I stand before my huge orchestra, looking around to make sure that they are ready to start. I lift my baton high and pause. I bring down the baton sharply, indicating that my orchestra should begin playing. This is a big section, so I conduct using strong gestures to suggest that the music should get louder and louder. The trumpets are not loud enough, so I encourage them to put in more effort. Suddenly, the music changes as we transition to a gentle stage. I gesture to my orchestra to quieten down. I place my fingers on my lips to warn the drummer to play softly. I point towards the violin section to remind them to join in. One of the violinists seems to have fallen asleep, so I stamp my feet, waving wildly to wake him up.

### *The hungry cat*

I prowl into the kitchen, looking around for food. I see my bowl. There is nothing there. I stretch and yawn. I notice my human owner. She is sitting on the floor working on her computer. I gaze at her adoringly … nothing! I jump up and start tapping her keyboard with my paw to get her attention. Nothing! She tells me to go away. I am angry. I can feel my body getting tense, and I think about how to get noticed. I stroll back over, take out my sharp claws and scratch her hand. Ha, ha, she has seen me now. She screams, and I scurry away quickly.

### *Written activity*

Students produce a further script, including the movements and gestures for a new character. They should produce something of a similar length and style to the characters in the previous practical exercise. Suggested characters:

1. The cook.
2. The artist.
3. The gardener.
4. The naughty dog.

# Improvisation

## 1. Group still images

Ask students to recall what makes an effective individual still image and what else they might consider when creating group still images. Make sure that you introduce:

1. **Levels**: In a group, it is important to use different levels. Students should avoid taking the same standing or seated positions.
2. **Connections**: They should consider the different ways they might connect in a still image. This could be a physical connection, such as shaking hands, or a connection through eye focus. (Advise students to look above or to the side of another student's eyes to help maintain concentration.)

Divide the students into groups of three or four to create several group still images based on titles. They will choose the characters involved, decide what they are all doing and how to use gestures. Start by exploring this example:

**Title***:* An Art Lesson Goes Wrong.
**Possible characters***:* Teacher and three students.
**What are they doing?** The teacher is trying to explain the task and maintain control, student one drops a pot of paint on the floor, student two is secretly trying to eat a bar of chocolate, and student three is drawing on a massive sheet of paper.
**Gestures***:* Teacher – hands in the air, desperately trying to get attention. Student one – trying to catch the paint pot before the paint spills. Student two – small, secretive gestures. Student three – huge, expansive gestures.

Having established the details, divide the students into groups of four to create this scene as a still image. They should imagine that they are producing something to be viewed in an art gallery, with the audience observing from all sides. Watch the work and provide feedback on students' use of levels, connections and gestures.

**Photo 1-2-3** Performing still images.

Allocate the groups further titles to create new still images. Give them about five minutes on each image. Suggested titles:

1. Auntie's 100th birthday party.
2. The busy hairdressing salon.
3. Summer airport madness.
4. The zoo.
5. A picnic in the rain.

To view the work, set up the performers in the middle of a circle of audience members who slowly walk around the still image to see it from all angles. Evaluate the work, examining the gestures in detail and assessing how successfully a group's still image has been created.

Students can now start developing their work to include some dialogue. Their still image is to be performed at the start of the scene and held for at least five seconds. A good strategy is to teach students to count pink elephants in their heads to ensure they don't rush through the counting process. One pink elephant, two pink elephants and up to five pink elephants secure an appropriate length of time to hold a still image. After the still image has been performed, the dialogue then begins. All characters can deliver two lines of dialogue, which can be of different lengths and performed in any order. You can limit the dialogue to one line per character or allow groups to create longer pieces if you wish. The work concludes with a repeat of the original still image.

## 2. Movement to music

This activity builds on the 'words or mime' warm-up exercise. Divide the students into groups of three, labelling themselves **A**, **B** and **C** to create a scene depicting three family members having breakfast together on **B**'s birthday. Start by giving each member of the group a role card or by projecting the roles onto a screen.

> Character **A:** You are the oldest child in the family. You are a positive, helpful, and considerate person. You are excited about going to an audition at school for the lead role in a play. You don't realize that your middle sibling, character **B**, is also auditioning. You are concerned that your

youngest sibling, character **C**, is experiencing difficulties at school. You have bought an exciting birthday present for **B.**

Character **B:** You are the middle child in the family. You often feel a bit left out. It is your birthday today. You are auditioning for the lead role in the school play, even though your oldest sibling, **A**, expects to get the part. You don't get on very well with your younger sibling **C**.

Character **C:** You are the youngest child in the family. You are quite lazy and are performing poorly at school. You think your older sibling **A** nags you. You have forgotten that it is your middle sibling **B**'s birthday, and you have not bought them a present.

Ask the students to discuss their roles with one another and to work out a clear story with four stages. With students of this age, it is helpful to give them an example of a four-stage drama:

1. **A** wishes **B** a happy birthday and gives them an exciting present which **B** loves.
2. **C** hears this and tells **B** that they had forgotten about the birthday. **B** is disappointed.
3. **A** complains to **C**, saying that it is not acceptable to forget about **B**'s birthday, and asks them about school. **C** tries to avoid talking about school
4. **B** tells **A** that they are auditioning for the play. **A** is annoyed. **C** finds it funny.

Students now improvise their scenes using dialogue. You can instruct them to use the example storyline or create their own four-stage version. Work closely with them as they will need support in structuring their work. It is helpful to ask them to share key moments of the work in progress.

For the next stage of the activity, students tell their stories through movement only, using a mixture of still images and mime work. They must carefully consider the gestures they employ to depict the different characters and their feelings towards one another. Since they are using movement solely to convey the characters' personalities and interactions, the movement scenes will probably be shorter. Stress that there should still be four clear stages to their work. Add background music to support the performances.

### *Written activity*

Using gestures as a performer can be very instinctive, and it is challenging to teach students how to articulate what they are doing and why in writing.

**Suggested title**: Select two moments from your movement performance and describe what you are doing in a way that would make sense to audience members if the lights went out.

To guide them, share this example:

- I point at my sister to show I am annoyed with her. I shrug my shoulders at my brother to show I don't care, and then fold my arms. I scratch my head to show that I am confused and wave my arms in the air to indicate that I am frustrated.

# Original script

## 1. First day

In this monologue, a young person describes a car journey as they travel to their first day at a new school. Read through the script, considering the references to different gestures in the speech. Students can rehearse the monologue individually or work in pairs, helping each other to ensure that all the gestures are accurately incorporated. Students can then repeat the sequence, performing the gestures only to background music.

### First Day

***Alex** is sitting in the back of a car, travelling to their new school. Deliver the monologue, ensuring you perform all the movements and gestures to bring to life what **Alex** describes.*

**Alex** The car is moving slowly. I am looking out of the window at the line of traffic crawling beside me. Suddenly, I see my friend sitting in the car next to me. I wave until I am seen. I produce a huge yawn to show how boring this journey has become to me. I tap my watch several times to indicate that I'm worried about being late. Something catches my eye in the opposite window, and I look out to see two people taking a massive group of dogs out for a walk. I count them on my fingers- one, two, three, four, five, six, seven, eight, nine. Nine dogs! How amazing! I twist around in my seat to see them disappearing into the distance as the car picks up more speed. My mum is driving the car. She asks me an unnecessary question, so I shrug my shoulders and look out of the window again. I see a young man playing a saxophone on the streets. I mirror what he is doing and imagine I am playing my own saxophone in the back of the car. I'm having a fantastic time, but my mum notices what I am doing in the mirror and tells me to sit still. I fold my arms tightly, annoyed that she has reprimanded me.

## 2. Copycat

In this scene, two characters meet outside the door to a house party and find that they are both wearing the same clothes. Examples of movement and gestures are specified throughout the script. Read through the dialogue and ask students to try out the different gestures. Discuss if there are places where they could add different or new gestures.

### Copycat

*Character **S** and Character **T** arrive at a party at the same time. They both discover that they are wearing the same outfit.*

*Pay careful attention to the directions on how you should use movement and gestures. Think about places in the text where you might use different gestures. The scene begins when characters **S** and **T** stand in front of each other and realize they are wearing the same clothes. You can decide the outfits, but they should be something unusual and unique. Both characters want to be the only ones wearing them. (Character **S** and Character **T** stand looking at each other.)*

**S** Why are you wearing the same outfit as me? *(Gestures with both hands towards **T**.)*

**T** Why are YOU wearing the same outfit as ME? *(Points to self and then points at **S**.)*

**S** I told you I was wearing this. *(Points at outfit.)*

**T** Did you? I don't remember that. *(Scratches head.)*

**S** I showed you a picture. *(Holds one hand out.)*

**T** Really? As I said, I don't recall. *(Folds arms.)*

**S** Yes, you do. You asked me all about it, where I bought it, and how much it cost. Now I know why! *(Uses lots of hand gestures.)*

**T** I think you must be confusing me with someone else. *(Shakes head.)*

**S** Don't lie about it. *(Points finger at* **T***.)*

**T** How rude! I don't lie. *(Points finger back.)*

**S** You are absolutely unbelievable! *(Throws arms up in air.)*

**T** Look, calm down. It's not the end of the world. *(Gentle arm gesture.)* There's no need to get so upset.

**S** But we look ridiculous wearing the same clothes. Everyone will laugh at us. *(Hands on head.)* Do you really want that?

**T** No, I don't. I agree with you about that. We can't both turn up looking like identical twins. *(Throws hands in air.)*

**S** Ok, so go home and get changed. *(Points in the direction of where* ***T*** *should go.)*

**T** Me? Why should I be the one to go home? Why not you? *(Shrugs shoulders.)*

**S** Because I bought the outfit first, and whatever you say, you know that's the truth. *(Points finger at* ***T****.)*

**T** But you live much closer than I do. It makes more sense if you go home and get changed. Neither of us would miss much of the party then. *(Folds arms.)*

**S** But that's just not fair. You have copied me, and I'm the one who's going to lose out. *(Stamps feet.)*

**T** Yes, but it's the sensible thing to do. (*Shrugs shoulders.*)

**S** I am not getting changed. I had this outfit first, so you should be the one to switch to something else. *(Folds arms.)*

**T** But I love what I'm wearing. I look so good in it. *(Waves arms about.)*

**S** Oh, and I don't? *(Points to self.)*

**T** I didn't say that. *(Lifts shoulders.)*

**S** So what did you mean? *(Points at T.)*

**T** Well, it's just the style, the fabric, the colour and the cut. It was made for me. You look good, but it looks so much better on me. *(Skips around playfully.)*

**S** You are unbelievably unkind, insensitive, rude and unfair. *(Stamps feet.)*

**T** I'm just being honest. *(Shrugs shoulders.)*

**S** You haven't shown much honesty today, that's for sure. *(Points.)*

**T** So what are you going to do? *(Hands behind back.)*

**S** Well, I'm certainly not getting changed. *(Folds arms.)*

**T** And neither am I. *(Folds arms.)*

**S** So we either go to the party looking like twins and get laughed at, or we don't go at all. *(Folds arms again.)*

**T** Ok, so what's it going to be then? *(Raises both hands.)*

### *Design activity*

This is a lovely opportunity for students to design the costumes for the characters in *Copycat.* You might also want them to start considering the different ways an identical costume can be worn. In this context, pose the following questions:

1. Are there items (such as shirts or blouses) that could be tucked in or worn out?
2. Are the costumes ironed or a bit creased?
3. Are the items clean or dirty?
4. Are there any missing items, such as buttons, on any part of the costume?
5. Do the costumes fit well, or are they ill-fitting?

### *Written activity*

**Suggested title**: Work through the script *Copycat,* providing reasons for the different gestures and what the audience learns about the characters' emotions.

To guide them, share this example:

- When character T scratches their head on the line, 'I don't remember that', they are showing the audience that the character is confused and wants to convince the other character that they are telling the truth.

## 3. A good friend?

In this pair scene, character **X** tries to console character **Y**, who has discovered that their trainers have been stolen. The scene is set on a beach on a summer's day. **X** and **Y** have become friends whilst on holiday, and as the scene develops, we find out that **X** has stolen the trainers. The script includes details of where gestures should be used, and it is up to the students to decide exactly what to do. It is advisable to have explored the first two original scripts, *First Day* and *Copycat,* before introducing this scene. Read through the script and begin discussing the movement and gestures students might choose to employ. Given the setting, several sound effects are also included that link to the next design activity.

### A Good Friend?

*Character* **X** *and Character* **Y** *met on holiday.* **X** *is consoling* **Y,** *who has had their trainers stolen. The scene is set on a beach, and sound effects are included.*

*The playwright has indicated where gestures should be used. It is up to you to decide what the gestures might be. You can also include other gestures and movements at different points in the text.*

*(Sounds of a light sea breeze and occasional seagulls can be heard throughout the scene.)*

**X** Are you ok? *(Gesture.)*

**Y** I'm so disappointed and upset. I loved those trainers. *(Gesture.)*

**X** I know. It's terrible. You just can't trust people. *(Gesture.)*

**Y** I only left them for a moment. I turned my back for a few seconds, and they were gone. Are you sure you didn't see anything? *(Gesture.)*

**X** No, I told you. I was looking at something in the other direction. *(Gesture.)* Whoever took them must have been so quick. *(Sound of ice cream van.)* Can I buy you an ice cream?

**Y** No, thanks. I've lost my appetite. I feel so fed up. *(Gesture.)*

**X** I wish I could help you, I really do. *(Gesture.)*

**Y** Sorry, I don't want to ruin your holiday *(Sound of a squawking seagull.)* That seagull sounds like how I feel. *(Sound of a car passing by with cheerful music playing.)* And that music is the opposite of how I feel.

**X** Why don't we go to the funfair? *(Gesture.)* That might take your mind off things.

**Y** Thanks, but I don't feel up to it at the moment. You go, please. *(Gesture.)* I don't expect you to sit around moping with me. I'll catch you later.

**X** I'm not leaving you alone. What sort of friend would do that? *(Gesture.)*

**Y** That's so kind of you. (Gesture.) I feel like I've known you for ages. *(Sound of a boat horn.)* I can't believe we only met a few days ago. *(Gesture.)*

**X** I agree. I'm so pleased that we ended up on holiday in the same place, at the same time. *(Gesture.)* It's been great fun.

*(Sound of the wind picking up.)*

**Y** What makes me so sad and frustrated is that I worked for months so I could buy those trainers. *(Gesture.)*

**X** Really? *(Gesture.)*

**Y** Yes, my family have very little money to spare for such luxuries.

**X** Oh I see, I just thought as you were on holiday here … I mean, it's pretty expensive. *(Gesture.)*

**Y** Oh no, my mum won a competition. *(Sound of dogs barking.)* We could never have afforded to come somewhere like this. *(Gesture.)*

**X** Oh, I see. I didn't know. *(Gesture.)*

**Y** Well, it's not the first thing you share, is it? I feel comfortable telling you now that I've got to know you better and trust you. *(Rumble of thunder.)* Oh, listen, I think there's a storm coming. *(Gesture.)* That's all we need.

**X** I have to tell you something. *(Gesture.)*

**Y** Go on. *(Gesture.)*

**X** You won't like it. It's awful. *(Sound of more thunder.)* And I am so sorry.

**Y** You're making me nervous. *(Gesture.)*

**X** I took your trainers. *(Sound of rain starting.)* And I am so, so sorry. I can't tell you how bad I feel. *(Gesture.)* I feel absolutely terrible. I'm so ashamed.

**Y** Are you joking? *(Sound of children screaming.)* Why on earth would you do that? *(Gesture.)* I don't understand.

**X** Because I was jealous as I wanted a pair like that, but my parents refused, and I just saw them, and I grabbed them, and then it was too late. *(Gesture.)*

**Y** I trusted you. I really liked you. I can't believe you would do this to me. *(Gesture.)*

**X** But I've come clean now. I've owned up. I've said I'm sorry. *(Sound of more thunder.)* I'm trying to be a good friend. *(Gesture.)* You must see that.

## *Design activity*

Given the number of sound effects in *A Good Friend?,* this is an excellent point to introduce students to the role of a sound designer in theatre. In this extract, several sounds have been incorporated to help establish the location and build tension. Explain that a sound designer selects the best sounds and then decides on the intensity at which they are played during the performance. In pairs, students work through the scene, determining whether the sounds should be played at very quiet, quiet, medium, loud or very loud volume levels. They can decide whether to add any other sounds to the script.

# 3

# SPACE – END-ON STAGE

## 'TAKE A BOW'

**Photo-1-3-1** End-on performance.

## Introduction

Students who go on to study drama at exam level need to be able to differentiate between various stage spaces and the challenges actors and designers face when working on them. Students may develop a basic understanding during practical activities, but dedicating more time to exploring this area when they are younger is helpful. In my experience, when I left this to the exam years, the exploration became rather hurried and superficial. We can have high expectations of this age group, and they enjoy examining the different options practically. As many younger students will have experienced the proscenium arch stage, the end-on stage is the focus in the first part of the book.

## Warm-up

### 1. Walk my way

Introduce the idea that performances are presented in different types of spaces, and the audience can be arranged in various ways. Ask for examples of plays students have seen and where they were seated in relation to the performers on the stage. Show students photographs of end-on and proscenium arch performances. Explain that they will be considering the challenges actors face when performing to audiences who are sitting directly in front of them.

Instruct the students to walk around the space. To start with, they can travel in any direction and should get used to moving around one another. Ask them to choose another student in the room to follow secretly. They must not get too close to them when moving and must not reveal who they have selected to follow.

For the next stage, determine which side of the space the audience is seated. With this in mind, students continue walking around their stage space following the same or a different student. This time, they need to be conscious that they have an audience sitting on one side. They can still move in different directions, but they must ensure they are aware of their audience and avoid turning their backs for too long. Split the class into two so that one half watches the other half perform this exercise.

## 2. End-on still images with dialogue

One of the challenges faced by younger actors is delivering dialogue in front of an audience in an end-on setting. Their instinct is to turn towards other performers when speaking, unaware of the impact of this on the audience in front of them. For this exercise, split your class into pairs to create several still images involving two characters. They must think carefully about their positioning, making sure that the audience can see their faces. If you have not covered the individual and group still image work in Chapter Two, stress that they both need to be still, take interesting positions and consider facial expressions. Possible ideas for still images:

1. Two friends who are gossiping.
2. Two friends disagreeing over what food to order at the takeaway.
3. Two friends examining an intriguing picture in a magazine.
4. Two friends playing a board game. (This is a particularly interesting one to stage, as students' first instinct is usually to face one another.)

Watch some of the work and point out good technique. Students can then select one of the scenes and develop it into a duologue, maintaining awareness of the need to connect with the audience.

## 3. Where am I?

Share Table 1-3-1 to introduce students to the terminology used for positioning actors on the end-on stage.

Position your students at the end of the room as the audience. Walk around the performance space and pause in different areas. Ask students to use the correct terminology to name the stage area you are in.

Assign each student a number from one to four. Task them to walk around the stage space in different directions, remaining aware of where their audience is seated. At a given point, instruct them to freeze and then join together with other students who have the same number in different areas of the space. Example of a set of commands:

1. Walk around the space, use different directions and remember where your audience is positioned.
2. Freeze until I tell you to move.

**Table 1-3-1**. End-on stage positions.

| | BACK OF STAGE | |
|---|---|---|
| UPSTAGE RIGHT<br>USR | UPSTAGE CENTRE<br>USC | UPSTAGE LEFT<br>USL |
| STAGE RIGHT<br>SR | STAGE CENTRE<br>SC | STAGE LEFT<br>SL |
| DOWNSTAGE RIGHT<br>DSR | DOWNSTAGE CENTRE<br>DSC | DOWNSTAGE LEFT<br>DSL |
| | **AUDIENCE** | |

3. When I tell you, the number ones move downstage centre, the number twos move upstage right, the number threes move stage left and the number fours move stage right.
4. Now, all move.

Once all members of the group have moved to the correct area, they should form an engaging still image. Remind them to think carefully about where their audience is positioned. Repeat the activity as many times as you want until you are confident that students understand the terminology.

## 4. What's my motivation?

Once students have familiarized themselves with the different areas of the stage, it is important to spend time considering what motivates an actor to move from one position on the stage to another, and how they move. Explain to your students that actors are not moved around like pieces on a chessboard and must have interesting reasons for moving around the stage. Start by asking them to walk around the space, avoiding one another and using all areas. Continue the activity by exploring different reasons for walking, such as:

1. Going to an important meeting.
2. Looking for something they have lost.
3. Training for a marathon walk.
4. Trying to avoid another person.
5. Rushing to catch a bus.
6. Looking for a clue during a treasure hunt.
7. Trying to avoid the sun and stay in the shade.
8. Taking a very strong dog out for a walk.

Follow up by asking for volunteers to move from one side of the space to the other with a specific purpose and motivation. Ask the other students to explain what they think is happening.

# Original script

## 1. Mini monologues

For this exercise, students explore short monologues. You can project a single monologue on a screen for all students to work on, give them copies of the five to choose their favourite, or distribute a different one to each student. Clarify where the audience will be seated, and ensure that students understand the abbreviated stage directions. They must follow these stage directions to be in the correct positions, but also consider why their character is moving from one area to another. Once the students have had about five minutes to rehearse, watch some of the work with the class sitting as an end-on audience.

### The clown

*This character plays the clown in class and often gets into trouble. When performing this monologue, follow the stage directions.*

**Clown** *(start USC)* I get into real bother all the time. I fool around and play the clown. *(Move to SC.)* My mum says she was the class clown when she was young, but she still gets angry when teachers complain about me. She says she wants better for me. *(Move to DSR.)* I don't plan to mess about. I usually do it because I don't understand the work. *(Move to DSL.)* If I start playing the clown and getting others to laugh with me, the teacher doesn't notice that I haven't done much work. It's easier than struggling with what I don't understand. *(Move to SC.)* I don't like getting into trouble, but I'm a little bit stuck now and don't know how to change things.

### The finalist

*This character is playing in their first final tomorrow. When performing this monologue, follow the stage directions.*

**Finalist** *(start USL)* I can't wait. It's tomorrow. *(Move to DSC.)* My big day. My first final playing in the top team. I have worked so hard this year to secure my place. There are so many brilliant players, so many I thought were better than me. *(Move to SC.)* However, I've trained really hard and I've been successful. I've had a bit of luck here and there, and I have scored some fantastic goals. *(Move to SL.)* I have been player of the match four times, and I've been injury-free. *(Move to DSR.)* Tomorrow is the final, and if we win it, we will lift the championship trophy. I can't tell you how excited I am. I can't wait.

### My first flight

*This passenger is recounting their experience of being on a plane for the first time as they prepare for take-off. When performing this monologue, follow the stage directions.*

**Passenger** *(start USR)* It was my very first flight. I was sitting by the window as we trundled along to the runway. I had listened carefully to the safety brief and was trying to remember how to tie my life jacket if I ever needed it. *(Move to SC.)* We seemed to spend ages bumping along, and I wondered how this massive monster of a plane was ever going to get off the ground. Then we turned and stopped. *(Move to DSC.)* There was a tremendous roar, and I felt like I was being pushed back in my seat. *(Move to DSR.)* We started moving faster and faster and faster and faster, and I couldn't believe we were ever going to take off into the air. *(Move to DSL.)* Suddenly, the nose went up, and I watched the buildings and the fields get smaller and smaller below me. I was flying.

### The puppy

*This new owner has just collected their first, very naughty puppy. When performing this monologue, follow the stage directions.*

**New owner** *(start USL)* Look at her. How cute is she? Our first-ever puppy. *(Move to SC.)* She has the loveliest little face, the brightest eyes and the softest fur. My puppy is the sweetest living creature on this planet. *(Move to DSR.)* Hold on, what does she have in her mouth? What is she chewing? Oh no, she has one of my EarPods! How did she get that? She's chewing it! She's going to ruin it. I'm trying to take it out of her mouth, but … arrrrrrhhhhh … her teeth are like little needles, and she won't let go of my fingers. *(Move to SL.)* That hurt. Now she is chasing around the room like a crazy thing. *(Move to SR.)* She's running and running and knocking over everything in her path. She's totally mad; she looks like she's laughing at us all. Now she's biting my brother's ankles. *(Move to SC.)* He's screaming in pain. He probably deserves it! *(Move USL.)* I think I'll get out of the room when I have a chance. (*Exits.*)

### It wasn't me

*Something has gone wrong, and* **Tally** *is explaining that they are not to blame. You can decide what it is the character is saying they didn't do and whether they are telling the truth. When performing this monologue, follow the stage directions.*

**Tally** *(start DSR)* No, I didn't do anything. It wasn't me. *(Move to SC.)* I promise you. I am telling the truth. I would never do anything like that, I really wouldn't. You have to believe me. *(Move to SL.)* Look, I wasn't even there; I don't think I have ever been there; I don't know what they're talking about. *(Move to SR.)* I know I got into a bit of bother in the past, but I wouldn't do anything like this. I don't want to be in trouble; it's very unpleasant being in the wrong. *(Move to USC.)* It's much nicer to do the right thing and not feel like you're going to get told off all the time. You do believe me, don't you? *(Move DSC.)* Please tell me you do.

### *Written activity*

Ask students to write a monologue of a similar length to those they have been practically working on, including clear stage directions. They can choose from one of the titles below:

1. I saw it happen.
2. A broken promise.
3. I want to be captain.

## 2. The treasure hunt

In this scene, two characters **J** and **K** are planning a treasure hunt for a birthday party. They are not very experienced and disagree on the arrangements. Read through the script with the students, clarifying where the audience will be seated.

### The Treasure Hunt

*Characters* **J** *and* **K** *are organizing their first treasure hunt for a party. They are not really enjoying the task and lack some confidence. When performing this scene, follow the stage directions carefully.*

*(At the start of the scene* **J** *and* **K** *are both standing SC.)*

**J** We could put the first clue over there. *(Pointing DSR.)*

**K** Where?

**J** Here. *(Moving DSR.)*

**K** We can't put a clue here. *(Follows DSR.)*

**J** Why?

**K** Because they have obviously planted some new flowers here. We can't have children trampling all over them. That will be a disaster.

**J** Ok, so what do you suggest?

**K** What about over here? *(Moving USR.)*

**J** You are joking. *(Following USR.)*

**K** No, I don't think we have time to joke. We need to get this sorted. The party starts soon.

**J** It's so muddy. We can't have all these children hunting about in the mud. They'll all be in their party clothes and will get absolutely filthy. Our names will then be mud!

**K** Ok. Fair point, I'll give you that. So, where should we start?

**J** What about over there? On that pretty bush. *(Moving DSL.)*

**K** That could work. *(Following DSL.)*

**J** Thank you. So, let's put the first clue here, in the middle of these flowers.

**K** Agreed. That's a good plan. Only another nineteen to go! So where next?

**J** What about going back in that direction, along that path over there? *(Pointing USR.)*

**K** You mean back to where they're planning on setting up the BBQ?

**J** Yes, somewhere around there.

**K** Don't you think the children might smell the food and decide that's more interesting than this treasure hunt?

**J** Ok, then, clever-clogs, you suggest somewhere better.

**K** I was thinking over here, near this garden swing. We could pin the clue on the bottom of the seat. *(Moving USC.)*

**J** Ok, yes, that's not a bad idea. *(Following USC.)* Rather good actually! You're getting better at this.

**K** Ok, so where next? Your turn to come up with the next spot.

**J** What about over here? *(Moving SR.)*

**K** You mean on the side of the tree? *(Following SR.)*

**J** Yes, we could pin the next clue there.

**K** Isn't a tree a bit obvious?

**J** We are in a garden, in the countryside. We can't avoid trees.

**K** Ok, there's no need to be sarcastic. It will have to do then, but not too high, as most of them are still very small.

**J** Agreed. Right, it's about time we moved to a different area of the grounds.

**K** Let's go that way beyond that bench over there. *(Pointing SL.)*

**J** Lead the way.
*(Both exit SL.)*

### *Design activity*

You can use *Treasure Hunt* to start exploring how to design a set for an end-on stage. Students choose the items of scenery they need to bring this scene to life, considering the best positioning for their audience. The set items should include:

1. Tree(s) and bushes.
2. A swing.
3. Flower beds.
4. Grass and mud areas.
5. Bench.

They can also select any props the actors might carry, such as the treasure hunt clues, a hammer and pins, and clipboards.

Using large sheets of paper to record their ideas, students plan their stage set and present their ideas to the class.

# Published script

## 1. *Dear England* by James Graham

This excerpt is from Act One, Scene Four of the 2023 edition of James Graham's *Dear England,* which was first performed at the National Theatre's Olivier Theatre. In his attempt to build a more cohesive and supportive football team, Gareth Southgate opens up about his missed penalty in the 1996 European Championship against Germany. In the original staging, the actor Joseph Fiennes delivered the speech from a downstage centre position to the audience members as if they were the players. It is a lovely, accessible extract for students to rehearse for a performance on an end-on stage.

Read the excerpt through, explaining how Joseph Fiennes used the stage space in the original performance. Discuss how they might use the different areas to perform on an end-on stage. They should also consider how to use tone of voice and volume to evoke sympathy from the audience for Gareth. Students can work individually or in pairs, helping one another.

### Context for students

This excerpt is from a play which explores the fortunes of the England football team under the management of **Gareth Southgate**. In this extract, he discusses how he felt when he missed a crucial penalty for England against Germany back in 1996, which knocked them out of the championship.

## Gareth

It was our biggest game in, like, thirty years. We were hosting the tournament, and everyone in the country was so - happy. There were parties, people were smiling …

We were against Germany. Of course. After extra time, it was 1–1, which meant … penalties.

All the other players before me, they all scored theirs, the first five. And Germany theirs. So it was sudden death. The first player to miss – their team was out. And there was a silence, in our huddle, 'Who's gonna go next'? Eyes of all England upon us. So I just – put my hand up.

And so I began that walk …

But all I was thinking about was what might go *wrong*. What if I tripped, scuffed the ball. My legs were so weak. The whistle went. My head, full of the fog of negativity, and other voices … I ran up, kicked the ball softly, like – hah, so so soft. And the keeper rolled gently towards it.

And I just wanted to disappear. I can't tell you … I knew I was responsible for ending millions of people's dream.

No one knew what to say to me, in the changing room, and I didn't want them to say anything anyway, I couldn't bear it.

I remember the pictures on TV of people *fighting*, smashing up city centres, rioting against police, in Trafalgar Square. Because of me …

The next day I avoided everybody – people who loved me. I couldn't look at them. And I wasn't offered any help. Mental health wasn't really … you know, back then.

It was a really, a very bad time. It just was. It nearly stopped me from saying yes to this job. Is the truth. Because I'm afraid of hurting people again, and hurting myself.

But I'm here. I haven't let those fears stop me doing what I love. So. There.

### *Written activity*

This is a good extract for students to discuss how and why they used the stage space.

**Suggested title**: Give four examples of how you moved around the space, where you were positioned and your reasons why.

To guide them, share this example:

- On the line 'And so I began that walk … ' I moved from centre stage to downstage centre. I wanted to show that I was walking to the spot where I would take the penalty kick. I wanted to be close to the audience to perform this very important moment.

## 2. *The Shy Manifesto* by Michael Ross

This play first opened at the Live Theatre in Newcastle in 2019 before touring throughout the UK. It is a coming-of-age play for one actor, presenting the experiences of a teenage boy (or a girl), and their attempts to defend their shy personality. The piece has some interesting messages for students of this age and is another excellent piece to practise performing on an end-on stage.

Discuss the excerpt with your students, making sure they understand the slightly heightened expression. You can decide whether students work individually or in pairs.

### Context for students

*The Shy Manifesto* presents the life of a young teenager who is proud of being shy. In this extract, **Callum** recounts an experience with his drama teacher, **Miss Cherry**, who was determined to cure him of his shyness by making him perform in a school production. **Callum** turns out to be quite good at acting, but when he observes **Miss Cherry**, he realizes that it is not good for a person to try to be something they are not, and he turns his back on the production.

**Callum** directs the speech to the audience. Work out how to stage this excerpt on the end-on stage, ensuring that you have clear reasons for moving around the space.



### Callum

Another such person determined to 'bring me out of my shell' was my Year 9 drama teacher – Miss Cherry. Miss Cherry was an altogether kinder, more compassionate figure than dreadful Libby, but she was equally misguided. She had somehow got it into her disordered mind that I had the makings in me of a fine actor – that an inner Laurence Olivier was just waiting for the right cue to burst onto the spotlit centre stage and dazzle the world. To this end she cast me in the school production without even asking me, let alone auditioning me. She merely took me aside after a drama lesson and told me the momentous news as if somehow expecting me to be delighted. Suffice to say, I wasn't too happy about this at all. The play was about a gaggle of convicts turning up on the golden beaches of Australia and mounting a production. My character was the well-meaning prison officer who hatches this hare-brained and inevitably doomed scheme to introduce high culture to

Australians. All through rehearsals I struggled with the artificial nature of acting, although the funny thing was I was actually quite good. Well, I mean to say I certainly wasn't awful. I could say my lines with a degree of confidence and feeling which surprised everyone in rehearsals. Miss Cherry rubbed her hands with glee, telling me how all the greatest actors were shy people, that she was once 'painfully shy' herself as a child but Dr Theatre cured her of her illness and was sure to do the same for me if I only succumbed to its treatment. Of course I had only to look at the supposedly cured patient to see the ineffectiveness of the medicine. Her personality was as mismatched as her bizarre multicoloured wardrobe. A collection of mannered tics that didn't quite cohere, a costume that didn't convince. I looked at her and saw the train wreck that occurs when a shy person tries so very hard to be the exact opposite of who they really are, and I was determined to avoid the same catastrophe.

So on opening night, as I entered onto the stage for my first line – I stared out at the audience and I suddenly froze, unable to speak. I had seen a ghost! Miss Cherry; the ghost of my un-shy future. I turned around and walked off stage, and legged it home.

# 4
# APPLYING SKILLS EXPLORED IN CHAPTERS ONE TO THREE
## 'SHOWTIME'

**Photo 1-4-1** Student applying skills.

## Introduction

In this chapter, students start to integrate what they have explored in the first three chapters by combining volume, tone of voice and gesture in performances on the end-on stage. The chapter consists of two improvisation tasks for students to work on in pairs, and three excerpts from published texts.

## Opening and ending a performance

Before embarking on these activities, this is an ideal time to explore ways to open and end a drama performance. Over the years, I have seen many student performances which start and finish weakly. Ending a piece of practical work often poses particular challenges with the cry of 'that's it' breaking the magic. Teach your students to appreciate that performers must always be confident in how their work starts and finishes.

## Opening a performance

When opening a performance, ask the students to consider:

1. Are all the performers onstage at the start? Are some performers onstage, while others are offstage? Are all performers offstage?
2. If performers are onstage, what are they doing at the start of the piece? Could the performance open with an interesting still image or a sequence of mime?
3. If performers are offstage, how do they move when they enter? What are they doing?
4. Who speaks first? What do they say? How do they say it?

## Exercises to explore the first moments of a performance

1. Ask the students to imagine that two performers are offstage, and the performance opens with an empty space. One performer enters from stage left. They are looking for something and appear very nervous. After about fifteen seconds, the other performer enters from stage right. They are feeling angry and confused. In pairs, students rehearse this opening. Watch some examples with accompanying music.
2. In groups of three or four, students create a still image that depicts a family having breakfast together. Confirm that holding a still image for about five slow counts is an interesting way to open a scene.
3. Students continue focusing on the family breakfast scenario and produce a short section of mime to be accompanied by music, presenting the characters in this setting.
4. Using the same scenario (or another), students face the audience and deliver one line of dialogue each, which expresses something about the way their character is feeling in that moment.

### *Design activity*

This is a convenient point to introduce students to elements of stage lighting. Discuss how house lights are used to guide audience members to their seats when they enter a theatre space. These fade as the stage lights come up, marking the beginning of the performance. Explain that the lighting designer collaborates with the director to select the colours and intensity of the lighting, creating a specific sense of time, place and atmosphere. Focusing on one of the opening moment exercises, students consider three questions:

1. How long does it take for the stage lights to come up at the beginning of the scene? Explain that it could be immediate, or the light could gradually increase over a few seconds. Discuss how the different alternatives might impact the audience.
2. What colours are used in the opening moment? In Part Two, various types of lanterns are explored in more detail. At this stage, introduce the LED lantern and gels as two ways of creating colour. Explain that the use of colour is usually subtle and mixed with white light to help create a mood. Introduce the following guidelines for creating atmosphere through colour:
   - All white light: cold, hard.
   - Some blue: cold atmosphere.
   - Some pink: warm atmosphere.

- Some light yellow/straw: warm atmosphere.
- Some orange: very warm.

3. How bright are the lights? A high intensity suggests daytime and helps promote a more positive, optimistic mood; a low intensity suggests nighttime and helps create a more tense and moody atmosphere.

### Ending a performance

When ending a performance, ask the students to consider:

1. Are all or some characters in the performance space? What are they doing? Could a still image or mime be used to end the performance?
2. Do the characters exit from the stage space at the end of the piece? How do they do this? What are they doing as they exit?

### Exercises to explore the final moments of a performance

1. In groups of three or four, students create a still image that could serve as the final moment of a pantomime of their choice.
2. In pairs, students imagine that they have just performed a scene between two friends who are saying goodbye to one another. They should work on the final exits from the stage, establishing that this is a difficult parting. They must retain the emotional energy as they leave the stage space. Add music to enhance their performances.

# Improvisation

## 1. The purgo robot improvisation

This improvisation features two people who live together (either friends or family members), contemplating whether to invite a robot called Purgo into their home to assist with cleaning, cooking and other tasks. The characters have opposing views, so start by dividing your students into pairs to decide who wants the robot and who is against the idea.

Students begin by improvising Scene One, which features the conversation between the two characters as they debate whether to book the robot. They should consider how to present their point of view and win the argument. At the end of the scene, the audience should learn that a decision has been reached to hire the robot.

Scene Two is set a month after Purgo arrived, and attitudes have now changed. The character who originally wanted Purgo now wants them dismissed; the character who was initially against Purgo now wants them to stay. Students should improvise this scene, deciding how it concludes. They must consider the following:

1. Each scene must start and finish with a still image which includes strong gestures showing how both characters are feeling.
2. In both scenes, they must ensure that they use varying tones of voice and volumes to convey each character's perspective.

3. They must ensure that their characters use gestures clearly and effectively in both scenes. They need to be able to describe the gestures they are using if asked.
4. The scene is to be performed on an end-on stage. They must consider the various sections of the stage they are using, ensuring they cover all nine sections during the two scenes. Remind them that they need to have reasons for moving from one part of the stage to another.

Watch and evaluate the performance work using the next written task to help structure your discussions.

### *Written activity*

'The purgo robot improvisation' serves as an excellent exercise to guide students to write about a combination of different elements in their performance work. At this stage, it is wise to structure the writing very carefully. Over the next two years, you will start preparing them to connect their discussion of different acting skills in more sophisticated ways.

Based on this exercise, set a longer written task in three parts that expands upon some of the activities students have already completed.

**Suggested title**: Evaluate how you used voice, gesture and stage space when playing your role in 'The Purgo Robot Improvisation'. Discuss what you hoped to show your audience.

The three stages are:

1. Students give examples of how they used tone of voice and volume in both scenes. They should provide reasons for their decisions and explain what they wanted to convey to the audience.
2. Students give examples of how they used gestures in both scenes. They should provide reasons for their decisions and explain what they wanted to convey to the audience.
3. Students give examples of where they were positioned in both scenes. They should provide reasons for their decisions and why they chose the different positions on the stage.

Depending on your group, you can choose to focus on one performance area or address all of them. Decide how many examples you would like your students to give in each stage of the piece of writing.

## 2. The case of the missing person

This is an exciting improvisation activity which enables students to apply many of the skills they have explored throughout the three preceding chapters. It is also designed to introduce students to the concept of teacher-in-role.

### Resources

You will need five large envelopes containing various items that belonged to a missing person. Overall, it does not matter what you include, but there should be a few items that help establish a narrative for what might have happened to the missing person. These items are as follows:

1. A letter signed by a character saying, 'I need my money back now'. (As teacher-in-role, you will be playing this character.)

2. Another note or card which includes the words 'this can't go on any longer' and is signed with a different name or initials.
3. An advert for a luxury holiday.
4. Adverts for designer clothes.
5. A book with an inscription inside saying 'We leave at 3 pm. Be ready'.

Other items could include coins, foreign notes, photos, newspaper clippings, theatre/cinema tickets, old sunglasses, takeaway leaflets, pamphlets, keys, birthday cards, invitations, old receipts, bits of jewellery, shopping lists and other notes. In short, include any old items which students can attempt to connect and build their stories around.

It is always helpful to have your own sense of what has happened to the missing person, particularly when you take on the role of one of the characters. You may find that students take the story in different directions, and you may wish to remain flexible, encouraging them to be creative. In my version of the events, I imagine that the missing person has run away to a luxurious, remote island with another friend to avoid settling their debts.

Start by introducing the scenario of a young person who has gone missing. It is your decision whether to choose a male or female and to name them. The students assume the role of detectives who have been employed to work in groups to solve the case. Begin outlining what has happened:

> On (date) at 10:15 am, (name of missing person) entered the car park of a large supermarket and parked their car. They were seen on CCTV entering the supermarket at 10:18 am. Upon further review of the footage, they were never seen again; however, the supermarket became very busy, which means they could have easily been obscured in the crowds as they exited. The next day, the supermarket manager notified the police that the car was still in the car park. When the police attempted to trace the car owner, they discovered that (name of missing person) had disappeared. The police searched the car and found several items. These have been organised into five separate packages. As members of a special squad of detectives, you have all been called in to examine the five packages one by one, to piece together what actually happened.

Divide your class into five groups. Spread the packages around the room and allocate one group to each package. Allow students to have about five minutes analysing each one. At the end of the allotted time, instruct them to return all items to the envelopes and rotate each group to their next package in the space. Once they have studied all of them, reconvene to share the initial theories.

For the next stage, inform the students that you will be taking on the role of the character who sent the letter requesting the return of their money. Explain that when you remove your jacket, add an item of clothing, or put on or take off glasses, you will no longer be their teacher but will instead be playing this different character. As the special detectives, they can ask you anything about the case. Stress that they will need to raise their hands to ask a question, and you will endeavour to answer all questions in turn.

Try to build a character who is complex and appears both suspicious and trustworthy, dishonest and honest. At the end of this activity, allow students time to draw together their theories and share their ideas again.

At this point, students work in their groups to create a polished improvisation based on the case. It should be in the style of a live television crime programme where they are seeking help from the public about the missing person. It should contain the following scenes/items:

1. An introduction to be given by one or more members of the group, presenting the main details of the case. Remind the students to think carefully about choosing appropriate tones of voice, volume and gestures to play these characters.
2. Four group still images which bring to life photos they should imagine they have been given of the missing person with family members and friends. They must work out what could be happening in these photos, the backgrounds of the different characters and what the still images reveal about the missing person. They must think carefully about using interesting gestures and constructing effective still images for an end-on audience.
3. Two conversations which have been recorded on CCTV two days before the disappearance, showing:
   - The missing person in conversation with the character who wants their money returned.
   - The missing person and another unknown acquaintance, in which the missing person asks to borrow money.

   In both scenes, students should pay close attention to the tone and volume of their voices and the use of gestures.
4. A concluding scene that includes an appeal to the public for any further information.

Stress to the students that all of the scenes must be performed to an audience sitting in an end-on configuration.

Watch and discuss the scenes, paying particular attention to whether they have applied the skills explored in Chapters One to Three.

Students usually want to know what happened to the missing person, and they enjoy hearing a conclusion at the end of all the activities. You might like to consider playing the role of the missing person to reveal what happened.

# Published script

## The director

Before commencing work on staging the published script excerpts, this is an interesting time to introduce the role of a director in theatre. In my experience, this early focus places a useful emphasis on different ways of creating theatre and structuring effective rehearsals. Students who go on to study the subject at exam level will be expected to consider how to stage extracts of texts from the director's perspective. The subject is further referenced at this point in Chapter Four in Parts Two and Three.

Start by asking students to discuss what might be listed on the job description for a theatre director. They usually base their responses on their experiences of performing in school productions. Share ideas and ask them to consider why the role of theatre director is significant. This list is not exhaustive, but might include:

1. To develop a clear understanding of the material to be staged.
2. To consider exits and entrances for actors.
3. To organize the actors in the stage space.
4. To help actors develop ways to speak and move.
5. To consider how the audience might respond to the performance.
6. To create a rehearsal schedule and make sure work is completed on time.

Explain that the job title of 'director' has not always existed. However, throughout history, there have always been individuals who organize, plan and oversee rehearsals, probably fulfilling many of the duties listed on their job descriptions. To illustrate, you could start by introducing the following areas of theatre history (suggested reading is included at the end of the book, if you want to explore any areas in more detail):

1. **Greek theatre:** examining how playwrights assumed responsibility for the rehearsals and sometimes even performed themselves.
2. **Medieval theatre:** focusing on how the clergy took charge of organizing religious plays.
3. **David Garrick**: exploring his dominance as an actor, playwright, theatre-manager and producer in the eighteenth century.

Confirm that they will be exploring different ways and styles of directing in the future. At this stage, they need to consider their job descriptions and fulfil their aims and intentions during rehearsals of the published excerpts.

You might decide to give students the experience of directing one another when exploring the two published excerpts. At this age, it is helpful to assign particular areas for individuals to take directorial responsibility for, such as:

- Tone of voice.
- Volume.
- Gesture.
- Movement around the space.
- Openings and endings.

## 1. *Alice* – Laura Wade

This is another extract from Act One of Laura Wade's adaptation of Lewis Carroll's *Alice in Wonderland*. First performed in 2010, it offers a contemporary twist on the original story. In Wade's version, Alice is a young Goth who is mourning the loss of her brother. This extract marks the first time she escapes her reality by meeting up with the White Rabbit, who, in this version, is wearing a white motorbike helmet.

Begin by reading the excerpt through with students, and then divide them into pairs for the activity. Discuss how they might use voice and gesture to play Alice and convey the craziness of the White Rabbit. Remind them to consider how and why they move around the stage space.

## Context for students

In this adaptation of the classic story *Alice in Wonderland,* **Alice** is a modern-day goth struggling to come to terms with the recent loss of her brother. As she attempts to deal with her demanding family and other guests at the funeral, like the original Alice, she escapes her reality into a new fantastical world. The first character she meets is the wonderful, mad **White Rabbit**, who, in this version, is dressed in a motorcycle helmet.



*After a moment, ALICE looks around her, finally realising the house has gone, that she's alone in a blank space, with no idea where she is.*

*A pair of long white ears appears through the seat of the armchair, followed shortly by a white motorbike helmet, (which the ears are growing out of), and underneath that, wearing the helmet, a man all dressed in white.*

*He sees ALICE.*

WHITE RABBIT: Right. Excellent. Here you are. All ready?

*The WHITE RABBIT climbs out of the chair.*

ALICE: What?

WHITE RABBIT: Good, I should go. Got your helmet?

*He looks down, realising he's got his jacket on back to front.*

Oh look at me.

*He clumsily takes it off and puts it back on the right way round during the next (without noticing that it's also inside-out).*

ALICE: Helmet?

WHITE RABBIT: Didn't they tell you?

ALICE: What, who?

WHITE RABBIT: Have you got any kind of hard hat with you?

ALICE: A hat?

WHITE RABBIT: Have you ever played that game where

everything you say has to be a question?

ALICE: Game?

WHITE RABBIT: Yup, yes, very good.

ALICE: I wasn't playing a –

That's still inside out.

WHITE RABBIT: Oh. Dear.

*He takes his jacket off again and turns it outside-out before putting it back on.*

So you haven't got a hard hat?

ALICE: No, um –

WHITE RABBIT: I'm sure you'll be fine, just look out for the cabbages. Pretty lethal if you don't see them coming.

Right, good, I must go.

*The WHITE RABBIT goes back towards the armchair, in a hurry.*

ALICE: Where are you going?

WHITE RABBIT: I've got to, um –

ALICE: You can't go, what am I supposed to –

WHITE RABBIT: You want me to stay here?

ALICE: I mean – I mean – what's going on? What is this?

WHITE RABBIT: Right right yeah yeah.

Yeah, I'm not really *supposed* to –

It'll get explained to you once you're inside.

ALICE: Once I'm inside what? I don't want to go inside anything.

WHITE RABBIT: I think actually, it's not really, um. Optional.

ALICE: What?

WHITE RABBIT: Don't shoot the messenger, OK? It's pretty – Difficult to explain.

ALICE: Sorry. Sorry.

Where's my family? Where's all our things?

WHITE RABBIT: Where they always were. Mostly.

ALICE: Are you being deliberately –

WHITE RABBIT: There's things I can't tell you yet.

ALICE: Why?

WHITE RABBIT: Because you've sort of got to work them out for yourself?

ALICE: OK. Well. I prefer having the answer and then working back from it, I'm that sort of –

*The WHITE RABBIT looks at his watch, trying to be surreptitious, but ALICE sees.*

Sorry, am I keeping you?

WHITE RABBIT: What?

ALICE: Tell me what's going on.

WHITE RABBIT: OK.

OK. You've gone into a kind of hole. A kind of –

It's called a rabbit hole. Hence the, um *(He points to his ears.)*

ALICE: What am I here for?

WHITE RABBIT: There's something you need to go through before you can go back.

ALICE: What if I don't want to 'go through' something?

WHITE RABBIT: You don't really have a choice. The longer you fight it, the longer you'll stay, actually. I'm told.

ALICE: Stay here. In this room?

WHITE RABBIT: Yup.

ALICE: With you?

WHITE RABBIT: Not so much.

ALICE: But I can't just –

You know my parents are going to be really cross if I've gone off somewhere, they'll be really cross at you.

WHITE RABBIT: I think they've got other things on their minds, haven't they?

*ALICE turns away from him. The WHITE RABBIT looks at his watch.*

ALICE: *(In a small voice.)* So what do I have to do?

WHITE RABBIT: Good question. Um.

*He tries to remember.*

Hang on – I wrote it down somewhere.

*He starts to go through his pockets. He pulls out various scraps of paper.*

Something about 'you've got to' – oh what was it?

*He looks at a piece of paper.*

Here we go – no that's a receipt for some beans –

Oh, what was it? I did say it shouldn't be my job to –

ALICE: I really quite need to know.

WHITE RABBIT: Yeah I know I know. Something about a *heart* – like, um, anyone who had a *heart*, or – total eclipse of the heart, or –

ALICE: Heart attack?

WHITE RABBIT: That's it! 'You've got to go right to the heart'.

ALICE: What does that mean?

WHITE RABBIT: You know, I'd love to stay here chatting but I've really got to get. On.

### *Written activity*

This excerpt presents valuable opportunities for students to evaluate the work of another student. At this stage, they should continue to consider each performance element individually. A similar three-stage structure to the one at the end of 'the purgo robot improvisation' is proposed:

**Suggested title**: Evaluate how a performer used voice, gesture and stage space when playing their role in *Alice*. Discuss what they communicated to the audience.

Use these three stages:

1. Students provide examples of how another student used tone of voice and volume when playing their character from *Alice*. They should explain what the impact was on the audience.
2. Students provide examples of how another student used gestures when playing their character from *Alice*. They should explain what the impact was on the audience.
3. Students provide examples of where another performer was positioned in their performance of *Alice*. They should provide reasons for their stage positions and examples of how they moved between them.

Based on your group, decide whether you want to focus on one of these performance areas or all of them. Determine the number of examples you would like your students to provide at each stage.

## 2. *The Tempest* by William Shakespeare

Start by reading Caliban's speech carefully to ensure that students understand Shakespeare's use of imagery. They should consider how they might convey both the beast-like exterior of Caliban and a more gentle and sensitive side. Discuss some of the ways they might employ different tones of voice and volumes, gestures and physicality for a performance on an end-on stage.

For this task, students can work independently or in pairs, directing one another. Alternatively, two or more students can deliver the speech to convey the two different sides of Caliban, drawing on some of the vocal techniques explored in the *Pied Piper: A Hip Hop Family Musical* activity in Chapter One.

### Context for students

*The Tempest* is set on an island controlled by **Prospero**, the former King of Milan. **Prospero** and his daughter **Miranda** were shipwrecked on the island after escaping from **Prospero**'s treacherous brother. **Prospero** has assumed power, and all the other characters are serving him, even though they were on the island before him. **Caliban** was born on the island. He is described as a 'strange beast', and **Prospero** imprisons him, considering him to be dangerous. In this speech, **Caliban** complains about being kept a prisoner. He explains that **Prospero** showed him kindness when he first arrived, and, as a consequence, **Caliban** guided him around the island and taught him how to survive. In this speech, **Caliban** uses some beautiful language to describe the island and express his anger towards **Prospero**.

Extract taken from The Arden Shakespeare edition (third series).

CALIBAN I must eat my dinner.
This island's mine by Sycorax, my mother,
Which thou tak'st from me. When thou cam'st first
Thou strok'st me and made much of me; wouldst give
me
Water with berries in't, and teach me how
To name the bigger light, and how the less
That burn by day and night. And then I loved thee
And showed thee all the qualities o'th' isle:
The fresh springs, brine pits, barren place and fertile.
Cursed be I that did so! All the charms
Of Sycorax – toads, beetles, bats – light on you,
For I am all the subjects that you have,
Which first was mine own king; and here you sty me
In this hard rock, whiles you do keep from me
The rest o'th' island.

## 3. *Protest* by Hannah Lavery

This is an interesting play that was performed at the Edinburgh International Children's Festival in 2023. It explores the lives of three young people who, facing a range of problems, strive to effect change. In this excerpt, they describe a protest they have initiated. Read through the piece discussing how students can apply the skills they have learnt over the year. The extract works for either gender.

### Context for students

In this excerpt, three young people describe a protest advocating for a kinder and more inclusive world. The speeches are directed to the audience.



**Alice** Gran has made us placards. One for each of us. Mine says, 'I am a girl, hear me roar'. I like that, and Hailey and I roar like lions.

*She roars.*

There are loads of kids from our year. Even Rory is here. Jade's nan has the school microphone and Mrs Lomax is helping her set it up. We all laugh when it does this big screech of feedback. Gran goes over to help. I watch them laughing. These three women.

**Chloe** My mum is holding my hand. She squeezes it tight as the park starts to fill up. I can tell she was worried nobody would come. But I have already counted one hundred and it's only 9.30. It will become two hundred by 10. I know it's not anywhere near the whole town but, as Lily says, ten is more than one and two hundred is way more than just me.

My brother comes in just before it starts. He is with his friends. He is waving his rainbow flag and has glitter on his face. He looks so happy. My beautiful boy, Mum whispers, and I look up to see her crying.

She says, it's all good tears. I squeeze her hand. Wave at my brother.

**Jade** My nan is up there at the mic. 'Funny to see her without Granda', I say. Dad says, 'Oh, he's here'. Then Nan begins to speak with this power in her voice. She asks us all to sit. And everyone does. There are loads and loads of folk here. She counts down from ten. And then at zero she says:

'Stand up for the planet, for our town'.

Then Alice's gran continues …

'Stand up for each other, for fairness, for kindness' –

**Alice** – and everyone stands and cheers, some folk are crying and some people are holding hands. Then Mrs Lomax plays her guitar and starts to sing and all the adults join in …

Then it's over.

# PART TWO

# AGES TWELVE TO THIRTEEN

## Introduction to Part Two

### Chapters One to Three can be delivered in any order. Chapter Four should be delivered last

This is a key year for developing students' drama skills and increasing their engagement with the subject. In my experience, I have found that this age group begins to connect more with drama as an academic subject, committing to the possibility of studying it at exam level if it is offered. It can also be the year when many schools reduce the amount of time allocated to the curriculum for teaching drama. Reflecting on my teaching experience, I was surprised to calculate that this age group faced a 50 per cent reduction in teaching time in 75 per cent of the schools where I worked. It is essential to maintain momentum by providing an exciting and aspirational curriculum that builds on and develops skills already acquired, allowing students to experience a real sense of achievement.

The structure of Part Two mirrors that of Part One. It comprises four chapters that focus on voice, movement and stage space, with a concluding chapter that integrates all the different elements explored in the first three. Chapters One to Three can be delivered in any sequence. Again, each chapter has been given a student-friendly title you may wish to use. The activities within each chapter are designed to be taught in the order they are presented, ensuring development and progression. Each chapter should take roughly six to ten weeks to complete. Similar to Part One, the four chapters include ideas for written tasks and design activities throughout. If you have not taught Part One, it will be beneficial to review the suggestions for organizing students into groups and showing practical work, which are outlined in the Introduction.

## Preparing for the future

This is a key moment to begin considering the future more broadly. I have always found that an engaging and challenging curriculum for younger students leads to a notable increase in the number choosing the subject at exam level. I also believe in the powerful impact of sharing and celebrating the wide range of drama work created by students with parents, guardians and colleagues, as well as highlighting some of the varied opportunities that studying drama offers. During this year or at the beginning of next year, you might consider organizing some of these activities:

1. Drama student showcases for audiences to observe examples of activities studied throughout the year, including, for example:
   - Spontaneous individual still images.
   - Spontaneous group still images using a ten-second countdown.
   - Individual and group mimes performed by the whole group to music.
   - Spontaneous monologues and pair scenes. The audience observes all students performing simultaneously (for about forty-five seconds), before you give as many of them as possible the chance to perform about twenty seconds of their work. Stop and start as necessary, overlap work, and even involve parents in performances if you wish.
   - Snippets of performances of original and published text extracts, allowing as many students as possible the chance to perform a short section.
   - Readings/performances of some of the creative written activities.
   - Presentation of work from the perspective of a set, lighting, costume or sound designer.
   - Short readings from evaluative work.

This event provides students with the opportunity to showcase examples of their practical work and challenges the misconception that drama is solely for those wanting to perform on stage. You will be able to explain how skills gained through teamwork, spontaneity, problem-solving, creating, evaluating and performing transfer to many areas of life and employment, as well as clarify that students also explore the roles of designers, writers and directors in their studies. You can emphasize that designers develop skills that can be applied in various creative arts and technology fields.

2. Drama information events for students and parents. These can be live or online events providing further insight into the opportunities afforded by studying drama and possible employment routes, and could include:
   - Performances of individual and group devised and scripted work by older students.
   - Short presentations on design areas by older students.
   - Short speeches by alumni who have pursued careers in different fields of the creative arts.
   - Short speeches by alumni who draw on their drama skills in other careers.

3. Theatre visits with optional creative and evaluative essay tasks, which could be compiled to create a new school publication.

# An introduction to evaluation

To continue to stretch this age group, the development of evaluative skills is essential. Your ability to ask good questions is at the heart of fostering these skills, and I hope that the skill-based approach allows you to frame effective questions. Avoid open-ended questions about what students liked or disliked, or what they thought worked or didn't work. Instead, be specific about the aspects you want them to evaluate.

## Examples of evaluative questions related to Part Two

1. Give one example of a moment when a performer used fast pace effectively. What did they do to make sure they were successful?
2. Give one suggestion for what you could have done to improve the pace of your work.
3. Give one example of a moment when a group used different levels effectively. What did the different levels tell us about the characters?
4. Give one suggestion of how a performer could have improved their position on the traverse stage. What difference would it make?

## Ensuring that all students are involved in evaluating work

1. Put two or three key questions on the board or screen and ask students to discuss in pairs.
2. Assign specific students the task of evaluating another group's work in detail. Share the areas you would like them to consider before watching the performance.
3. To promote self-evaluation, start by dividing your students into pairs. Give one student in each pair a list of carefully focused questions which you have prepared. The student assumes the role of an award-winning theatre critic interviewing a famous actor. After approximately five minutes, ask the critics to share some of their findings, then switch roles and repeat the exercise.

# 1

# VOICE – PACE

## 'I'M TALKING'

**Photo 2-1-1** Experimenting with pace.

## Introduction

In this first chapter exploring voice, the focus is on how an actor uses pace when creating dialogue and performing text. There is a particular emphasis on how to deliver fast-paced dialogue whilst maintaining control and clarity. At this age, students often create scenes that are lengthy and repetitive; therefore, activities are included to help them develop clear and well-structured scenes. To ensure progression and development, continue working through the activities in order throughout the chapter. However, since the improvisation exercise is challenging, you may want to consider exploring some of the text-based exercises first.

## Games

### 1. Round the circle

This is a simple activity which requires concentration and focus. Students start by standing in a circle. Introduce the idea that they should say their full names one after the other, using a fast pace. Emphasize the importance of stating their name clearly, ensuring that they articulate every syllable distinctly.

The sense of fast pace is not achieved by how quickly an individual speaks, but by how quickly one name follows another. The next person to deliver their name should try to overlap their first syllable with the last syllable of the previous person's name. The aim is to avoid using any pauses between the end of one name and the start of the next. Aim to go all the way around the circle. You will probably find that the delivery of individual names becomes increasingly fast as students attempt to overlap. Stop the activity and remind students of the need to articulate clearly, whilst trying to eliminate all pauses.

## 2. Speak to the rhythm

Establish a four-beat rhythm by:

**Beat one**: Slap both hands gently on the front of the legs.
**Beat two**: Clap hands together.
**Beat three**: Click the right fingers together.
**Beat four**: Click the left fingers together.

If students are unable to make a noise when clicking fingers, they should still perform the action. Start by practising the rhythm. You will find that students often tend to get faster and faster, so work on maintaining the pace you want to establish. Explain that they will go on to introduce their names during the four beats, but are only allowed to speak when they click. It is worth demonstrating the basic principles:

1. For a one-syllable name, hold the sound over the two clicks (beats three and four).
2. For a two-syllable name, syllable one is pronounced on the first click and syllable two on the second click.
3. For a three-syllable name, syllable one is pronounced on the first click, followed quickly by syllable two and syllable three on the second click.
4. Longer names are delivered quickly over the two clicks.

Begin by going around the circle and asking each student to deliver their first name only on the clicks. Once the rhythm has been established, ensure that the four-beat rhythm does not increase in speed. Stress that once the activity commences, they cannot omit a set of beats, and the next person must always speak on the next set of clicks.

To develop the game, students speak more quickly during each set of clicks, stating their own name and passing the turn to another student by including that student's name as well. For example:

Beat one
Beat two
On clicks three and four: **Omari** says- 'Omari to Ashley'.
Beat one
Beat two
On clicks three and four: **Ashley** says- 'Ashley to Laila'.
Beat one
Beat two
On clicks three and four: **Laila** says- 'Laila to Eden'.

This age group can usually cope with this rhythm; however, if you want an easier version, you can split the delivery of the names over two sets of beats. For example:

Beat one
Beat two
On clicks three and four: **Omari** says- 'Omari'.
Beat one
Beat two
On clicks three and four: **Omari** says- 'to Ashley'.
Beat one
Beat two
On clicks three and four: **Ashley** says- 'Ashley'.
Beat one
Beat two
On clicks three and four: **Ashley** says- 'to Laila'.

To ensure that you set the correct rhythm, establish a rule that you always go first. If a student makes a mistake, stop the activity and start again. Avoid turning this into a competition where mistakes lead to elimination, as students who are out can quickly become disengaged. The class will experience a greater sense of achievement when they collaborate to succeed.

## 3. Passing rainstorm

In this activity, you will lead the students through a sound sequence designed to evoke the build-up and passing of a rainstorm. Sit in a circle with your students. Explain that you will start by performing a simple action, such as clapping your hands. After about two seconds, the person on your right will join in with you by copying and performing the action in the same way. Two seconds later, the person on their right will copy and join in, and so on. Stress that they are only allowed to copy the person on their left, and they must not be tempted to copy you (unless they are directly on your right). Once the first action has travelled about a third of the way around the circle, you will initiate a new action, leading to overlapping actions. Remind them that they are only allowed to follow the person to their left (after two seconds) and must ensure they perform the action in the same way and at the same pace. It is worth passing a few actions around the circle before starting to create the whole sequence. The order of actions for the passing rainstorm is:

1. Tap one finger gently and slowly on the other hand.
2. Click fingers on one hand together slowly.
3. Tap two fingers on one hand slightly faster and louder.
4. Clap both hands together at medium volume and pace.
5. Bang hands on knees faster and at medium volume.
6. Clap hands together fast and loud.
7. Bang hands on the floor fast and loud.
8. Clap hands together fast and loud.
9. Bang hands on knees fast with medium volume.
10. Clap both hands together at medium volume and pace.

**Photo 2-1-2** Rainstorm game.

11. Tap two fingers on one hand fast and loud.
12. Click fingers on one hand together slowly.
13. Tap one finger gently and slowly on the hand.
14. Fold arms (again, this should be copied one at a time around the whole circle to complete the sequence).

# Warm-up

## 1. Spontaneous monologues

Start by discussing why a playwright might include a monologue in a play and what it can reveal to an audience. Explain that they are going to create their own monologues by thinking on their feet and being spontaneous.

Ask students to spread out in the space, facing in one direction, to perform three spontaneous monologues to an imaginary audience in front of them. Stress that they are going to be working at the same time and that you are not going to pick on any individuals to perform on their own. They must concentrate and try to block out what others are doing and saying around them. The monologues end when you count down from five, and they must finish by taking an interesting final still image position. All three monologues present characters in significant or exciting situations and should be delivered at a fast pace. It is essential that they do not rush and must ensure that every word is delivered clearly, as they practised in the games they played. The sense of fast pace will be achieved by eliminating any gaps or pauses in their speeches. The monologue instructions are:

1. You are in a game show and have thirty seconds to tell the audience as much about yourself as you can. It can be real or made up.
2. You are the ideal candidate for a job (ask the students to suggest what the job could be). Convince the audience in front of you that the role should be given to you.
3. You have just seen something astonishing (again, discuss what this might be, for example, a UFO, a famous person shopping). Tell the audience all about it.

**Photo 2-1-3** Spontaneous mono work.

After the entire class has simultaneously performed these monologues, you might decide to ask brave volunteers to perform their work individually. Alternatively, you can ask all students to polish one monologue and then share it with a partner. Look for examples that demonstrate the effective use of a controlled, fast pace.

## *Written activity*

Creative task: Working individually or in pairs, students produce the script for one of the spontaneous monologues they have rehearsed. Alternatively, you can give them a choice of new titles. Emphasize that they must write something intended for performance at a fast pace. Students can then spend time rehearsing their own written monologue or that of another student. Suggested new titles:

1. You have entered a competition for designing new trainers and have won.
2. You have just won the 100 metres race, beating a rival who once told you that you were no good at running.

# 2. The birthday party

Give all students a copy of the script or project it onto a screen. Sitting in a circle or another formation where a clear order has been established, all students are responsible for delivering one line of dialogue. Similar to the 'round the circle' game, students must ensure that their line is delivered accurately and that a fast pace is achieved by overlapping the lines. The symbol / is placed in each line of text to indicate to the next person when to begin performing their line. Emphasize that the person speaking must finish their line with confidence, even when the next person starts to speak.

### The Birthday Party

I don't know what we should buy her. She seems to have everything / a person needs.
I have a great idea. I bet nobody else will ever think / of the same thing.
You are such a show-off, and I'm not sure if we should listen / to you at all.
I agree with you. Do you remember what you bought for Jay? That was / a disaster.

Look, I don't think we should start arguing about it. We need to work / together here.
Absolutely, I have some excellent brochures where we might find something / unusual and unique.
I'm not sure about your brochures. Everything is ultra expensive in them, I seem / to remember.
Have we even decided on a budget? I don't remember what we discussed about the / price of the gift.
Seriously, I'd rather not give anything. I've already bought my own present / for her.
Why have you done that? I thought we had all agreed that we could afford something special if we clubbed / together.
There's no point wasting time searching for the perfect gift if we then find out that people have just done / their own thing.
I can't see how we will ever agree, there are too many of us trying / to decide.
Let's not give up now. We need to be positive. I am sure we can / sort this out.
It might be her next birthday by the time we make a decision. I'm all for doing / my own thing.
We seem to be going round and round in circles. I'm not sure what to say.

When the script comes to an end, the next person in the group should restart the extract. Allow students to have as many turns as you feel are necessary to establish the appropriate pace. This exercise serves as a good starting point for further exploration of the various methods playwrights employ to convey overlapping dialogue and a fast pace. There are numerous examples of such dialogue in Caryl Churchill's *Love and Information*, introduced in Part One, Chapter One, providing several accessible and appropriate scenes for this age group to explore.

### *Written activity*

Creative task: Ask students to write a script for two characters who are attempting to tell one another about something they consider to be very important. Both characters are excited about their own story and constantly interrupt each other, cutting one another off. Take some time to discuss ideas for the stories. Students can work independently or in pairs. They should present their work in the same format as *The Birthday Present* script.

# Improvisation

## 1. Getting to the heart of the matter

This exercise is designed to encourage students to consider the overall rhythm and flow of their work while developing an improvisation with a clear structure and effective pacing. Divide your students into pairs and describe this scenario:

Character **A** and character **B** have just completed a half-marathon, raising money for charity. Feeling very proud of themselves, they decided to go into a supermarket on their way home to buy some food, as they were both extremely hungry. They chose a few items before realizing that the supermarket only accepted card payments. Unfortunately, they only had cash. They returned the items to the shelves and left the supermarket. As they walked down the road, **A** noticed that **B** was eating a chocolate bar, which had been stolen from the supermarket. This is where the improvisation starts. Share these character details with the students:

Character **A** is very law-abiding. They are aware that there are cameras everywhere and are worried that the theft has been recorded, and they will both be caught and end up in trouble.

Character **B** is driven by pure hunger. They feel they have completed a good deed by running a half-marathon and raising money for charity. They believe they deserve the chocolate bar and that the supermarket won't notice. Besides, with supermarkets making millions in profit, it really shouldn't matter.

Give the students about eight minutes to improvise this scene. You can spend time reviewing a few examples of their work, but the next stage of the exercise is the most crucial.

Explain that they are now going to reshape their improvisation to get to the heart of the drama and create a piece of work which is clear and structured. They should use their initial improvisation to build a scene with a total of sixteen exchanges. Clarify that each performer will deliver a total of eight exchanges. An exchange could be as simple as one word or as complex as several different sentences combined. The exchanges should vary in length to create a performance with an exciting pace and rhythm. Explain that sixteen one-word exchanges would not enable them to communicate any detail; sixteen long exchanges could become repetitive and lack direction. While they are working, continue to offer guidance to ensure they are using exchanges of different lengths. Watch and evaluate the work.

Repeat the exercise, limiting it to a total of eight exchanges.

## 2. It all goes round and round

These activities are designed to help students explore the overall shape of a drama, specifically focusing on developing scenes with a cyclical structure. Teach the following exercises in order:

1. Divide students into groups of three. Ask them to create an interesting still image depicting three friends on holiday together. They are staying at a resort with supposedly guaranteed sunshine, and it is pouring with rain. They are feeling bored and dissatisfied. Remind them of the elements that constitute a successful still image as discussed in Part One, Chapter Two, including the creation of interesting shapes, the use of different levels, the connection of characters and the consideration of expressive facial expressions. Once the groups have created their still image, explain that this will serve as the starting and ending moments of their scene. They should now improvise the dialogue to be delivered between the two still images. To control the length of the scenes, you can use the 'getting to the heart of the matter' method and limit the total number of exchanges.
2. Divide the students into pairs to build a short scene consisting of ten exchanges (five each). The scene must open and end with the same line – 'I can't believe you did that'. Students create the eight other exchanges, which come in the middle of the scene.
3. For this next exercise, divide the students into pairs to improvise a short piece of dialogue consisting of a total of eight exchanges between characters **A** and **B**. In this exchange, **A** is contending that **B** does not deserve the medal they are wearing. **B** disagrees. Start by discussing who the characters might be, when the scene could be set and what the medal might have been awarded for. Help students develop clear and concise dialogue. Explain to them that this eight-exchange piece of dialogue is to be used as the opening and final moments of a more extended scene. The drama begins with a performance of the short piece of dialogue, followed by a flashback to reveal what actually happened. At the end of the piece, they complete a full circle

and repeat the opening section of eight exchanges. It is up to them to determine the length of the flashback, but remind them to create clear, structured dialogue applying some of the techniques they have explored.

Once the students have completed these three exercises, discuss the potential impact of the cyclical structure on an audience. Chapter Four of this part includes an excerpt from Willy Russell's *Blood Brothers,* which serves as an interesting example of a play with this type of structure.

## 3. Order out of chaos

Divide the class into groups of three or four. For this activity, students spontaneously improvise different scenarios from various viewpoints, which will naturally result in fast-paced, overlapping dialogue. Read a scenario aloud to the entire class, then distribute the role cards to the individuals assigned to specific roles. Alternatively, you can explain the roles to those playing the different parts. Work through all scenarios.

## Scenario one: A Controversial School Announcement

For as long as anyone can remember, chips have always been served on Fridays. An announcement was given out in assembly this morning that chips are now banned. It is breaktime, and some students and staff members are discussing the situation.

## Characters

**Student one:** Since you are not allowed chips at home, having them on Fridays at school is a real treat. You are very annoyed about this sudden decision and want to take action to have chips reinstated on the menu.
**Student two:** You are delighted with this decision. You are part of the healthy eating group at school and have been campaigning for a healthier menu.
**Headteacher:** You have made this decision, and you genuinely believe that you are doing what is best for your students.
**Chef:** You are against this decision. You believe that eating chips occasionally will not hurt young people. You do not like banning foods.

## Scenario two: The Bus

A group of students are queuing for the bus. They all arrived at the bus stop at roughly the same time. When the bus arrives, there is only one place left to travel. They all have to persuade the driver to give them the final spot.

## Characters

**Student one:** You have to get on this bus. You have promised your family that you will get back home early to care for your baby brother. You cannot let your family down.
**Student two:** You have an interview for a part-time job. You need to get on the bus to get home, change, and travel to the interview. You have to get this job.

**Student three:** You are in big trouble with your family and have been grounded. You need to get home on time; otherwise, your punishment will be extended.
**Bus Driver:** You don't care who gets on, but it can only be one person. Your bus is running late, so a decision needs to be made quickly.

## Scenario three: The Penalty

The score is 0–0 in an important football match. In the final minute of extra time, a penalty is given by the referee as a player tripped up an opposing team member in the penalty area.

## Characters

**Referee:** You have awarded the penalty, and you are convinced you are right, as you clearly saw one player trip up the other one.
**Player one:** You are the player who is accused of tripping up another player. You are sure that you didn't do this and are convinced that the other player pretended to fall over.
**Player two:** You are the player who was tripped up. You are convinced the other player tripped you up on purpose.
**Goalkeeper:** You are the goalkeeper who will have to try to save the penalty. You don't think it is fair and are confident that the player fell over on purpose.

Allow the students time to spontaneously rehearse each scenario and then watch examples of their favourite. You will probably find that the work is quite chaotic, making it difficult for the audience to hear all the different views. Discuss how playwrights carefully consider how they structure scenes to convey a sense of fast pace and chaos without losing audibility, coherence and clarity.

In groups, students should take one of these scenarios and work on a polished improvisation. They should aim to incorporate the different points of view through overlapping dialogue to create a sense of chaos. They must ensure that the audience can hear what is happening and does not become confused. It can be helpful for students to order and write out the structure of their scene before they start improvising. You can also suggest that they apply the structured dialogue techniques explored in the 'getting to the heart of the matter' and 'it all goes round and round' improvisation exercises.

Watch and evaluate the work, focusing specifically on constructive ways to improve it, in preparation for the next written activity.

### *Written activity*

The focus of this activity is to reflect on ways to improve the quality of practical work. This involves considering strategies to enhance both rehearsal practices and performance skills. Related to the 'order out of chaos' exercise, discuss how students could improve their work, drawing out some of the following suggestions:

1. Ensure that all group members have a chance to share and discuss ideas.
2. Establish a plan for how the group use the time allocated to a task.
3. Take time to try out an idea rather than just talking about it.
4. Rehearse a scene in sections, consolidating one part before progressing to the next.

5. Ask your teacher or another student to watch your work to ensure that you are achieving your aims.
6. Ensure that you articulate every word when trying to achieve a fast pace.
7. Rehearse the overlapping dialogue sections multiple times to ensure the timing is accurate and precise.
8. When overlapping with another performer's words, ensure that the first words are delivered clearly and are not gabbled.
9. Think about an interesting start and/or finish to the scene.

**Suggested title**: Based on your 'order out of chaos' improvisation, give five suggestions for how you might improve your work.

# Original script

## 1. It wasn't me

In this monologue, **Parker**, age thirteen, attempts to convince a friend that they did not eat the last piece of birthday cake that had been set aside. Students can work independently, considering where the silent character would be positioned on stage. Alternatively, they can work in pairs, taking turns to play **Parker** and the silent character. The monologue must be delivered at a fast pace, maintaining clarity and clear diction.

### It Wasn't Me

*A friend has accused* **Parker** *of stealing and eating the last piece of birthday cake, which was put aside for another guest. In this fast-paced monologue,* **Parker** *tries to convince the friend that they did not eat the cake.*

*When delivering this monologue, use a fast pace while ensuring that all words are clearly articulated for the audience. Determine the stage position of the friend who has made the accusation. You should direct the monologue towards where you decide the friend is positioned. It is up to you to decide whether* **Parker** *is telling the truth.*

**Parker** You think I ate the cake? I didn't eat the cake; I would never eat the cake, as it wasn't mine to eat. I know that, you know that, we all know that. The cake was meant for someone else. Frankly speaking, I'm rather upset that you would think that I would steal and eat the cake you made, so kindly shared with all of us, and which we all really, really loved. So, thank you for making the cake, which, as I said, I did absolutely love, but it was very rich and creamy, which I liked, but I couldn't have eaten another slice, even if I had been offered another slice, as it would have been far too much, even for someone like me who loves cake. Thinking about it, I'm a bit upset that it would even cross your mind that I would steal something because I am not a thief, and I try to respect other people. I am very aware that you, my friend, spent a long time making this cake and slicing it up carefully so we all got a piece and nobody was left out. It actually makes me feel sad, disappointed, grumpy and a little bit angry that you would think so badly of me over a piece of birthday cake.

## 2. The comedians

In this scene, two competing solo comedians, **Lee** and **Tee**, have been asked to explain to a team of judges why they should be selected for the prestigious position of hosting a variety show in a theatre venue. This might be a useful time to find a theatre in your area to study and even visit with your students.

The text is fast-moving with overlapping dialogue. The overlaps are indicated with the symbol /. Start by reading through the dialogue in class, so that students are clear about where the overlaps occur.

## The Comedians

**Lee** *and* **Tee** *are two solo comedians. They are competing for the job of host for a variety show, which is to be recorded for television in a famous theatre. The judges are unable to decide who to give the job to, so* **Lee** *and* **Tee** *have been asked to put forward their cases.*

**Lee** *and* **Tee** *are on stage at the same time, talking out to the judges, who, you should imagine, are sitting directly in front of you.* **Lee** *and* **Tee** *are competing for the job, so the dialogue is fast-paced with many overlaps, which are indicated with the symbol /. Be careful not to speak too quickly, or your words might get lost. Make sure you finish your lines clearly and confidently, even when the other performer overlaps with you.*

**Lee** I'm obviously the right person for the job. I'm much more experienced than Tee. You know you can always rely on me. I have already shown / that I can do it.

**Tee** I think Lee has actually revealed why I'm the one for the job. I'm fresh, new, exciting. Audiences don't want the same thing over and over again. They don't need experience, they / like change.

**Lee** Audiences like what is funny. And let's be honest here. Tee isn't funny / and I am!

**Tee** Let's not get personal, / that's not acceptable!

**Lee** I'm not being personal, / I'm trying to …

**Tee** Oh yes you / are.

**Lee** Oh no I'm / not.

**Tee** Oh yes you are. Saying I am not funny is personal, rude / and unkind.

**Lee** What I mean / is that …

**Tee** I know what you / mean.

**Lee** If I can finish / I think …

**Tee** Go on then. Say what / you think.

**Lee** What I meant and maybe I didn't express it / very well …

**Tee** You certainly / didn't.

**Lee** You have an unusual style. You are creating the image of a grumpy, complaining / comedian.

**Tee** It's my unique / style.

**Lee** Yes, it's your unique style, but it's maybe not a style which is right for a family variety show. I offer something a bit lighter / and upbeat.

**Tee** Silly is what you mean. Old-fashioned, daft / and silly.

**Lee** I'm not silly. I am sunny, enthusiastic / and upbeat.

**Tee** Yes, as I said, you are daft, silly and past your sell-by date. Do you think audiences want to come to the show and see you smirking and giggling / all night long?

**Lee** Smirking and giggling! Well, at least that's better than looking miserable / and moody.

**Tee** I am not / miserable!

**Lee** Tell me a joke!

**Tee** What?

**Lee** Tell me a joke.

**Tee** Why is the moon so grumpy?

**Lee** Go on, why is the moon so grumpy?

**Tee** Because, it's going through one of its phases!

**Lee** See, a miserable, grumpy joke.

**Tee** You tell a joke then.

**Lee** Ok, here we go. Where do polar bears keep their money?

**Tee** I dread to think.

**Lee** (laughing and smiling) In a snowbank!

**Tee** That's so cheesy and out of date. That's precisely what I mean. This role requires someone with a bit more gravitas / than you.

**Lee** Well that certainly isn't you.

**Tee** Oh yes it is!

**Lee** Oh no it isn't!

**Tee** Oh yes it is!

**Lee** Oh no it isn't!

**Tee** Hang on, hang on. One of the judges is saying / something.

**Lee** They have come to a / decision.

**Tee** They have made up / their minds.

**Lee** I can't / wait.

**Tee** It's bound to be me. *(The first long pause as Tee and Lee look towards the judges.)*

**Lee** I don't believe / it.

**Tee** I don't believe / it.

**Lee** They don't want either of us!

**Lee** & **Tee** What are we going to do?

## *Design activity*

*The Comedians* is an entertaining excerpt that can help students develop their understanding of ways of using costumes to enhance a performance. To build on their work from last year, introduce them to the following fabrics and what they might communicate on stage:

1. Velvet might suggest flamboyance, theatricality and wealth.
2. Silk might suggest wealth, lightness and refinement
3. Synthetic materials such as nylon, acrylic and Lycra might suggest fun, relaxation, informality and a contemporary context.
4. Denim might suggest timelessness, a relaxed attitude, a modern context and approachability.
5. Leather/faux leather might suggest boldness and strength.

For this task, students should work in pairs to determine the costumes for **Lee** and **Tee**. They should consider and be prepared to explain their reasoning for:

1. The clothes the two characters wear.
2. The colours of the costumes.
3. Condition of clothes and how the costumes are worn (e.g. neatly or untidily).
4. Fabrics.

## 3. The most important decision in the world

In this group scene, four new party planners have been brought together to arrange a special sixteenth birthday party. They have been given the freedom to choose the theme, venue, entertainment and catering. The text includes many overlaps indicated by the symbol /. Spend time reading and discussing the script so that students get a sense of the pace and challenges of organizing four characters.

### The Most Important Decision in the World

*Four new party planners* **J, K, L** *and* **M** *have been given the task of arranging a sixteenth birthday party. They can spend as much money as they wish, and need to make decisions regarding the party's location, theme, entertainment, food and drink. The scene is set during their first meeting.*

*Consider where you position the characters for the meeting. Note that the symbol / is used to denote when dialogue overlaps. Think carefully about creating a fast pace, ensuring that all the lines are delivered clearly.*

**J** I am really enthusiastic about the concept of taking them all to a theme park. Money is no object, meaning we can hire the whole place, and they will never have to queue / up for anything.

**K** I don't think that will work. Some sixteen-year-olds hate theme parks, and there will be no atmosphere if we ban the public from / attending.

**L** I agree. I'm totally against a theme park. Horrible places! I've been thinking that we could fly them to a Caribbean Island and party there. That's something they will / never forget.

**J** Isn't that a bit too much for a group of / sixteen-year-olds?

**M** I agree, and I also think that all that time spent in an airport and sitting on a plane is just a waste. I was hoping for something a bit more unique and unusual. I suggest they walk up Ben Nevis, the highest mountain in Scotland and the United Kingdom, eat cake up there and then walk down and have a barn dance / in a …

**K** Oh, let me guess, they could have a barn dance in a barn! / How original!

**M** There's no need to be rude. I haven't heard you come up with any ideas of your own. All you do is rubbish others. It's time to share / your brilliant thoughts.

**K** I'm thinking that we could set up an area with ten-pin bowling, ice skating, a few favourite fun fair rides like dodgems, a merry-go-round, / crazy golf.

**J** Surely that's too many different things and none of them are particularly special / or original.

**L** Which is why I came up with the Caribbean / Island idea.

**J** Which we don't like. We have ruled / that out.

**L** Have we? I didn't know it was / ruled out.

**K** Rule it out. It's / dreadful.

**J** What about a disco? / That's fun.

**M** Not exciting enough. What about a band? A well-known / one?

**L** That's a possibility. But, how will we ever choose one that they / all like?

**K** Why don't we hold that thought and consider a theme for a moment? Maybe that will help us get / on track.

**J** Glamorous. That / always works.

**L** No, it's a bit obvious nowadays. How about fancy dress? / That's fun.

**M** Yes, but rather boring. They will have gone to endless fancy dress parties. I was thinking about a colour theme. How about green? / That would work.

**K** Hardly! Most people would turn up hating what they were wearing. We need something that all of them / would enjoy.

**M** Well, go on then. What do / you think?

**K** I was thinking of a broader theme that they could interpret in / different ways.

**L** I thought we were all doing that! / But go on.

**K** I was thinking carnival. That gives them loads / of choice.

**J** I still prefer glamorous, or maybe Hollywood would be a different way of / putting it.

**L** Well, that certainly wouldn't work if we were all stuck up / Ben Nevis.

**M** Why don't we think about food for a moment? Maybe we can all agree / on that.

**J** Fish and / chips.

**K** Italian, pizzas and pasta / dishes

**L** Street food. We could have a variety of / different foods.

**M** I am still keen on the outdoor theme, bangers and mash / style food.

**J** What about drinks?

**K** Mocktails and fancy / drinks.

**L** A bar with everything we can offer, except alcohol / of course.

**M** Hot chocolate, tea, / coffee.

**J** We are not going up Ben / Nevis!

**L** We don't seem to be agreeing on / anything.

**K** That is the first thing anybody has said that I do actually / agree with.

**M** Well, what are we going to do?

**J** We could do something totally new / and radical.

**M** Go / on.

**L** What are you thinking?

**J** We could just ask them what they want!

# Published script

## 1. *Elmina's Kitchen* by Kwame Kwei-Armah

Kwame Kwei-Armah's *Elmina's Kitchen* premiered at the National Theatre's Cottesloe Theatre (now Dorfman) in 2003. It is set in a West Indian restaurant in Hackney, London and explores how the owner, Deli, attempts to protect his son, who is drawn to the culture of crime surrounding him. It is a play for older students to study in more depth, but there are also accessible sections for this age group. In this short speech, Deli answers the phone to take a food order, and a sense of familiarity and routine prevails. Students can work independently or support one another in pairs to deliver the speech using a fast pace, conveying a sense that Deli has spoken these words many times in the past.

### Context for students

This excerpt is from the play *Elmina's Kitchen*, which explores the lives of a group of people who work in a restaurant in East London. In this speech, **Deli**, the restaurant owner, is on the phone taking a call regarding an order. He has probably taken many similar calls, so work on delivering the piece clearly with a fast pace.



**Deli**

Hello! Elmina's Kitchen, takeaway and delivery, how can I help you? … Chicken? We have jerk chicken, curried chicken, fried chicken, brown chicken, stew chicken and our new vibe is sweet and sour chicken. Yeah, West Indian style … Yeah, yeah … Where'd you live, bra? Berringham Road, seen, gonna be forty-five minutes, you alright wid dat? … What's your name? Badder youth? Seen, Badder, that'll be five pounds fifty cash handed over to my delivery boy before he takes the food out of the heated rear box, yeah? Nice.

## 2. *Dance Nation* by Clare Barron

This American play was first performed in New York in 2018, opening a few months later at the Almeida Theatre in London. It explores the lives of a group of thirteen-year-olds taking part in a dance competition. Written to be performed by adults, the play conveys the ruthless nature of the dance world and portrays the insecurities of the teenagers. There are some interesting monologues and group scenes to explore with older students, which could be performed in practical exams. This particular excerpt from the start of Scene Four is the opening exchange between four girls after a dance audition. It is an excellent example of overlapping dialogue and, in this context, the gender of the performers is irrelevant. Clare Barron sets out clearly when characters speak at the same time; the lines are short and the piece is fast-moving.

Begin by reading through the text, checking to ensure that students understand where the lines overlap. Working in groups of five, they should stage the dialogue, ensuring that the pace is fast and the lines are delivered clearly. Watch and evaluate the performances.

### Context for students

This excerpt is from the play *Dance Nation*, which examines the lives of a group of teenagers immersed in the competitive dance world. In this section, they are chatting after an audition.



| | |
|---|---|
| **ASHLEE**<br>If I get a dog, it's gonna be a wolf dog | |
| **CONNIE**<br>A what? | |
| **ASHLEE**<br>A wolf dog | |
| **CONNIE**<br>That's bad for the wolves | **SOFIA**<br>What's a wolf dog? |
| **ASHLEE**<br>No it's not | **AMINA**<br>Half-dog, half-wolf |
| **CONNIE**<br>Ask Maeve. She's really into wolf preservation | |
| **ASHLEE**<br>Maeve | **MAEVE**<br>I'm really into what? |
| **CONNIE**<br>Wolf preservation | |
| **MAEVE**<br>Oh. Yeah | |
| **ASHLEE**<br>I wanna get a wolf dog | |
| **MAEVE**<br>That's bad | |

**CONNIE**
See

**ASHLEE**
Why is that bad? / They're beautiful

**MAEVE**
It's bad for the wolves. They're not pets. / They're wild animals

**SOFIA**
I'm not into wolf preservation. I'm into wolf extinction

**CONNIE**
Okay, you freak

**ASHLEE**
Wait. Are you serious?

**SOFIA**
I'm not really into wolf extinction. I just think they're scary

**ASHLEE**
They're not scary

**MAEVE**
I want to walk to school with wolves

**CONNIE**
No you don't

**MAEVE**
Yes I do! I want to walk to school with the wolves howling / in the mountains

## 3. *Happy To Help* by Michael Ross

This play premiered at the Park Theatre in Finsbury Park, London, in 2016. It is a comedy that presents a group of characters employed at the Frisca supermarket and explores the impact of large retail stores on society. This exchange between the store manager, Vicky, and the young shelf stacker, Josh, offers excellent opportunities for students to practise using a fast pace. Start by reading the text and discussing where and why a fast pace might be appropriate. Students work in pairs to bring the text to life.

### Context for students

In this excerpt, **Vicky**, the store manager of a supermarket called Frisca, requests a meeting with **Josh**, the young shelf-stacker. **Vicky** is challenging and unsympathetic; **Josh** is young and hopeful. The gender of the characters is irrelevant.



**Josh** *enters the office.*

**Josh** Hi, Vicky.

**Vicky** Josh. Good of you to pop by. Want to go and grab yourself a cup of tea or coffee?

**Josh** I'm alright, thanks.

**Vicky** You sure?

**Josh** Yeah, I'm fine, thanks.

**Vicky** OK. Take a pew. So. Josh. Thank you for popping in to see me. I won't keep you long, just wanted to have a little chat. Just a general chit-chat about things, OK?

**Josh** OK.

**Vicky** Josh, can I ask you a personal question?

**Josh** OK.

**Vicky** Are you happy?

**Josh** Am I happy?

**Vicky** Yes. Are you happy?

**Josh** In the job, you mean?

**Vicky** Job, life, home. Are you happy in yourself?

**Josh** More or less.

**Vicky** Is that a yes?

**Josh** Yeah. Yes.

**Vicky** OK. Good.

**Josh** Why?

**Vicky** I just wondered.

**Josh** Do I look sad?

**Vicky** No, you don't look *sad*. It's not that you look *sad*.

**Josh** Good. Because I am happy, Vicky.

**Vicky** Pleased to hear it.

**Josh** (*pointing to the slogan on his name badge*) I'm 'Happy to Help'.

**Vicky** (*pause, cold as ice*) Right. Was that a joke?

**Josh** (*suddenly uneasy*) Erm. Well …

**Vicky** You think it's funny?

**Josh** No, no.

**Vicky** You think this job is a joke?

**Josh** No, I don't, I don't, Vicky.

**Vicky** You think Frisca is one big joke?

**Josh** Not at all.

**Vicky** You think it's a joke that we're in a recession and mums are struggling to put food on the table? You think it's a joke that we're trying to help those mums by rolling back prices throughout our stores? That's the Frisca *mission*. Do you think our mission is funny, Josh?

**Josh** I don't, Vicky, I don't think it's funny.

**Vicky** (*sweetly*) Well I'm glad to hear that, Josh.

**Josh** (*timidly*) Sorry, but what's the problem, Vicky?

**Vicky** (*pointedly*) Who mentioned any problem?

**Josh** Sorry, I don't understand. Have I done something wrong?

**Vicky** Do you think you've done something wrong?

**Josh** (*increasingly paranoid*) I do the job, don't I? I'm here every day. I'm on time.

**Vicky** Yes, you are.

**Josh** I work hard. I think I do a good job.

**Vicky** That's nice.

**Josh** I'm a good shelf-stacker.

**Vicky** You are a good shelf-stacker. You're a very good shelf-stacker.

**Josh** Thank you, Vicky.

**Vicky** One of the best.

**Josh** And I'm good with the customers. I've had high scores from the secret shoppers.

**Vicky** There was that one time –

**Josh** There was one time, but that was my very first day, I was new, I thought she said pasta not pesto, I had no idea what pesto was but I asked another member of staff who did know –

**Vicky** That's good.

**Josh** – which is what we're supposed to do –

**Vicky** It is, yes.

**Josh** – so I think I did everything right in the circumstances –

**Vicky** In that scenario, perhaps.

**Josh** – but I've learnt from my mistakes.

**Vicky** I'm very pleased to hear that.

**Josh** I've never had negative feedback from anyone I've worked with.

**Vicky** That's true.

**Josh** Nobody has any complaints about me.

**Vicky** (*pointedly*) As far as you know.

**Josh** Has someone complained about me?

**Vicky** Don't worry, nobody's complained about you.

**Josh** If anyone's complained about me, I've a right to know about it, haven't I?

**Vicky** Yes, you do.

**Josh** I've never had a disciplinary.

**Vicky** You're in a band, aren't you, Josh?

**Josh** (*thrown by the question*) Yeah.

**Vicky** What are you called?

**Josh** 'Wild Fluctuations in Tone'.

**Vicky** Is that what you want to be when you grow up? A rock star?

**Josh** When I *grow up*? (*Laughs.)* Either that or a train driver.

**Vicky** (*humourlessly*) Is that a yes?

**Josh** I'd like us to be successful, yeah.

**Vicky** So you could just jack in the day job?

**Josh** Well …

**Vicky** So you could abandon us?

**Josh** (*laughs*) *Abandon*? That's a bit –

**Vicky** Just say yes.

## *Written activity*

Creative task: Students write Josh's monologue, imagining that it is performed at the end of this exchange with Vicky.

# 2
# MOVEMENT – LEVELS
## 'HIGHS AND LOWS'

**Photo 2-2-1** Exploring levels.

## Introduction

The exercises in this chapter continue to develop students' awareness and understanding of how to use movement in performance. The focus is on how to employ different levels to create visually exciting, practical work that communicates meaning to an audience. Remind students to draw on the movement focus explored in last year's lessons, and to continue integrating strong gestures into their work. All activities in this chapter should be taught in the order they are presented to ensure the best experience and progress.

## Games

### 1. Jump, sit, clap, touch

This is a version of the game *Stop, Go, Jump, Clap*, in which students walk around the space performing the four actions when instructed. Once the students become familiar with those commands, they move on to perform the opposite action to the command given. Stop means go, go means stop, jump means clap and clap means jump. You might want to use this original version as a starter activity.

When playing this new version, students perform a series of commands issued by you, requiring them to use different levels. Stress that by varying levels used in performance, they will create more visually exciting work for an audience. In this game:

- Jump means jump as high as you can.
- Sit means sit on the floor.
- Clap means clap your hands above your head.
- Touch means touch the floor.

Once the students are familiar with performing these actions, they progress to performing an opposite action to the command given:

- Jump means sit on the floor.
- Sit means jump as high as you can.
- Clap means touch the floor.
- Touch means clap your hands above your head.

## 2. Teacher says to you

This game is a more advanced version of the one introduced in Chapter Two of Part One, based on the childhood game *Simon Says*. As advised, consider replacing 'Simon' with your name or a significant name from the school. With this age group, instruct students to perform a series of physical tasks which require them to use a range of different levels. The students should only perform the instruction if preceded by the command 'teacher says'. Deliver these instructions as quickly as possible. Examples of instructions:

1. Tap the floor.
2. Put both hands in the air.
3. Jump up and down.
4. Curl up into a small ball.
5. Stand as tall as possible.
6. Touch your toes.
7. Sit on the floor.
8. Lie on the floor.
9. Sit on a chair.
10. Stand on a chair.
11. Crawl under a chair.
12. Lie flat on the floor.

You can also connect this game to the 'jump, sit, clap, touch' exercise, asking students to perform an opposite level for every instruction given.

## 3. Low, middle, high

Students individually decide whether to sit on the floor, sit on a chair, stand up or stand on a chair (if appropriate in your drama space) to create still image positions which convey different characters. Stress that there is no correct way to capture these characters, and that you hope and expect they will make different decisions. After each example, ask individual students to explain why they made particular choices. Suggested characters:

1. An airline pilot.
2. A singer.
3. A three-year-old.
4. A teacher.
5. A student.
6. A magician.
7. A traffic warden.
8. A baby.
9. A ninety-year-old.
10. A King or a Queen.
11. A famous scientist.
12. A sportsperson.
13. A politician.
14. An astronaut.

Develop this activity by reading out a list of emotions and feelings. Students now select the most appropriate level to create a still image of a character experiencing that emotion. As an example, explain that the emotion of anger could be expressed on a high level to show that the feeling is powerful. Alternatively, they could choose to use a low level to suggest that anger can sometimes be held inside and is under the surface. Suggested emotions:

1. Anger.
2. Sadness.
3. Happiness.
4. Jealousy.
5. Courage.
6. Weakness.
7. Determination.
8. Amusement.
9. Fear.
10. Suspicion.

# Warm-up

## 1. Find a group

Ask the students to walk around the space, ensuring they spread out, cover all areas, and move in different directions. To challenge them, describe different reasons for moving, such as:

1. Sauntering as if they are reluctant to get to their destination.
2. Running late for an appointment.

3. Feeling lost.
4. Feeling excited about getting somewhere.
5. Feeling scared.

When you call out a number, students should form a group with that many members. (If the group doesn't divide exactly by the given number, they can create groups that are as close to the number as possible.) As soon as the groups are established, students organize themselves using as many levels as possible. Share examples of work where levels have been used creatively and effectively.

## 2. Packing a suitcase

In this activity, students mime packing a large suitcase for a trip. They must aim to use as many different levels as possible. You can ask them to invent their own story about where they are going and what they will be taking, or you can provide a common background. Suggested story:

> You have won a competition and are going on an all-expenses-paid holiday to Spain. As part of the trip, you will spend time in a beach resort where the weather is forecast to be lovely. You will also climb a mountain, where you can expect cooler and possibly wet weather. Think carefully about what you need to pack.

To prompt students to employ a range of different levels, it can be helpful for them to base their mime on their own bedrooms and where items are stored.

Instruct students to take a visually interesting and creative still image starting position. When they begin moving, the mime continues until you count them down to a final still image finishing position. This activity will be enhanced by adding background music.

There are several ways to share this work. You could ask one half of the class to watch the other half. You could watch a small group of three or four individuals perform simultaneously. This particular method enables the class to observe how individual mime sequences naturally combine to form an interesting group piece.

### *Design activity*

This is a good point to continue exploring set design. Working in pairs, students decide on the different pieces of scenery they require to perform the 'packing a suitcase' mime accurately. Explain that there are no restrictions and they can include wardrobes, cupboards, drawers and other items. Once they have planned and shared their ideas, ask them to imagine how this set could be cleared quickly to make way for a new scene set in an entirely different location. Through discussion, cover the following ideas:

1. A well-trained, large stage crew could move the different items off the stage. Explain that this can be quite cumbersome, given the potential size of some of the scenery.
2. Large items such as wardrobes could be on wheels to be manoeuvred off stage quickly by one or two members of the stage crew.

3. Several large items of scenery could be placed on a wheeled platform known as a truck, which can be moved by the stage crew or on an electrical runner. Confirm that this is an efficient way of moving several difficult items offstage quickly.
4. Many students will have seen pantomimes where characters are flown through the air on wires. Explain that flying scenery on and off stage quickly is possible by employing systems which are operated electronically or by using ropes controlled by the stage crew.

Once students have been introduced to the different options, they can work with their partner to determine the methods they would use to clear their set as quickly as possible.

## 3. Mirroring

This exercise requires your students to be completely focused and in control. Divide them into pairs, labelling themselves **A** and **B** to face one another. Explain that **A** is to perform some simple movements slowly, which **B** will mirror. Start by demonstrating the exercise with one of your students. Model simple arm movements such as lifting one arm into the air, moving it to the side, and bringing both hands together. Demonstrate other movements such as turning one's head slowly to the right, then to the left, stepping back slowly, and touching the floor. It is also worth trying out the activity with all the students following your lead. Stress that all movements must be performed very slowly, so that students appear to be in complete unison with one another. Start by asking the **A**s to lead and the **B**s to follow.

Continue by switching the leader. Once students are confident with the exercise, ask them to repeat it. They can decide who starts as leader, but they are now able to change who controls the movement at any point. These changeovers must be seamless and not apparent to anyone watching. If they are doing this correctly, they should almost feel as if they have become one.

For the next stage of the exercise, students continue to work in pairs. This time, the student who is following should attempt to find an opposite action to the leader's movement. For example, suggest that touching the floor would be a good opposite movement to raising an arm in the air. Demonstrate the technique to the students before they attempt the task.

## 4. Parts on the floor

This is an interesting exercise designed to encourage students to create more abstract images and innovative shapes using different levels. Divide the class into groups of four to produce a still image which has a total number of body parts on the floor. If they have been given number ten, for example, their task will be to create a still image with a total of ten body parts on the floor. Guide them through the rules:

1. If a performer lies flat on the floor, that will be equal to one body part.
2. If a performer lies flat on the floor with their knees raised and both feet on the floor, that will equal three body parts.
3. If a performer sits on a chair with two feet on the floor, that equals two parts.
4. If a performer sits on a chair with two feet on the floor and the tip of every finger touching the floor, that will equal twelve parts (two feet and ten fingertips).
5. If a student stands on a chair, that will equal no parts on the floor.

Answer any questions students might have about the rules before they start working. Stress that they should concentrate on creating an interesting shape and should not worry about inventing characters or telling stories. They must include different levels and attempt to make connections between the group members. Assign each group a number between ten and twenty, and confirm that they should create their shape using that number of body parts on the floor. They can achieve this in any way they wish. Watch the work, highlighting any interesting shapes and levels.

## 5. Still images with levels

This exercise builds on the still-image work undertaken in Part One. It is always helpful to remind students of the different elements which combine to make successful individual and group still images:

1. **Balance**: Still images must be held, so it is vital to choose a position which can be controlled.
2. **Shape**: It is essential to consider the shape of the position taken.
3. **Facial expressions**: Characters come to life with interesting facial expressions.
4. **Eyes**: Fix eyes on a particular point in the room.

Whenever you work on still images with any age group, it is helpful to revise the basic rules by practising a quick sequence of individual positions. Examples of more demanding titles for this age group are:

1. You are walking along a street on a very windy day.
2. You are pulling on a very tight pair of shoes.
3. You are stroking a cat.
4. You are tasting some very hot, delicious food.
5. You are reading a notice to hundreds of people.
6. You are at a silent disco.
7. You are tiptoeing up some stairs.
8. You are parachuting out of an aeroplane.

Divide the students into groups of three to five to create several group still images based on different titles. In addition to applying the same rules as when working individually, they should also consider how all group members connect in their images. This might be through a physical connection, such as shaking hands, or through eye contact. Stress that you want them to pay particular attention to how they use different levels. Allow each group access to two chairs, which they can opt to position themselves under, sit on or stand on (if appropriate in your drama space), as well as stand, sit or lie on the floor. Whenever possible, all students should be on a different level in each group image. When introducing a title, you might choose to spend some time discussing the types of characters they could depict and the ways and reasons for using different levels. This age group can be stretched to consider how levels can also convey feelings, emotions and relationships between characters. Give them about two minutes to create each image, followed by a final ten-second countdown to take their frozen position. Identify any areas for further improvement, ensuring that different levels have been used. When the students have explored each title, ask them to pick their favourite one to show to the rest of the group. They should perform in the middle of the circle whilst the other class members walk around and view the still image from all sides. This is an excellent exercise to instil performance discipline and concentration. Suggested titles:

1. A busy restaurant kitchen.
2. Emergency evacuation of an aircraft.
3. A ski resort.
4. A newspaper office working to meet a deadline.
5. A carnival.
6. A courtroom.
7. Backstage at a theatre performance.
8. The gym.

# Improvisation

## 1. The excuse

In pairs, students improvise a scene featuring one character who is making excuses for missing the other character's party. Read out or project this information:

> Character **A** spent many weeks organizing a special party to celebrate the end of the school year and the holiday. Character **A**'s best friend, character **B**, did not turn up for the party and sent no apologies or excuses. This scene is set the day after the party.
>
> Character **A:** You were very excited about the party, having spent a long time organizing it. All your school friends attended except for your best friend**, B,** and you do not know why. Although you enjoyed the party, you still felt sad that your best friend did not share it with you. You are worried about them, as it is very unusual for them not to be in contact with you.
>
> Character **B:** You completely forgot about the party. You spent the evening watching television. You feel very guilty for forgetting, so you have decided to invent another excuse.

Spend time talking to the class about the type of excuses **B** could invent. Explain that two chairs must be used in the improvisation and that the characters must always be on different levels. They must try to vary the levels as much as possible, carefully considering why their characters might change positions. When your students are rehearsing, point out any examples of creative changes of level to the rest of the class.

Watch and evaluate some of the work. Discuss how the use of different levels communicates meaning to the audience.

## 2. The advisor

In pairs, students improvise a scene between two siblings. The older sibling is concerned about the younger sibling and is advising them about their future. Share this information with the students:

**Photo 2-2-2** Exploring levels.

Character **X** is the older brother or sister of character **Y**. **X** is very concerned about **Y**. **X** feels that **Y** is doing poorly in all areas of their life, such as schoolwork, hobbies, and friendships.

Character **Y** is very happy with their life, but they are frustrated that their older sibling, character **X,** always interferes and thinks they know best.

Only one chair can be used in this improvisation, and either character can sit or stand on it (if appropriate in your space). Students can also choose to stand up or sit on the floor. Stress that the two characters must be on different levels at all times, changing as many times as possible in creative and appropriate ways.

Watch and evaluate the work, considering how the levels help convey different meanings and ideas to the audience.

# Original script

## 1. The Moon

In this monologue, the students play the role of **Moon,** a personified character who is portrayed as bored, kind-hearted and considerate. You might like to refer to Shakespeare's personification of the sun and moon in Act Two, Scene Two of *Romeo and Juliet*, and provide students with a brief outline of Lorca's *Blood Wedding*, explaining how he personifies the Moon as a dangerous and cruel character. There is also the chance to explore Ian Wooldridge's stage version of George Orwell's *Animal Farm*.

For this exercise, students can work independently or in pairs to stage all or part of the monologue. They require a chair to realize the different levels specified in the text. (You will find some references to standing on the chair; change this to standing on the floor if this is not appropriate in your space.) Read through the monologue with students and discuss what the different levels might communicate to an audience. Students can also stage the monologue, making their own decisions regarding their use of levels. You might decide to add some background music to enhance the atmosphere.

### The Moon

**Moon** *is a young , impatient, kind and considerate character. It is a cloudy night, and* **Moon** *is feeling bored.* **Moon** *is speaking to the audience.*

*For this performance, you have one chair. Follow the stage directions to ensure that you use the different levels in the performance to help convey how* **Moon** *is feeling.*

**Moon** *(sitting on the floor)* Oh, it is such a tedious night. There is absolutely nothing for me to do. Why are there so many clouds below me? I can't see anything, and I am totally redundant. Come on, wind, where are you hiding? Blow the clouds away to reveal the little people below me. They need me. *(Standing up.)* Just a minute, I think I felt a slight breeze. Was there a momentary gap in the clouds? Did I see a glimmer of light below me? *(Sit on the chair.)* No, I must have been mistaken. There's nothing. Just clouds and more clouds and perpetual darkness. Those poor humans down there are forced to struggle in the pitch dark without me. They are all alone, and I'm stuck up here, trapped with this wall below me. There's nothing I can do. *(Stands up.)* Sun always tells me to be patient, but it's different for Sun. Sun can burn the clouds away. I don't have the powers to do anything like that. *(Stands on chair.)* Oh, but look, something is changing. Gaps are appearing, and I can see below. Yes, I can spy the land and sea and all the human beings scuttling about. They are so happy to see me. I can keep them safe and help them find their way. I am up here! I am shining bright! I will look after you. I will take care of you. I will reveal the way. *(Standing on the floor.)* You down there, watch out. You almost didn't notice that bike heading towards you … Thank goodness I am here to protect you. Take care of yourselves, little people, and know that I am up here, always in your service, your very own moon. *(Sit on the chair.)*

## *Design activity*

This speech presents a lovely opportunity to explore how lighting can enhance a performance. In Part One, students started considering the colour and intensity of lights. For this activity, introduce them to a range of different lanterns:

1. **Fresnel**: This is a very versatile light, as the beam can be adapted to cover different areas. The edge of the light is soft, so it is easy to use several fresnels to cover a larger stage space. Alternatively, you can focus a single fresnel on one performer to create a spotlight effect with a very soft edge.
2. **Spotlight**: This is a powerful light which creates a spot with a hard edge. It is effective for highlighting one performer.
3. **Birdies**: These are very small, compact lanterns which can be used to create a general wash of light on a stage. Because they are small, they can be positioned on the edge of the stage. If directed from a low level at a performer, shadows are created behind them, which can be very effective.

Working individually or in pairs, students make and justify the following lighting decisions for a performance of *The Moon:*

1. The types of lanterns to be used.
2. Any colours.
3. The intensity of the light.

If you have added music to the performance of *The Moon,* this is also a good time to introduce students to the idea of sound coming from different directions. Explain that most theatres have several speakers so that all audience members can experience the sound surrounding them. The speakers can be turned on and off at different times, creating the impression that the sound is coming from various directions. In this context, if background music and sounds are played from different speakers, it might help create the illusion that the moon is moving around the sky.

### *Written activity*

For this written task, ask the students to discuss their performance of Moon's Speech, giving reasons for the changes in physical levels.

**Suggested title**: Give five examples of how you used levels to play Moon and what this conveyed about Moon's character.

To guide them, share this example:

- When playing Moon, I sat on the floor at the start of the speech to show the audience that Moon was feeling bored, frustrated and tired because I was not able to see the world below me because of the clouds.

## 2. Two into three won't go

This scene is for three performers and explores what happens when three friends arrive at their holiday accommodation. It is a sequential scene set in real time. Three chairs are needed for the performance, and levels are indicated throughout the script. This is a good point to introduce some of Stanislavski's theories to your students. Start by reading the script through and discussing the potential impact of the different levels on the audience. At the end of the reading, work through the Stanislavskian-inspired activities before students bring the script to life.

#### Two Into Three Won't Go

Character **D,** character **E** *and* character **F** *are friends who have gone on a holiday together to Greece. They have just arrived at their accommodation and have been shown to their three rooms. Two rooms are large and have views of the sea. The other room is very small and has a view of the car park.*

*The scene is set in the corridor outside the bedrooms. There are three chairs. Follow the directions which indicate how the chairs are used and when the characters stand and sit. Notes about characters:*

Character **D:** *You have known* **E** *for a long time and consider them your best friend. You get on well with* **F,** *but they can be bossy. You haven't been abroad before.*

Character **E:** *You have known* **D** *for a long time and get on well, although they can be a bit clingy. You haven't known* **F** *for so long, but feel you have a lot in common. You want to impress* **F**. *You have been to Greece before.*

Character **F:** *You get on well with* **E** *and feel they could become your best friend. You only know* **D** *because they are friends with* **E**. *You like* **D,** *but you don't think that you have much in common with them. You have been abroad several times.*
*(At the start of the scene, all three characters are standing.)*

**E** I'm not sure how we sort these bedrooms out. I thought they were all supposed to be exactly the same.

**D** *(sitting down on chair)* You organised the holiday, so you should probably take one of the nicer rooms.

**F** Yes, absolutely. Obviously, you should have the best room. I wouldn't be here if it weren't for you.

**E** Well, that's kind of you, but that doesn't resolve who should get the other room.

**D** We could take turns. Spend half the week in one room and then switch. That would be the fairest way.

**F** That never works. It's always such a nuisance moving everything around. I've tried that before. It just doesn't work.

**E** *(sitting next to* **D***)* Would you mind taking the smaller room?

**D** Really?

**E** I didn't think you would be particularly bothered. We'll only be sleeping in our rooms at night. I'm sure we will be out and about exploring most of the time.

**D** *(standing up)* To be honest, I'm not sure why any of us should have to agree to the tiny room. We were told that we would all have a room with a view of the sea. Perhaps we should speak to a member of staff again.

**F** *(sitting down)* I don't think there is any point in a further confrontation. They made it quite clear that they only have these rooms left. And remember, they have offered us a complimentary drink to make up for it.

**D** *(sitting down)* How does one complimentary drink make up for it? I honestly think I will get claustrophobic stuck in there all week.

**E** (*standing up*) Look, there's no point moaning. I don't think they have another room. They would have given it to us if they had one.

**D** *(standing up*) But how can a complimentary drink fully compensate for looking out onto a car park when a sea view was promised? You enjoy your drinks from your luxury rooms, with beautiful views. I'm sorry to moan, but I'm so disappointed.

**E** I'm amazed that you are so upset about it.

**D** I have never been away before.

**F** *(standing up)* Honestly? You have never been on holiday before?

**D** Well, I've been away, but this is the first time I have ever been abroad.

**F** Seriously?

**D** Yes.

**E** *(sitting down)* Look, I'll take the smaller room.

**F** (*sitting down)* That's not fair! You planned the whole trip.

**E** I've been to Greece before. It's fine.

**F** Well, I've been abroad loads of times, so I think I should take the smaller room.

**E** No, you can't do that.

**F** Why can't I?

**E** Well, I don't want you to. Is that a good enough reason?

**F** That's so kind of you. But you should have the best room.

**E** I insist. This is our first holiday together, so I want you to have a lovely room and a wonderful experience.

**F** That's so sweet of you.

**E** *(standing next to* **D)** So, you can have the other sea-view room. Happy?

**D** I don't want to take it off you.

**E** Well, I can't see another way around it.

**D** Well, there is one other way.

**E** Look, I don't want to discuss it anymore.

**F** *(standing up)* We could just toss a coin.

**D** What?

**E** That's an interesting idea. That seems a fair way. Leave it to chance.

**F** Or we could choose straws?

**E** Yes, either way would work.

**D** *(sitting down)* Look, I'll take the smaller room. It doesn't matter.

**E** (*sitting down)* Are you sure?

**D** Yes, it's fine. I'm sure we will spend most of our time swimming in the sea anyhow. It won't matter that I can't see it from my room.

**E** Thank you.

**D** It's fine.

**F** I prefer a swimming pool myself, actually.

**D** I'm surprised.

**F** I'm not a big fan of the sea.

**D** Except to admire it from your gorgeous room!

**F** I just don't like swimming in it.

**E** *(standing up)* Yes, I know what you mean.

**D** I thought you loved the sea?

**E** I like it, yes, but swimming in a pool can be more relaxing somehow.

**F** Yes, that's what I think. No terrifying sea creatures to worry about.

**E** Oh I know. In a pool, you can swim around without a care in the world.

**D** *(standing up)* You have always said that swimming in the sea is a beautiful experience.

**E** I can't recall ever saying that.

**F** It doesn't sound like something you would say.

**D** Ok, well … should we go for something to eat or explore a little?

**F** *(sitting down)* I'm exhausted, actually. I'd like to unpack and take a quick nap.

**E** *(sitting down)* Yes, I agree, that sounds like a good idea.

**D** *(sitting down)* Well, I'll hang around on my own then until you have both recovered.

# Exercises based on the theories of Stanislavski to use before staging *Two Into Three Won't Go*

Before embarking on these exercises, make sure you have read and discussed the scene. Divide the students into groups of three and allocate them their character roles **D**, **E** or **F**.

## Character development- profiles

Ask students to fill in a character profile. You can either prepare a document or provide them with various headings and ask them to create their own version. Suggested areas to consider:

- Name.
- Age.
- Family background.
- Friendship groups.
- Hobbies.
- Favourite TV programme.
- Favourite Food.
- Education.
- Holiday experiences.
- Ambition.
- Happiest experience in life so far.
- Motto.
- Type of clothes you would wear for a special occasion.

## Character development- hot seating

This is an extension of the profile exercise. To demonstrate, take on the role of another character linked to the scene, such as the manager of the hotel who has to deal with the request for an alternative room. The students pose questions about your character's background, hobbies, interests, ambitions, and so on. Always stay in role to answer, showing that questions cannot be avoided when on the hot seat. Stress that by thinking quickly, they will build background and detail about their character, which they can change and adapt later if they do not feel they have made the right choices. Volunteers can answer questions posed by the rest of the class before dividing the group into pairs to hot seat one another. Students can switch partners several times.

## Magic if

Introduce the concept of Magic if, explaining that Stanislavski asked his actors to think about what they might do if they found themselves in particular situations. Working in their groups of three, students now take on the roles of **D**, **E** and **F**. Either allocate them a set of situation cards or read out each scenario separately. Speaking from their characters' point of view, students discuss how they would respond if they found themselves in these situations:

1. You are walking along the road and you see a £10 note on the ground. Ahead of you is an old lady who seems to be looking for something, but you can't be sure. What do you do?
2. You have accepted an invitation to a party and are not feeling well. It's a cold night, and there is something fantastic on television. You know that if you don't go, a meal prepared for you will go to waste. What do you do?
3. Your neighbours are having a party on a Tuesday evening. It is very noisy, and you haven't been invited. You have an important commitment tomorrow. What do you do?
4. Your friend gives you a present. You open it and find that it is something special you bought for them last year. What do you do?

## Emotional memory

This is always a challenging area to introduce to students, as it can trigger reactions. To work with this age group, keep the exercise very focused. Start by explaining that Stanislavski asked his actors to draw on their own lives, experiences and emotions when playing a character. As a simple example, explain that if an actor were playing an angry character, Stanislavski would want them to recall and draw on a time they felt angry in their own lives. He believed they could harness this emotion to play their part more believably and convincingly on stage. Relate this exercise to the script and highlight that the three friends are disappointed when they arrive at their hotel, as they have been allocated a smaller room with no sea view. In their groups of three, students discuss times when something has not lived up to expectations and has disappointed them. Share some of the examples.

Once you have worked your way through the exercises, students can now work on staging the script. After watching the performances, discuss whether they found that any of the exercises helped them improve their work.

You can also ask students to restage the script, making their own decisions about the use of chairs and different levels.

# 3
# SPACE – TRAVERSE
## 'CATWALK'

**Photo 2-3-1** Performing on a traverse.

## Introduction

Having introduced students to end-on staging and stage positioning in Part One, Chapter One, I always enjoy studying the traverse stage with this age group. Students typically find this particular space exciting to work in and enjoy activities that allow them to explore it in challenging and creative ways. Two original scripts and three published excerpts offer a variety of opportunities for them to experiment with performing to an audience on two sides.

## Warm-up

### 1. Catwalk spots

Start by dividing the class into two groups and seating them on either side of the performance space, facing one another. As you move around the space, explain that they will be exploring a new type of stage called a traverse, where actors perform in the middle of two banks of audience members. Discuss the ways models at fashion shows move on the traverse (catwalk), ensuring that all audience members have a good view of the clothes being presented. As you speak to your students, ask them to consider what it feels like to be sitting in this formation, observing you as you walk around the space. Try to draw out some of the following points:

1. It is exciting to be in a different formation.
2. At times, audience members find that they are very close to the performers.
3. The proximity between audience members and performers changes.
4. At times, the backs of performers can be turned towards the audience. (It is worth emphasizing that audiences can cope with seeing performers' backs turned during a performance.)
5. You get to see things from different angles.
6. It can be interesting/distracting to face a bank of audience on the other side.

Select three students from each side of the audience (six in total) to spread out in the performance space. Ask them to walk around the space, maintaining an equal distance apart and being aware that audience members are watching them from two sides. When they become familiar with moving in the space, instruct them to create either an individual still image or perform a mime depicting a character in different situations. They must remember that they have audience members on both sides and consider how to position themselves to connect with as many individuals as possible. They should also experiment with applying the most appropriate facial expressions when performing. After each still image or mime, students switch positions to experience working in different areas. Suggested characters for still images:

1. You are late for an appointment and want the bus to stop for you.
2. You are a juggler in your first circus performance.
3. You are playing a musical instrument of your choice in an audition.
4. You are taking a very strong, almost out-of-control dog out for a walk.
5. You have been told to clean your teeth and don't want to!

Suggested miming topics:

1. You are vacuuming your friend's expensive carpet after dropping a bag of flour on it.
2. You are laying a table for an important banquet.

Ask the audience to give examples of what they think worked effectively in the space. Choose another six students to attempt the same exercise. Alternative still image characters:

1. You are watching a scary film with someone you want to impress. You are trying not to show you are terrified.
2. You are on an outside tightrope when the wind picks up.
3. You are conducting an orchestra and really want to scratch your head.
4. You are crossing the winning line of a marathon, in the pouring rain.
5. You are styling your hair, and it just won't do what you want.
6. You are tossing a pancake, and it gets stuck on the ceiling.
7. You are about to attempt your first dive off the top board of a swimming pool.
8. You are driving a racing car in an important race.

Alternative miming topics:

1. You are walking through freezing water.
2. You are painting a high wall.

3. You are cutting someone's hair in a salon.
4. You are putting the cover on a king-sized duvet.

Repeat this exercise until every student has had the opportunity to work in the space. Draw attention to any particularly effective techniques which enable all audience members to connect with the performance.

Ask for individual volunteers to attempt a spontaneous monologue performance with the audience on both sides. Highlight any good practice. All students should then find a space on the traverse stage to perform one of the monologues simultaneously. Suggested topics:

1. Tell the audience about a favourite holiday (real or imaginary).
2. Tell the audience how to play a game of your choice.
3. Tell the audience about a favourite hobby (real or imaginary).
4. Tell the audience how to make a cup of tea.
5. Tell the audience what you did at the weekend (real or imaginary).
6. Tell the audience how to get from the room you are working in to another space.

## 2. Catwalk still images

Divide the class into groups of two to four to create group still images to be performed on the traverse stage. If you have already completed Chapter Two, students will have gained experience in creating group still images. If not, confirm that they must apply all the rules they learnt last year when working on still images (strong facial expressions, good balance and shape, fixed eye contact, different levels and connections). They must carefully consider where to position their still image and how it will work for an audience seated on both sides of the performance area. Suggested titles:

1. A school exam.
2. A beach resort, as it suddenly starts to rain.
3. A passenger flight during turbulence.
4. A celebrity trying to go unnoticed in a shopping centre.
5. A lion escaping on a packed day at the zoo.

Each group presents their still image. Evaluate how effectively they work for the audience.

# Original script

## 1. It can't be

For this exercise, students work in pairs to stage the text. They must follow the instructions on where to position themselves in the traverse space. For the final part of the scene, they take responsibility for determining how to use the space. Before reading the text, introduce the students to Table 2-3-1, which outlines how the stage has been divided and labelled.

Once the students are familiar with the stage labelling, read the text through as a class. When exploring end-on staging in Part One, students were encouraged to consider why they transitioned from one area to another. One of the biggest challenges when moving around the traverse stage is to make

**Table 2-3-1** Traverse stage positions.

| | | | | |
|---|---|---|---|---|
| | | **ONE HALF OF THE AUDIENCE** | | |
| A | D | G | J | M |
| B | E | H | K | N |
| C | F | I | L | O |
| | | **OTHER HALF OF THE AUDIENCE** | | |

sure that movement doesn't become too mechanical. Remind students that they must consider why their character might move from one part of the stage to another.

## It Can't Be

**Sam** *and* **Taylor** *have not seen each other since they were seven years old, when* **Sam** *moved to a new town. They had promised to stay in touch, and* **Taylor** *sent several letters and cards for four years, but never received a reply. They are now fourteen years old, and* **Sam** *has suddenly returned to the area, joining* **Taylor's** *school. By chance,* **Taylor** *has been asked to be* **Sam's** *buddy to help them settle in. At first, they don't recognize one another.*

*When performing this scene, follow the directions, which indicate which part of the stage you should be positioned in. You always face each other when talking.*

*At the start of the scene,* **Taylor** *is at position B;* **Sam** *is at N. In the script, you are told when you move to a different part of the stage. It is up to you to decide how quickly or slowly you do this. Consider why and how you move, and try to make it look as natural as possible. For the final part of the script, you decide where and why you move.*

**Taylor** Hello, welcome. *(Move to H.)* I've been chosen to show you around. Sam, isn't it?

**Sam** *(move to K)* Yes, that's right. It's really good to meet you. What's your name?

**Taylor** *(move to I)* Tee.

**Sam** That's quite an unusual name.

**Taylor** *(move to H)* I guess so. It's not my full name. I shorten it nowadays.

**Sam** *(move to L)* So what's your full name then?

**Taylor** I don't use my full name anymore.

**Sam** Oh go on, tell me. I've always wanted to have a more unusual name.

**Taylor** It's Taylor.

**Sam** *(move to G)* You're kidding me! Taylor? I once had a best friend called Taylor.

**Taylor** *(move to L)* Seriously? When was this?

**Sam** Up until I was about seven.

**Taylor** *(move to N)* Really! And where was this?

**Sam** *(move to H)* This town. I used to live here, and we moved away. My dad was promoted. We've come back again.

**Taylor** *(move to K)* Well, I once had a best friend called Sam.

**Sam** You did?

**Taylor** I did.

**Sam** *(move to A)* I can't believe it. This is unreal.

**Taylor** *(move to G)* I hardly recognise you.

**Sam** I hardly recognise *you*.

**Taylor** *(move to E)* This is like something that happens on television, and we would laugh and say it could never happen in real life.

**Sam** It's good to see you.

**Taylor** Yes.

**Sam** Is that all you have to say?

**Taylor** *(move to O)* You never wrote back.

**Sam** What?

**Taylor** I said, you never wrote back.

**Sam** *(move to E)* I never received any letters.

**Taylor** *(move to M)* I wrote to you for four years. I sent cards, letters, and even some gifts.

**Sam** I didn't get anything.

**Taylor** *(move to J)* Honestly?

**Sam** *(move to I)* Yes, I promise. I was heartbroken. I remember waiting every day, waiting and waiting.

**Taylor** *(move to A)* You could have written to me. You must have known my address.

**Sam** *(move to N)* I remember you said that you would write first. I asked my mum and dad if I could get in touch, but I think they felt that, as we hadn't heard from you, your parents must have decided it was best for you to get to know other children and move on with life. My parents told me to make new friends and forget the past.

**Taylor** *(move to E)* No, my parents would never have wanted me to lose touch with you. They knew you were my best friend. I was distraught.

**Sam** When did you stop writing?

**Taylor** I was eleven, it was when I started this school.

**Sam** *(move to K)* Oh wow. You wrote for years.

**Taylor** I never forgot you.

**Sam** I never forgot you. I wonder what happened to all your letters?

**Taylor** *(move to H)* Who knows? It's a mystery. Maybe I had the wrong address. I'm glad you're well, and it's good you're back here.

**Sam** *(move to G)* I expect you have a new best mate now?

**Taylor** *(move to I)* I have lots of friends, but I am not sure if I have one best friend.

**Sam** Same as me.

**Taylor** Really?

*(For the final part of the scene, you now decide where you should be positioned on the traverse stage, and why you move.)*

**Sam** Yes, my family have moved around so much. I never seem to fit in properly.

**Taylor** Do you want to do something together after school? I can show you how the town has changed.

**Sam** I'm not sure if I will be allowed.

**Taylor** Why?

**Sam** My parents were terribly angry with you when you didn't write.

**Taylor** But I did write.

**Sam** Yes, but I'm not sure if they'll believe you. I know what they can be like.

**Taylor** Well, I know my parents will accept that you didn't reply because you didn't get my letters. I don't see why this has to be a problem.

**Sam** I was so upset.

**Taylor** So was I.

**Sam** I stopped talking for a few weeks.

**Taylor** That's awful. But this isn't a competition.

**Sam** I know. What a mess.

**Taylor** Can't we both explain calmly to our parents what happened?

**Sam** I'm not sure it will work.

**Taylor** We can try.

**Sam** I don't know.

**Taylor** So we're going to leave it then? We're going to give up on our friendship again?

**Sam** I don't know what to do.

**Taylor** You do believe me, don't you?

**Sam** What?

**Taylor** You do believe I wrote, don't you?

**Sam** Yes, I think so.

### *Written activity*

For this task, students explain and justify their decisions regarding the use of different areas of the stage space in the latter part of the script.

**Suggested title**: Give four examples of where and why you moved around the stage in the second half of the script. Provide reasons for your decisions and explain what you intended to convey to the audience.

To guide them, share this example:

- On the line 'I'm not sure if I will be allowed', I quickly moved to point M on the traverse stage. I wanted to move as far away from Taylor as possible to show that I didn't completely trust them, and I needed space to think about the situation.

## 2. Spud is innocent

In this monologue, a defence lawyer tries to persuade a jury that Spud the puppy is innocent of all charges. Students can work individually or in pairs, directing the speech to an imaginary jury on both sides of the traverse. They should consider how they use the different sections of the stage space.

### Spud is Innocent

*You are playing the role of the* **Lawyer** *who is defending Spud the puppy in court. Spud has been accused of being disorderly and breaching the peace. Imagine that the jury is seated on either side of the traverse stage. Consider how and why you move around the different areas of the performance space to address them.*

**Lawyer** Members of the jury, I urge you to think very, very carefully. Here before you is poor, innocent Spud. A puppy who has done nothing wrong, except to be a puppy. You have heard testimony from spoiled adults who were, quite simply, too lazy to care for and exercise little Spud. They should be standing before you, facing charges of negligence and lack of responsibility. Spud admits that he pulled the stuffing out of all the cushions, chewed up the shoes, scratched the paintwork, smashed the valuable lamp, stole the sausages, howled all night, and nibbled the adults' toes; however, this is not his fault, and he indeed has not committed a crime. Spud is just a puppy, and puppies need exercise. Can he be blamed for having energy? Can he be blamed for being excitable? The only answer is no! Members of the jury, I urge you to do the only thing possible and throw this ridiculous case out of court and find poor Spud not guilty.

# Published script

## 1. *The Comedy of Errors*- William Shakespeare

This is a fun and accessible excerpt from Act One, Scene Two of Shakespeare's *The Comedy of Errors.* It is the first exchange between Antipholus of Syracuse and Dromio of Ephesus in the play. The characters are talking at cross purposes, and it opens up exciting opportunities for movement around the traverse stage. Start by discussing the context of the extract, then read it through to ensure students understand the mix-up. Divide the class into pairs to stage the scene using the different sections of the traverse stage explored in earlier exercises. Given the references to physical reprimands, it is essential to state that there should be no actual physical contact. Work through these comedy movement exercises before students start staging the text:

1. **Slow motion argument**: In pairs, students work on a slow motion sequence, imagining that they are throwing mud pies at one another. They must not make contact, and all the actions should be performed with slow, sustained dynamics as if they are moving through sticky mud.
2. **Chasing**: In a circle, one student chases another. The size of the circle should remain constant, and the distance between the two students must always remain the same. Students create a comedy run by lifting their knees high when moving.

Students must consider how they might use the different sections of the traverse stage so both sides of the audience can enjoy the scene. Clarify that either gender can play the roles. It is often helpful to use five students to visually represent the five key characters discussed in the 'context for students' section to ensure they understand the situation.

## Context for students

*The Comedy of Errors* is one of Shakespeare's famous comedies, packed full of humorous encounters resulting from mishaps and mistaken identities.

The play is set in Ephesus, where **Antipholus of Ephesus** lives with his wife, **Adriana**, and his servant, **Dromio of Ephesus**. Unbeknownst to them, **Antipholus of Ephesus**'s twin brother **Antipholus of Syracuse** has arrived in town with his servant **Dromio of Syracuse**, who is the twin of **Dromio of Ephesus**.

Despite the dangers of coming from Syracuse to Ephesus, as the towns are at war, **Antipholus of Syracuse** and **Dromio of Syracuse** are there to search for their twins, whom they have not seen since they were very young.

This extract is the first exchange in the play between **Antipholus of Syracuse** and **Dromio of Ephesus**. Earlier, **Antipholus of Syracuse** sent his actual servant, **Dromio of Syracuse,** to the bank to deposit their money. A few moments later, **Antipholus of Syracuse** spots **Dromio of Ephesus** and assumes it is his own servant, **Dromio of Syracuse,** returning. **Antipholus of Syracuse** is concerned to find out what has happened to the money. **Dromio of Ephesus** has been sent to find **Antipholus of Ephesus** to ask him to return home for dinner, as his wife, **Adriana**, is waiting for him. Naturally, he thinks **Antipholus of Syracuse** is his boss **Antipholus of Ephesus**. In short, both characters believe they are talking to a different person, resulting in a scene filled with chaos and confusion.

Extract taken from The Arden Shakespeare edition (third series).

ANTIPHOLUS OF SYRACUSE

He that commends me to mine own content  
Commends me to the thing I cannot get:  
I to the world am like a drop of water  
That in the ocean seeks another drop;  
Who, falling there to find his fellow forth,  
Unseen, inquisitive, confounds himself.  
So I, to find a mother and a brother,  
In quest of them, unhappy, lose myself.

*Enter* DROMIO OF EPHESUS

Here comes the almanac of my true date.
- What now? How chance thou art returned so soon?

DROMIO OF EPHESUS

'Returned so soon'? Rather approached too late!
The capon burns, the pig falls from the spit;
The clock hath strucken twelve upon the bell;
My mistress made it one upon my cheek.
She is so hot because the meat is cold;
The meat is cold because you come not home;
You come not home because you have no stomach;
You have no stomach, having broke your fast.
But we that know what 'tis to fast and pray
Are penitent for your default today.

ANTIPHOLUS OF SYRACUSE

Stop in your wind, sir; tell me this, I pray:
Where have you left the money that I gave you?

DROMIO OF EPHESUS

O, sixpence that I had o'Wednesday last
To pay the saddler for my mistress' crupper?
The saddler had it, sir; I kept it not.

ANTIPHOLUS OF SYRACUSE

I am not in a sportive humour now;
Tell me, and dally not: where is the money?
We being strangers here, how dar'st thou trust
So great a charge from thine own custody?

DROMIO OF EPHESUS

I pray you, jest, sir, as you sit at dinner.
I from my mistress come to you in post;
If I return, I shall be post indeed,
For she will score your fault upon my pate.
Methinks your maw, like mine, should be your clock
And strike you home without a messenger.

ANTIPHOLUS OF SYRACUSE

Come, Dromio, come, these jests are out of season;
Reserve them till a merrier hour than this.
Where is the gold I gave in charge to thee?

DROMIO OF EPHESUS

To me, sir? why, you gave no gold to me!

ANTIPHOLUS OF SYRACUSE
Come on, sir knave, have done your foolishness,
And tell me how thou hast disposed thy charge.

DROMIO OF EPHESUS
My charge was but to fetch you from the mart
Home to your house, the Phoenix, sir, to dinner;
My mistress and her sister stays for you.

ANTIPHOLUS OF SYRACUSE
Now as I am a Christian answer me
In what safe place you have bestowed my money,
Or I shall break that merry sconce of yours
That stands on tricks when I am undisposed.
Where is the thousand marks thou hadst of me?

DROMIO OF EPHESUS
I have some marks of yours upon my pate,
Some of my mistress' marks upon my shoulders,
But not a thousand marks between you both.
If I should pay your worship those again,
Perchance you will not bear them patiently.

ANTIPHOLUS OF SYRACUSE
Thy 'mistress' marks'? What 'mistress', slave, hast thou?

DROMIO OF EPHESUS
Your worship's wife, my mistress at the Phoenix;
She that doth fast till you come home to dinner,
And prays that you will hie you home to dinner.

ANTIPHOLUS OF SYRACUSE
What, wilt thou flout me thus unto my face,
Being forbid? [*Strikes Dromio.*]
There, take you that, sir knave.

DROMIO OF EPHESUS
What mean you, sir? For God's sake hold your hands!
Nay, an you will not, sir, I'll take my heels. [*Exit.*]

ANTIPHOLUS OF SYRACUSE
Upon my life, by some device or other
The villain is o'er-raught of all my money.
They say this town is full of cozenage -
As, nimble jugglers that deceive the eye,

Dark-working sorcerers that change the mind,
Soul-killing witches that deform the body,
Disguised cheaters, prating mountebanks
And many such – like liberties of sin.
If it prove so, I will be gone the sooner.
I'll to the Centaur to go seek this slave;
I greatly fear my money is not safe. *Exit.*

### *Design activity*

In pairs or small groups, students design the costumes for Dromio of Ephesus and Dromio of Syracuse. They need to have similar costumes and hairstyles to establish that they are twins, but there must also be distinct differences so the audience can tell them apart. Spend time considering how they might differentiate between the two characters. Discussion might include:

1. **Colour**: One Dromio could wear a red top and blue trousers, while the other could wear a blue top and red trousers.
2. **Pattern**: Striped or spotted designs could help differentiate between costumes of the same style and colour.
3. **Condition**: As Dromio of Syracuse has been travelling, that costume could be tatty and worn.
4. **Hairstyles**: They could have the same hairstyle in a different colour or different styles in the same colour.
5. **Accessories**: Glasses, sunglasses, scarves, gloves, jewellery could all help differentiate between the two characters.

Students consider and present their costume ideas to the rest of the class.

### *Written activity*

For this activity, students will further develop their skills in evaluating the performances of their peers. Allocate each student another pair to observe.

**Suggested title**: Choose three moments to illustrate how the two performers successfully used the traverse stage to present the exchange between Antipholus of Syracuse and Dromio of Ephesus.

To guide them, share this example:

- I liked the way that the actor playing Dromio of Ephesus crawled from one end of the traverse stage to the other. I found the sequence extremely amusing, as it highlighted his lower status compared to Antipholus of Syracuse. The entire audience could see clearly.

## 2. *Earthquakes in London* by Mike Bartlett

This Mike Bartlett play was first performed at the National Theatre's Cottesloe Theatre (now Dorfman) in 2010. Spanning a period from 1968 to the distant future, the play explores a range of themes, including climate change and corporate corruption, through the interconnected lives of three sisters and their complex relationship with their father. It is an exciting text for older students, also offering some interesting excerpts for this age group. The fast-moving scenes, set in numerous locations, were originally performed on a traverse stage with two additional platform stages positioned at either end of the traverse.

This excerpt is from the epilogue, featuring Emily, the daughter of one of the three sisters, and Tom, who was first introduced at the beginning of the play as a young activist involved with another sister. This epilogue brings a sense of hope and optimism to the end of the play as Emily leaves to walk barefoot to London to protest. Having witnessed the collapse of society throughout the play, the final sight of a young person finding the drive and determination to make a difference in the world is powerful. There are several themes and ideas in the play which you might want to explore with students.

After reading and discussing the excerpt, students should consider how to bring the text to life on a traverse stage.

## Context for students

This is an exciting play that spans from 1968 to the distant future. Many of the earlier scenes in the play are set in 2010, introducing us to one of the central characters, **Freya**, who is heavily pregnant. This scene is set sixteen years later, when **Freya**'s daughter, **Emily**, has just turned sixteen. In this excerpt, she is speaking to a family friend, **Tom**. **Emily** is a symbol of hope at the end of the play as she sets off barefoot to walk to London to protest. The playwright is using **Emily** to illustrate how young people can make a positive impact on the world's future. The production was originally performed on a traverse stage. Stage the scene, thinking carefully about how and why you move around the traverse.



*The kitchen of a large house in the west Oxfordshire countryside.*
*Night. On the table there is food out.*

*It is sixteen years later.*

**Emily** *is packing food into a backpack.*

*Some of it doesn't fit. In the rearranging, we see a map, a torch.*

*A knock on the door.*

**Emily** *goes and opens it.*

**Tom** *enters, now thirty-five, a man, rather than a boy. He is dressed much better, ready for a long walk. He is sure of himself.*

**Emily** Shhh- / Dad's asleep – you look nervous.

**Tom** You've barely left the town on your own before, you don't know what it's like.

**Emily** I've done my research.

**Tom** You should let me come with you.

*She smiles. Touches his arm.*

**Emily** I'll be fine.

**Tom** And what are you wearing?

**Emily** Do you like it? Before she died, Mum told Dad it was her favourite dress. Dad gave it to me this afternoon, for my birthday. I like the pattern. How about you? Did you get me a present?

**Tom** *gives her a small bag.*

**Tom** Papers, ID, map, new phone.

**Emily** Good.

**Tom** All in the bag, as ordered.

**Emily** Perfect. I'm thinking maybe I should go barefoot …

**Tom** It's a long way.

**Emily** It is, and people should notice.

*She takes her shoes off.*

Definitely barefoot.

**Tom** You'll call me if you get into trouble?

**Emily** There won't be trouble.

**Tom** There might be, maybe we should tell your dad what you're doing. If he wakes up and you're gone –

**Emily** When did you care what he thought?

**Tom** This is different.

**Emily** I've told them for years, over and over, when I'm sixteen, this is what happens. At dawn, I'll be on my way. Not my fault if they never believed me.

**Tom** At least leave a note –

**Emily** Right. Toothbrush, bag, towel.

*She puts the backpack on.*

**Tom** Speech?

**Emily** Don't need a speech. It's all up here … Tom! I'm half your age and you look petrified.

**Tom** It's ridiculous.

**Emily** You know what I can do?

**Tom** Yes.

**Emily** And you trust me?

**Tom** Of course.

**Emily** Then smile. It'll be fine. Now, how do I look?

*He looks at her, takes her in.*

**Tom** Emily Sullivan.

Magnificent.

*She smiles.*

*He smiles too.*

*She looks at him, goes to the kitchen blackboard, and writes, in large letters.*

*'Gone to London'*

## 3. *Red Velvet* by Lolita Chakrabarti

*Red Velvet* was first performed at the Tricycle Theatre (now Kiln) in Kilburn, London, in 2012. It explores the career and prejudices faced by Ira Aldridge, the first Black actor to portray Othello in England. Structurally, it is an interesting piece, starting and concluding at the end of Ira's life in 1867, and flashing back to his performances as Othello in the 1830s. The selected excerpt is from the end of the play, revealing the resilience Ira developed following an attack on a theatre where he performed as a boy. Working in pairs, students should explore how to perform the excerpt on the traverse stage. Two texts are recommended in the *Further Reading* section if you wish to explore the life and work of Ira Aldridge further.

### Context for students

In this speech, **Ira Aldridge**, a nineteenth-century Black actor, recounts his experience of a fire that broke out during a production in which he performed as a boy. Consider how you will bring his story to life on a traverse stage.



**Ira**

Look, you and I, we don't have the ease of following in footsteps. We stand apart, I see that. It's a, a lonely path and putting your head above the parapet is a, it's a courageous thing … When I was a boy, there was this man, William Brown, spent his life savings on a house. It was rundown, basic but he had such passion he turned his own house into a theatre. He would serve cakes and punch in the back yard in the interval. His friend, Jimmy Hewlett, was an actor – untrained, unpolished, worked as a tailor uptown in the day but was burnin' up with talent. They had no one to follow either. You see Jimmy was cuttin' an' stitchin' in the day, Mr Brown did odd jobs, I was at school but evenings we rehearsed and played *Romeo and Juliet*, *Richard III*, *Henry V*. I was fourteen. We were rough but we had passion … we became real popular. Powers that be didn't like it though and one night while we playin' in our tumbledown theatre and our homemade costumes, they set fire to that house. It burned like paper. The drier the wood, the quicker it burns. The noise was deafenin' – screams, the flames catchin' further, shoutin'. Couldn't see my way out, couldn't breathe and just when I thought I was done, Mr Brown grabbed my hand, pulled me up from the floor and dragged me out into the open air. I was gaspin', chokin' on the smoke. Seems like yesterday but look what he did. We just in the fire, Pierre … I've given everything to get here. I have pushed and forced and played my way in.

# 4
# APPLYING SKILLS EXPLORED IN CHAPTERS ONE TO THREE
## 'MIX IT UP'

**Photo 2-4-1** Students applying skills.

## Introduction

In this chapter, students have the opportunity to connect everything they have explored in the first three chapters, combining their work on pace and levels, in performances on a traverse stage. They should also be prompted to consider how they apply tone of voice, volume and gesture, as explored in Part One. The chapter includes two improvisation activities for students to work on in pairs and small groups, along with three excerpts from published scripts.

## Improvisation

### 1. A taste of drama machines

This is an excellent exercise that allows students to explore and connect some of the skills they have developed in Chapters One and Two, applying them to a performance on a traverse stage.

For this activity, students create a repetitive vocal and movement sequence to convey and capture the mood and flavour of a starting title. Divide the class into groups of three or four. To help them fully understand this new technique before creating their own original machines, begin by introducing the practice title *The shopping centre*. All members of the group start by choosing an interesting character whom one might discover in a shopping centre, such as:

1. A disgruntled shopper who can't find what they want.
2. A nervous shop assistant who has just started work and hasn't been told what to do.
3. A bored security guard who wants to be a famous musician.

When students have selected their characters, they then create one or two lines of appropriate dialogue. For example:

1. Next time I'm going to do my shopping online. This is an absolute nightmare.
2. Please don't ask me because I won't know. I'll look the other way; just leave me alone.
3. I shouldn't be here. I should be in the studio recording my amazing video to go with my hit single from my latest album.

Once the dialogue has been established, students work on a repetitive, mechanical-style movement sequence incorporating different levels, to be performed whilst delivering their lines. For example:

1. Start by sitting on the floor, stand up, turn to the other direction, reach out, sit down again.
2. Start in a standing position, sit on the floor, reach forward, stand again, and turn 360°.
3. Raise both hands, turn left, then right, turn in a full circle, and touch the floor.

Once all members of the group have perfected their individual combined dialogue and mechanical movement sequences, they should begin linking everything together to create a group essence machine. To start, they perform their sequences one at a time. They then explore ways of connecting the end of one performer's sequence to the start of the next one. This could involve overlapping the dialogue and linking the beginning of one movement sequence to the end of another. Emphasize that the whole sequence should resemble a moving, complex machine with several interconnected parts.

When you feel that your students are confident in structuring a group machine, introduce the new starting titles. As the work is to be performed on a traverse stage, they must carefully consider positioning and movement. Suggested titles:

1. Questions to the Prime Minister in the House of Commons.
2. A mountain rescue.
3. The disorganized neighbourhood street party.

Once they have connected their sequences, they can begin experimenting with the pace of the performance, imagining that their machine starts slowly, gradually builds up to a fast pace and then slows down again. Watch and evaluate the work.

## 2. A different world

This activity provides students with experience of improvising a more naturalistic style scene, building on the skills they have developed throughout the year. Divide the class into pairs, labelling themselves **A** and **B**. The scene takes place in the present year, where **A** is a contemporary. **B** is from 1963 but has somehow ended up in the current year. Confirm that there is a red telephone box at one end of the traverse, which, in this contemporary context, no longer functions but has been left on display. There is a bench at the other end of the traverse. In this scene, **B** asks **A** for some coins to use a phone box to call home. **A** explains that the phone box no longer works, but is happy to lend their mobile phone for **B** to use. Spend time discussing the social, cultural and historical contexts to help students appreciate the different experiences the two characters have encountered.

Students improvise the scene, exploring ways to maintain a fast pace, using different levels and connecting with an audience on both sides. Remind them to consider volume, tone of voice and gestures, as studied in Part One. Watch and evaluate the work.

# Published script

## The director

Before exploring the three published excerpts, this is a good point to continue examining the role of a director in theatre. In Part One, students learned that throughout history, individuals played a crucial role in bringing a play to life on stage. At this point, highlight how directorial approaches truly started to develop in the twentieth century and went far beyond merely organizing actors in the stage space and planning rehearsals. In the twentieth century, directors developed a range of techniques to help actors understand their characters and determine the most effective ways to portray them in performance. Directors began to focus more deeply on interpreting plays and characters, as well as developing the best acting techniques. Stanislavski's approaches have already been introduced in Chapter Two and are revisited in the exploration of the next published excerpt in this chapter.

Since many of the theatre practitioners discussed in drama courses are male, this is an excellent point to introduce the contemporary director, Katie Mitchell. Influenced by Stanislavski's work, she has become renowned for her in-depth exploration of characters in a play and her multi-layered productions. Her use of film and projection is also an interesting area to explore. In her 2006 production of *The Waves* and 2007 version of *Women of Troy,* both staged at the National Theatre, she utilized live projection to convey characters' deep emotions, enabling the audience to observe subtle and nuanced facial expressions. There are many examples of theatre productions that have also used film and projection, and you might want to consider exploring the following:

1. *Brief Encounter*- Kneehigh (adapted from David Lean's 1945 film based on Noël Coward's *Still Life)*- 2008.
2. *Small Island* by Helen Edmundson (based on Andrea Levy's novel)- National Theatre- 2019.
3. *Life of Pi* adapted by Lolita Chakrabarti (based on Yann Martel's novel)- Crucible Theatre- 2019.
4. *Romeo & Juliet*- Jamie Lloyd- Duke of York's- 2024.
5. *Evita*- Jamie Lloyd- London Palladium- 2025.

There are examples of materials you might like to draw on in the *Further Reading* section.

## 1. *Di and Viv and Rose* by Amelia Bullmore

Amelia Bullmore's *Di and Viv and Rose* was first performed at the Hampstead Downstairs in 2011 and was subsequently revived on the main stage in 2013.

The three characters, Di, Viv and Rose, first meet at university in 1983, and the play traces their relationship up until 2010. It is an interesting focus on three young women who appear dissimilar but connect at university, and despite their lives taking them in different directions, the bonds between them remain strong. The play is clearly a study of female friendship, but it is possible to explore and perform this excerpt with both boys and girls.

Having studied some of Stanislavski's techniques in Chapter Two, consider the following exercises to explore his ideas further:

1. **Concentration**: Begin by asking the students to sit in a part of the space where they can concentrate. Ask them to choose a spot very close to them, such as their watch or a specific part of their clothing. Explain that you want them to concentrate on this spot for a short period. Aim for about thirty to forty-five seconds of silence. Continue by asking them to focus on a spot that is approximately three metres away. Give some examples of where this spot might be from your perspective. Aim to hold the silence for about thirty to forty-five seconds. Finally, ask them to select a spot that is about ten metres away, giving examples from your perspective. Hold the silence for about thirty seconds. At the end of the activity, ask the students to identify the point they found easiest to focus on. There is no correct answer, but you will probably find that most students choose the closest point because they have experienced fewer distractions. Explain that Stanislavski used this exercise to help prepare actors to immerse themselves in their performances, block out the audience and become absorbed in their character.
2. For this **concentration** exercise, students find their own space, sit on the floor and imagine that they are inside a large cardboard box. From this position, they should be able to imagine feeling the top, bottom and sides of the box with their hands. Ask them to close their eyes and imagine that they are inside the box, feeling all sides with their hands. When you sense they are all concentrating, they should progress to imagine that the box is lined in:

   - Sandpaper.
   - Velvet.
   - Ice.

   Stressing that there is no correct answer, students share which lining they found it easiest to imagine. Explain that they could only succeed in this exercise if they had actually experienced touching cardboard, sandpaper, velvet and ice. Confirm that Stanislavski wanted his actors to draw on their own life experiences and use these when performing.
3. You can also revisit the technique of **emotional memory**. This excerpt centres on young people meeting one another and forging friendships, and allows students to discuss times when they have made new friends. Divide the class into pairs to draw on their own experiences to improvise a scene involving two people who meet for the first time and begin to form a friendship.
4. Divide the group into threes to play Di, Viv and Rose. Students create their own profile sheet, developing the backgrounds of their characters. You can decide to mix them up, so, for example, students playing the same characters work and plan together.
5. **Hot seating**: Students walk around the space, and upon your signal, they pair with the nearest person and take turns hot seating each other.
6. **Magic If**: Once the students have had time to develop their characters' background, ask them to reflect on some of the experiences the characters face in this excerpt. Drawing from their own lives, how do they feel if they:

- are in a new situation where they don't know another person?
- are away from home, for example, on a school trip?
- see another person who dresses in a very original, unique way?

Students need to consider carefully how they use pace appropriately to deal with the quick transitions between different sections of dialogue, and to build the energy and vitality of these young people. They must also find ways to utilize different levels and devise inventive reasons for moving around the traverse stage. For this exercise, the characters can be portrayed as male.

## Context for students

This play explores the lives of three young women who meet at university and remain connected throughout their lives. The excerpt is taken from the first scene, where the three girls meet and begin to build their relationship. **Rose** is an art student; she is creative, outgoing and warm. Her stepfather, Charlie, buys the house where the three girls live together. **Viv** studies sociology; she is focused and passionately committed to her studies. **Rose** comments that 'she dresses like it is the war'. **Di** is reading business studies; her main love and focus is sport.



*Lights up on* **Rose***, on the payphone.*

**Rose** Hello Charlie! – Fine, thank you. – How's Mum? – Oh well, give her a kiss when she wakes up. – The course is fine. We've had to buy tons of books. They're so expensive. – Art history books especially are because of the pictures.

**Viv** *appears, with a ten-pence piece in her hand, as before. She watches* **Rose**, *as before.*

**Rose** Oh. Well. Not so good. Honestly Charlie, they're all peculiar. There's one girl. A dentist student. Dental student. Once a week, she goes to Asda, which is a supermarket, and she buys a pack of cheese, and she cuts it into seven pieces, and she wraps them up in cling film and she writes Monday, Tuesday, Wednesday, Thursday, Friday, Saturday, Sunday on them! There's one girl in the flat who's nice. Di. I tell you something amazing. There's a girl in the flat next door who dresses like it's the war.

**Viv** Are you going to be long?

**Rose** *turns and sees* **Viv.**

**Rose** Oh. Hello. I think it looks brilliant, by the way. (*Back to Charlie.)* Guess what? The girl who dresses like it's the war's standing right beside me. Waiting for the phone. – Quite, mustn't hog it, better let Mrs Miniver have a go. Bye, Charlie. Bye.

*She puts the phone down.*

All yours.

*Blackout.*

*Lights up on* **Di**, *on the payphone.*

**Di** Thanks for the parcel, Mum. It came today. – I had a bit just now with a cuppa. Excellent. And one of my flatmates – she's really into cooking – she said it was the best Dundee cake she'd ever had. – Rose. – No, I don't like the others much. – There's a girl next door who's interesting. Viv. I'm having a drink with her tonight. – The Sports Centre's excellent. I'm on the hockey team, the netball team and the soccer team. – Yep. Lots of boys about.

**Rose** *appears, with bike.* **Di** *waves.*

**Di** Okay, Mum, I'll phone you Friday. Ta-ra.

**Rose** Di! I'm cooking tonight!

**Di** Can Viv come?

**Rose** Of course. Who's Viv?

**Di** Next door.

**Rose** Oh war-time Viv! She's scary.

**Di** She's a laugh!

**Rose** She doesn't like me.

**Di** She doesn't know you.

**Rose** Why does she dress like that?

**Di** She does Sociology.

**Rose** Let's have Viv over then. It's channa dhal and chapatis.

*Blackout.*

*Lights up on* **Di. Viv** *appears.*

**Di** Do you fancy eating at my place before we go out? Rose is cooking.

**Viv** The annoying one?

**Di** She's all right.

**Viv** What's she cooking?

**Di** I can't say it, but it'll be good.

**Viv** Okay. See you in a bit.

**Di** See ya.

*Blackout.*

*Lights up on* **Viv***, holding a bottle wrapped in tissue.* **Rose** *appears.*

**Rose** Hello!

**Viv** I'm Viv.

**Rose** I'm Rose.

**Viv** I brought a bottle.

**Rose** Thank you. I hope you found us all right.

**Viv** Di did me a map.

**Rose** Perfect. Come in.

*Blackout.*

*Lights up on* ***Rose*** *and* **Di** *(plus bike).*

**Di** He can just buy a house? An extra house?

**Rose** Apparently he can. Charlie says property's the thing.

**Di** I think that would be excellent.

**Rose** Really?

**Di** Yeah.

**Rose** Will you ask Viv? I would, but she doesn't like me.

**Di** Why do you want to share a house with her?

**Rose** She will like me. It's better if you ask. You ask.

**Di** Do you like her?

**Rose** I think she's what we need.

*Blackout.*

*Lights up on* ***Viv*** *and* ***Di****, with bikes.*

**Viv** She's annoying.

**Di** I like her.

**Viv** Really annoying.

**Di** We wouldn't have to live in each other's pockets.

**Viv** Has the stepdad bought somewhere already?

**Di** He's still looking.

**Viv** What if it's a dump?

**Di** He won't make his money back if he buys a dump, will he?

**Viv** I'll think about it.

*Blackout.*

*Lights up on **Rose** on payphone.*

**Rose** Three bedrooms is perfect, Charlie, because I've got two very good friends. Di, who I live with who does Business Studies and is very sporty and her mum makes that cake. And my other very good friend is Viv, who's extremely clever and does Sociology and dresses like it's the war and lives next door. – Yes I know we're all eighteen, Charlie, but we're very mature for our age.

*Blackout.*

## *Design activity*

Interesting design work can stem from studying this excerpt. Students can research the type of staging and props which help to establish the 1983 setting. They can also explore how they would distinguish between the years 1986, 1987, 1988, 1998, 1999 and 2010 in England, and 1998 in New York, as specified by Amelia Bullmore.

They should also consider how to design for a traverse stage. Make them aware of the challenges posed by sight lines and warn that placing a tall piece of scenery in the middle of the traverse stage would obstruct the view of some audience members. They are still able to use trucks and flying, as explored in Chapter Two. Suggest that they consider using low-level scenery, placing significant items at either end of the traverse. Build on the idea of using projection behind the two banks of audience as an efficient way of moving between different locations and years on a traverse stage. Working in groups of three, students should:

1. Present their ideas for scenery and projections required to stage this excerpt.
2. Present ideas for projections they might use to differentiate between the different years the play is set.

# 2. *Dear England* by James Graham

This excerpt is from Act One, Scene Two of the 2023 edition of James Graham's *Dear England,* which was first performed at the National Theatre's Olivier Theatre. Chronicling the experiences of the England football team under the management of Gareth Southgate, this excerpt focuses on his attempt to convince the psychologist Dr Pippa Grange to be part of his new training approach with the England team members. This section is an exciting opportunity for students to apply some of the skills they have developed throughout this part of the course.

Start by reading the excerpt and exploring the relationship between the two characters. Students are allowed to use two chairs positioned at either end of the traverse. Discuss ways they might use these to incorporate different levels throughout the piece to reveal the relationship between Gareth and Pippa. Reflect on how they might apply their work on pace to help communicate Gareth's enthusiasm for persuading Pippa to join the team.

### Context for students

This excerpt brings together two real-life individuals, **Gareth Southgate**, the England Manager, and the psychologist **Dr Pippa Grange**. In this exchange, **Gareth** tries to persuade **Pippa** to work with him in training the England players. Up to this point, women would not have been actively involved in training the men's team, and using psychology would have been unheard of. **Gareth** and **Pippa** respect one another, but **Pippa** remains quite undecided about whether she should accept the role.



**Gareth** Doctor Pippa Grange?

**Pippa** Oh. 'Gareth Southgate'.

**Gareth** Hah. Gareth's fine without the Southgate, hi.

**Pippa** Well, Pippa's fine, without the Doctor. Hello. Uh, are we – did we -?

**Gareth** Yeah, sorry, I hope this doesn't feel like an ambush or a tackle from behind at ten yards. I know we've been calling, trying to … I'm just a fan of your work.

**Pippa** Huh, well. Now I really feel bad declining your interview – thank you. It's just – I don't think it's for me, I'm sorry.

**Gareth** I get it. I sort of think that's why we think it *is* for you, huh.

I know that football hasn't always been as welcoming to, to psychologists, as other sports –

**Pippa** I *was* a performance psychologist, now I'm more of a – 'culture coach'. Not focused on individual performance, so much. More transforming the whole culture of a place.

**Gareth** … Ok. Well. That's exactly why I'm here, Pippa. I've been put in a car already going at 100 mph whose entire engine I want to change but I'm already driving it, so I need changemakers, from the outside. If we get through qualifiers, if I survive, I plan to build a new team, new people. For, a New England.

And I suppose also, to say it out loud, as a woman you'd –

**Pippa** That bit I'm used to, believe me, being the sole female in teams of men. Although the England changing room, I mean … Jesus, I can only imagine –

**Gareth** And you'd be right. You'd be bang on. There's a lot about this game I don't like or agree with, Pippa. It's – it can be stubborn, cruel. But what can I say, I love it.

**Pippa** Ok. And what are you asking help for, then? Brass tacks.

**Gareth** … I'd settle, right now, for the team feeling better. They're not in a good way, they're … (*Referencing her*.)

Doctor, doctor, they're not very well. Hah.

The pressure they face – they're not handling it. It's … all the things I think you know about …

**Pippa** And *you* know about. Right? What *you* went through.

*A moment,* **Gareth** *not necessarily having expected to go 'here'.*

**Gareth** Well. Exactly. And I don't want any of these young men to go through that.

**Pippa** I am sorry, that must have been, just, huge. All those years ago.

**Gareth** Honestly, thanks, but, it's Ok.

I'm Ok I am. I-I-I actually am. And I know by saying 'I-I-I' three times, it makes it sound like I'm not, but …

**Pippa** (*studying him, a small smile*) Hmm.

**Gareth** 'Hmm', is that a good 'hmm', or?

**Pippa** … 'England', you say.

**Gareth** Yeah. Yeah, come help fix England with me.

**Pippa** … Can I think about it?

**Gareth** … Yeah. Of course.

## 3. *Blood Brothers* by Willy Russell

Willy Russell's *Blood Brothers* was first performed at the Liverpool Playhouse in 1983. Although not specified in the text, references suggest that it is set in Liverpool from the late 1950s/early 1960s to the early 1980s. Although often used as an exam text, there are some wonderful scenes for younger students to explore.

Explain to the students that adult actors play the roles of Edward and Mickey throughout the play, from the age of seven up until they are grown up. Read the text through and start discussing the various ways they might apply the skills they have developed over this part of the course. For example, a fast pace is appropriate to convey the excitement and exuberance as the two children get to know each other. Consider how young children are constantly on the move, providing reasons for using different levels. Similarly, the characters' energy and movement provide believable reasons for adjusting their positioning on a traverse stage. They can also draw on their work from last year on volume, tone of voice, and gesture.

### Context for students

This play explores the relationship between two twin boys who are split at birth. **Mickey** is raised by his real mother; **Edward** is adopted and brought up by another family. Despite an agreement by the adult women to keep them apart, the boys find themselves in situations where they are drawn back together. In this scene, seven-year-old **Mickey** and **Edward** meet again after being separated as babies.

*Bored and petulant,* **Mickey** *sits and shoots an imaginary* **Sammy.**

**Edward,** *also aged seven, appears. He is bright and forthcoming.*

**Edward** Hello.

**Mickey** (*suspiciously*) Hello.

**Edward** I've seen you before.

**Mickey** Where?

**Edward** You were playing with some other boys near my house.

**Mickey** Do you live up in the park?

**Edward** Yes. Are you going to come and play up there again?

**Mickey** No. I would do but I'm not allowed.

**Edward** Why?

**Mickey** Cos me mam says.

**Edward** Well, my mummy doesn't allow me to play down here actually.

**Mickey** Gis a sweet.

**Edward** All right. (*He offers a bag from his pocket.*)

**Mickey** (*shocked*) What?

**Edward** Here.

**Mickey** (*trying to work out the catch; suspiciously taking one*) Can I have another one. For our Sammy?

**Edward** Yes, of course. Take as many as you want.

**Mickey** (*taking a handful*) Are you soft?

**Edward** I don't think so.

**Mickey** Round here if y' ask for a sweet, y' have to ask about, about twenty million times. An' y' know what?

**Edward** (*sitting beside* **Mickey**) What?

**Mickey** They still don't bleedin' give y' one. Sometimes our Sammy does but y' have to be dead careful if our Sammy gives y' a sweet.

**Edward** Why?

**Mickey** Cos, if our Sammy gives y' a sweet he's usually weed on it first.

**Edward** (*exploding in giggles*) Oh, that sounds like super fun.

**Mickey** It is. If y' our Sammy.

**Edward** Do you want to come and play?

**Mickey** I might do. But I'm not playin' now cos I'm pissed off.

**Edward** (*awed*) Pissed off! You say smashing things, don't you? Do you know any more words like that?

**Mickey** Yeh. Yeh, I know loads of words like that. Y' know, like the 'F' word.

**Edward** (*clueless*) Pardon?

**Mickey** The 'F' word.

**Edward** *is still pulled.* **Mickey** *looks round to check that he cannot be overheard, then whispers the word to* **Edward**. *The two of them immediately wriggle and giggle with glee.*

**Edward** What does it mean?

**Mickey** I don't know. It sounds good though, doesn't it?

**Edward** Fantastic. When I get home I'll look it up in the dictionary.

**Mickey** In the what?

**Edward** The dictionary. Don't you know what a dictionary is?

**Mickey** Course I do … It's a, it's a thingy, innit?

**Edward** A book which explains the meaning of words.

**Mickey** The meaning of words, yeh. Our Sammy'll be here soon. I hope he's in a good mood. He's dead mean sometimes.

**Edward** Why?

**Mickey** It's cos he's got a plate in his head.

**Edward** A plate. In his head?

**Mickey** Yeh. When he was little, me mam was at work an' our Donna Marie was supposed to be lookin' after him but he fell out the window an' broke his head. So they took him to the hospital an' put a plate in his head.

**Edward** A plate. A dinner plate?

**Mickey** I don't think so, cos our Sammy's head's not really that big. I think it must have been one of them little plates that you have bread off.

**Edward** A side plate?

**Mickey** No, it's on the top.

**Edward** And … and can you see the shape of it, in his head?

**Mickey** I suppose, I suppose if y' looked under his hair.

**Edward** *(after a reflective pause)* You know the most smashing things. Will you be my best friend?

**Mickey** Yeh. If y' want.

**Edward** What's your name?

**Mickey** Michael Johnstone. But everyone calls me Mickey. What's yours?

**Edward** Edward Lyons.

**Mickey** D' they call y' Eddie?

**Edward** No.

**Mickey** Well, I will.

**Edward** Will you?

**Mickey** Yeh. How old are y', Eddie?

**Edward** Seven.

**Mickey** I'm older than you. I'm nearly eight.

**Edward** Well, I'm nearly eight, really.

**Mickey** What's your birthday?

**Edward** July the eighteenth.

**Mickey** So is mine.

**Edward** Is it really?

**Mickey** 'Ey, we were born on the same day … that means we can be blood brothers. Do you wanna be my blood brother, Eddie?

**Edward** Yes, please.

**Mickey** (*producing a penknife*) It hurts y' know. (*He puts a nick in his hand.)* Now, give us yours.

*He nicks* **Edward'***s hand, then they clamp hands together.*

**Mickey** See, this means that we're blood brothers, an' that we always have to stand by each other. Now you say after me: 'I will always defend my brother.'

**Edward** I will always defend my brother …

**Mickey** And stand by him.

**Edward** And stand by him.

## *Design activity*

This excerpt again allows students to consider how costumes can help communicate the connections and differences between two characters. Working in pairs, students design a costume for both Mickey and Edward, researching the type of clothes worn during the late 1960s and early 1970s period. There should be some similarities in their costumes to highlight that they are twins. Mickey's costume should also indicate that his family is struggling financially; Edward's costume should suggest that he is from a more affluent family.

## *Written activity*

This task can be set after working on any of the three published excerpts in this chapter. Students will evaluate their own performance by discussing their use of voice, movement and stage space. Think about whether you want them to concentrate solely on the areas studied this year or whether you also want them to include discussion of tone and volume of voice and gesture as explored last year. This activity builds on the evaluation students wrote after working on the published script in the final chapter of Part One. At that stage, skills were discussed and evaluated discretely. Building on that experience, this is a good time for students to start familiarizing themselves with how to combine various areas of their performance in evaluative writing. Explain that, as actors speak and move simultaneously, it is more efficient and interesting to link things together when writing.

**Suggested title**: Evaluate how well you performed your character from (*name of text*). Give examples of how you used pace, levels and the stage space and what you intended to show the audience. Give suggestions for how you might improve your work.

To prepare them for this challenging piece of writing, students benefit from recording their ideas on a structured document, noting different moments from their performance.

**Table 2-4-1** Performance record sheet for evaluative writing.

| **RECORD OF MY DECISIONS WHEN PERFORMING *(character)* FROM *(text)*** | | | | |
|---|---|---|---|---|
| **LINE FROM SCRIPT** | **VOICE-PACE** (and tone and volume if you choose) | **MOVEMENT-LEVELS** (and gesture if you choose) | **STAGE SPACE-TRAVERSE** | **REASONS-** WHAT I WANTED TO SHOW THE AUDIENCE |
| E.g. 'I never wanted to go there in the first place'. | Fast pace. Annoyed and frustrated tone. Loud volume. | Standing up from seated position. Fling arms in air. | Move from position B at one end of the traverse to position H in the very middle. | I wanted to show the audience that I was angry and determined. |
| E.g. 'I don't understand what you mean by that'. | Slower pace. Anxious and guilty tone. Quiet volume. | Sit down on floor. Fold arms. | Sit on floor in position F. | I wanted to show the audience that I felt worried and that I had been caught doing wrong. I wanted them to see that I felt nervous and defensive. |

Depending on your students, decide how many moments you want them to record. Explain that these notes form the ingredients for the written activity. Students start by specifying the line(s) from the script they are discussing, then explain what they wanted to convey to the audience, discuss the skills they used to achieve this, and finally provide a recommendation for improving their work.

To guide them, share these two examples (using the two lines from the examples in table 2-4-1):

1. When I performed the line, 'I never wanted to go there in the first place'. I wanted the audience to understand that I felt annoyed and was determined to make my point. I spoke at a fast pace with a loud volume, and I stood up quickly after sitting on the floor. I moved quickly from the end of the traverse to the middle of the stage, flinging my arms into the air as I travelled. To improve my work, I could articulate my words more clearly when speaking at a fast pace.
2. When I performed the line, 'I don't understand what you mean by that'. I wanted the audience to see that I was worried about being discovered for doing something wrong. I wanted them to appreciate that I had become very defensive and longed for others to leave me alone. I spoke in a quiet and slow voice, sitting down on the floor to show that I wanted to be left alone. I folded my arms as a barrier between my character and others. To improve my work, I should ensure that I speak loudly enough to be heard by the audience on both sides of the traverse.

# PART THREE

# AGES THIRTEEN TO FOURTEEN

## Introduction to Part Three

### Chapters One to Three can be delivered in any order. Chapter Four should be delivered last

Part Three is designed to stretch and challenge students aged thirteen to fourteen by building on the skills developed over the last two years. An ambitious set of lessons ensures that students can progress to any offered exam courses with confidence. In the introduction to Part Two, you will find suggestions for promoting drama as an exam subject and highlighting potential career paths, which will be helpful to consider if you haven't already done so. I firmly believe that we must never underestimate the capabilities of this age group in tackling complex ideas. With this in mind, I have included some activities that, in the early stages of my career, I would have only delivered to older students. Most of us will also encounter students who do not continue with the subject at exam level, either because it is not offered or they have opted not to pursue it further. Whatever situation you find yourself in, we must ensure all our students have a positive experience of our subject, building skills they can develop further and transfer to other areas of their lives.

Students who find the performance aspect of the drama course challenging often become more evident at this stage, and others who demonstrate particular flair as designers emerge. You will find suggestions for offering more experiences to students who might choose to focus on design rather than acting in future practical performance exam tasks.

The structure mirrors the first two parts of the book. The first three chapters focus on voice, movement and stage space, while a concluding chapter integrates all the elements explored throughout. You can deliver Chapters One to Three in any order; chapters have been given titles which you may choose to use. The activities within each chapter are designed to be taught as they are presented, ensuring development and progression. Creative and more complex evaluative-style writing tasks are included to prepare students for further study. It should take about six to ten weeks to deliver each chapter.

# 1
# VOICE – PAUSE
## 'SILENCE IS GOLDEN'

**Photo 3-1-1** Student using pause.

## Introduction

In this chapter, you will continue to explore how actors use their voices with a particular focus on how to apply pause. Students often find using pause in their performance work to be one of the most complex challenges. It is a brave and sensitive performer who dares to hold a long pause, filling it with what is most appropriate to convey meaning to the audience. Very often, in the heat of a performance, rehearsed pauses become shorter and shorter. Pausing can become repetitive as students start mirroring one another, resulting in dramas that settle into a regular, monotonous rhythm lacking variety.

The activities have been designed to be delivered in the order presented to ensure progression. However, given the sophistication of the 'it's difficult to say' exercise from the improvisation section, you could choose to explore this after the activities based on original and published scripts.

## Games

### 1. Taking / the ... register

As you did in the study of tone of voice and volume in Chapter One of Part One, use the taking of the register to start exploring the current focus. Ask your students to pause for varying lengths of time before responding when their name is called. To help them consider the different pausing options, share some of the ways playwrights indicate pauses in texts:

1. **Beat**: A very short pause, which is like one beat of a drum or a knock on the door.
2. **Short pause**: A slightly longer pause. In performance, silently use the count: one pink elephant, two pink elephants.
3. **Pause**: A medium-length pause. In performance, silently use the count: one pink elephant, two pink elephants, three pink elephants, four pink elephants.
4. **Long pause**: In performance, silently use the count: one pink elephant, two pink elephants, three pink elephants, four pink elephants, five pink elephants, six pink elephants, seven pink elephants.
5. **Silence**: The most extended pause. How long do you dare hold a pause? Count up to and beyond eight pink elephants.

You can practise setting the correct pause lengths with a simple clapping game. Students stand in a circle, poised to clap. Announce one of the pause instructions, and from the moment you have spoken the instruction, the pause starts. Count the correct number of pink elephants aloud together, then clap. Once you are confident that you have established the length of pauses, continue the activity without counting aloud.

When calling the register, establish a rule that students must use a pause of a different length than the person before them before responding. Explain that pauses of varying lengths help make a performance more exciting and engaging for the audience. Stress that it is vital to consider what they will do during their pause. It is not enough for a performer to stop and wait. They must use their performance skills to fill the pause, providing insight into what they are doing, thinking or feeling. Discuss and demonstrate some examples of what they could consider doing, including:

1. Looking for something.
2. Controlling feelings of anger.
3. Controlling feelings of sadness.
4. Showing that they find it difficult to know what to say.
5. Showing that they are distracted or are daydreaming.
6. Finishing an activity such as sending an e-mail, watering a plant, or tidying.
7. Thinking deeply.
8. Showing they are feeling confused.

This could become a regular activity at the start of every lesson, allowing students to explore how to use pauses in a variety of ways.

## 2. Count the class

This game demands concentration and focus. If there are twenty students in the class, the aim is for each individual to call out a number from one to twenty. Any student can decide to start the game by stating 'one'. If more than one student calls the number simultaneously, you must restart the game. When a student has called out the number one, they cannot call out another number. Out of the remaining nineteen students, another student must call out the number two. If any students speak together at any point in the game, you must start again. To be successful, students need to be patient and observe one another. Pauses of varying lengths will naturally occur, filled with concentration and intensity. Completing this activity can be challenging; therefore, if students are unsuccessful, revisit it at the start of another lesson.

# Warm-up

## 1. It's my chair

In pairs, one student sits on a chair and the other tries to persuade them that they need the seat. There must be no physical contact at all during the activity, and the person sitting on the chair should never agree to stand up. Discuss the reasons that one could use to persuade another to give up a chair and the reasons that one might give to refuse. Allow students a few minutes to improvise the situation and then switch the roles around. Ask students to select about thirty seconds of their work and watch some examples, discussing the persuasion and refusal methods used. You will probably find that the performances do not include many moments of pause.

Students should now repeat the activity, incorporating pauses of varying lengths to enhance their attempts to persuade and refuse. Discuss some examples of how pauses might be used to achieve this. These could include:

1. Staring angrily.
2. Looking sad.
3. Thinking about how to react.
4. For the persuader, walking around the chair, thinking about what to do or walking away.
5. Looking confused as to what to say next.
6. Pretending to text or phone someone.
7. Eating something.

Give students time to rehearse the scene and then watch examples.

## 2. Spontaneous pausing monologues

In this exercise, students work individually to perform three spontaneous monologues. This builds on the monologue work they undertook as a warm-up exercise in Part Two, Chapter One. Revise the basic principles of spontaneous monologues, which should now also incorporate short pauses, pauses and long pauses. Recap the pink elephant counting method as outlined in the 'taking / the … register' game. The three scenarios are:

1. You are trying to tell your best friend that you don't think their new hairstyle suits them. Your friend is very sensitive and you don't want to hurt their feelings, but you also want to be honest.

2. You are telling a parent/guardian that they should get changed before going to a school event, as you find their choice of outfit very embarrassing (too formal, too trendy, too young, too colourful). You respect them and are concerned that they will be upset, but you are determined not to be seen at the event with them looking like this.
3. You are telling a friend that you have broken their precious laptop. You borrowed it and promised to keep it safe. You can't afford to repair it, but you know that they have money to do so. You are concerned because they do become angry in challenging situations. In the past, they broke your phone.

After the students have spontaneously improvised the three situations, ask them to pick one. They should now spend time perfecting it, ensuring that they have included pauses of different lengths. Emphasize the importance of conveying their intentions clearly during these pauses. They can all perform simultaneously before splitting into pairs to share their work. After each performance, the observers discuss what was communicated to them during the different-length pauses and how these enhanced the drama. Ask volunteers to perform for the whole class and evaluate their use of pause and the impact on the audience.

## *Written activity*

Creative task: Students work individually to write a responding monologue. This could be:

1. The monologue from the perspective of the individual who has just been told that their new hairstyle does not suit them.
2. The monologue from the point of view of the parent/guardian who has just been told that they should get changed.
3. The monologue from the point of view of the individual who has had their broken laptop returned.

Students can then work practically on their new monologue (or one written by another student), incorporating pauses. Design students can create an appropriate costume for the performance.

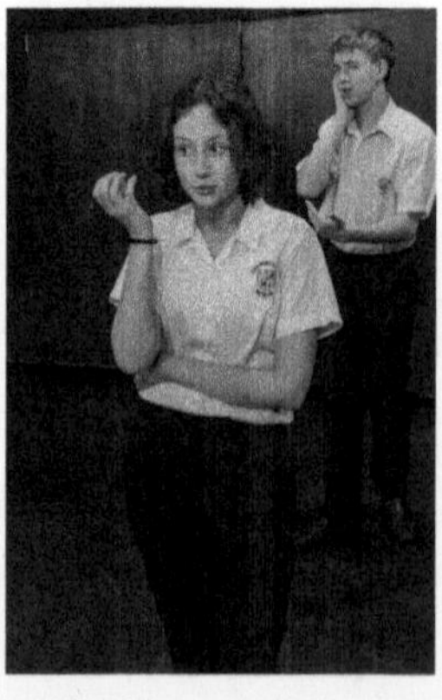

**Photo 3-1-2** Using pause in monologues.

# Improvisation

## 1. Monologues to pair work

In pairs, students develop one of the three 'spontaneous pausing monologues' from the warm-up section. They should experiment with different length pauses to create a fully developed scene for two. Recall the work covered on using different volumes and tones of voice from the first part of the book, as students may forget to maintain vocal variety when concentrating on applying pause, and delivery can become flat. Watch and evaluate the work.

## 2. Telephone conversations

To develop students' confidence in using pause, introduce the idea of improvising just one side of a telephone conversation. In these calls, students should imagine that the person at the other end of the line has a great deal to say. They need to consider carefully how to use dialogue and pause to enable audiences to get a sense of what the other person is communicating and how their character feels and responds. Read out the instructions to students and then give them time to improvise each call spontaneously. Suggested conversations:

1. You are phoning a friend. You are very excited, believing you have found the perfect holiday deal. You are trying to share all the information, but your friend keeps interrupting you to ask endless questions. Remember that the audience can't hear what the other person is saying, so you need to use pause to communicate your responses and frustration with their interruptions. Later in the conversation, your friend tells you that they don't want to go on the holiday at all. Consider how you might suggest this to the audience, and how you use pause to convey your shock and upset.
2. In this conversation, a very assertive friend has phoned you about a school project you have been set to work on together. Your friend is telling you what they expect you to do and when you need to complete it. You are trying to be polite, but also want to make it clear that you disagree with the ideas. In your dialogue and through the use of pause, you need to show how frustrated and annoyed you feel. The audience should get the impression that the person at the end of the line is very forceful and is not considering what you want.
3. In this phone call, you are the boss on a Zoom call with two of your employees. You are trying to organize the annual summer holiday rota. You are not permitted to go on holiday at the same time, and at this point, you all want the same dates. Imagine that one person on the call is very demanding and is unwilling to compromise; the other doesn't appear to be listening properly, and you are forced to keep repeating yourself. The audience should see that you are attempting to behave professionally, but should also sense your annoyance and frustration with the others on the call. Think carefully about how you use pause throughout.

After their first spontaneous attempts, give students time to polish and perfect one call. It is sometimes helpful for them to work in pairs (or threes for conversation three), improvising both (all) sides of the conversation to get a clearer sense of the appropriate length of the pauses and what to do during them.

### *Written activity*

For this activity, students write about some of the ways they used pause and what they wanted to convey to their audience.

**Suggested title**: Based on any of the telephone conversations, give five examples of how you used pause and discuss the intended impact on your audience.

To guide them, share this example:

- In the telephone conversation with my assertive friend, I used long pauses to convey my frustration and to show the audience that the character at the end of the line was dominating the discussion. I furrowed my brow and bit my lip to indicate how annoyed I felt. I wanted the audience to feel sorry for my character and hope that they would have a chance to speak.

## 3. It's difficult to say

Divide the class into groups of three. Individual design students can also work with a group of three actors on the activity described after the improvisation instructions. Read out the background information:

> This scene takes place in a meeting between a group of filmmakers planning to remake the classic film *Jaws*. Character **A** is the producer who is financing the film. Character **B** is a well-known film star who has been hired to play the lead role of the shark catcher. Character **C** is the assistant director who has had a successful career but lacks sufficient experience to be the principal director. All of them have important conditions and issues to discuss in the meeting.

Students start by casting the roles. Each student in the group is then given a role card. Alternatively, you can speak to all the **A**s, then the **B**s and then the **C**s together in groups. The exercise works best if they have not heard all the detailed information about the other characters before starting to improvise.

> Character **A**: You have always had a desire to perform in a film. You have never acted, but you are somewhat weary of being the one who pays for everything while remaining unseen on the screen. If you agree to finance this hugely expensive film, you want the lead role, and you plan to inform **B** that they are no longer needed. This will be challenging as you like and respect **B.**
>
> Character **B**: You have been offered another extremely tempting and lucrative role in a different, high-profile film. You respect **A** and **C,** and don't want to let them down, but you are seriously considering dropping out.
>
> Character **C**: The original producers of Jaws have approached you, now willing to produce and fund this film on the condition that **B** is in the lead role. They have offered you the role of principal director. You are delighted and can't wait to direct **B**. However, your initial task is to inform **A** that they are no longer required to produce or assume any other position. This will be difficult as you like and respect **A**.

Once you have set up the background, students improvise the scene spontaneously. Remind them to remain conscious of incorporating pauses of varying lengths. Allow about five to eight minutes for this first attempt. Bring the students together to discuss how their scenes developed, what happened and how they used pauses. Allow them an extra fifteen to twenty minutes to refine and polish the scenes, carefully considering the structure and how they include pauses of varying lengths. Students perform sections of their work, demonstrating their best use of pause.

### *Design activity*

Students design the set for a professional performance of the 'it's difficult to say' improvisation. They should consider the following areas:

1. The items of scenery needed to help establish that this is a meeting between professional people.
2. The items of scenery needed to indicate that the scene is set in the film industry.
3. Any personal props the different characters might carry and use.
4. The colours in the set and what these choices might convey to an audience about the scene.

# Original script

## 1. A wise choice?

In this two-scene script for pairs, students continue to explore how to apply pause in dialogue and revise how to deliver fast-paced dialogue as explored in Part Two, Chapter One. In Scene One, character **A** persuades character **B** to leave home, move to a different part of the country and take a job in their company. Scene Two explores the consequences when **A** decides things are not working out and fires **B**. Capturing the excitement of both characters in Scene One, a fast pace is used in several places. The use of the symbol / indicates where dialogue overlaps. In Scene Two, the awkwardness and tension between the two characters are expressed through pauses of varying lengths. Start by reading the text with students, examining the various ways the pauses can be interpreted and performed. Discuss what they might want to convey to the audience about the two characters in these pauses. You might also want to set up improvisation tasks to explore what happened between the two characters at school and last month, as referenced in the extract.

### A Wise Choice?

**A** *and* **B** *have been friends for a long time.* **A** *now runs their own business in a different part of the country. In Scene One,* **A** *is trying to persuade* **B** *to leave home to start a new job at this company. Scene Two is set about a year later.* **A** *has now decided to terminate* **B***'s employment.*

*Scene One builds on previous work examining the use of fast-paced dialogue. The symbol / is used to indicate where dialogue overlaps. In Scene Two, you have the opportunity to practise your work on applying pauses. Throughout the text, you will find that pauses of different lengths are indicated. Think carefully about how to use them and what you can reveal to the audience about the two characters during them.*

## Scene One

**A** So, what do you think? I urge you to do this. I am convinced that you will be absolutely/ brilliant.

**B** I don't know … it's such a major move. There is so much / to consider.

**A** The role is perfect for you, absolutely perfect. It will be a significant step forward in your career.

**B** I enjoy what I am doing now. I've been given extra / responsibility.

**A** But there's no real future where you are now. You'll have more opportunities in my team. You can go places I / promise you.

**B** I realise that. / It's just …

**A** So, what's holding you back? You need to be courageous, / move on.

**B** It's the change, the upheaval of moving, starting in a new place. I'm scared / I suppose.

**A** Don't be scared. I did it. I've made a real success of it. / You can too.

**B** I'm not the same as you. I'm not as confident or as ambitious / as you.

**A** It means we will see more of each other again. That would be great / wouldn't it?

**B** Yes, I know, but I'm wondering / if it will be …

**A** Yes, go on. What are you / thinking?

**B** Well, won't it be a bit awkward? You will be my manager. That seems / strange.

**A** What, because we are friends?

**B** Yes, exactly.

**A** Look, you're good at your job … you have the potential to do well with me. Yes, I'll be your manager, but probably only until you find your feet and then you can move on if you prefer. I know you will excel. I'll support you. It's not going to affect our friendship. We have been friends for / too long.

**B** I want to do it. It's / just …

**A** Go on. Tell me. You need to be honest. What's the / problem?

**B** It's just that time when we were at school / in our exam year.

**A** Why are you bringing that up again? I can't believe you still even / remember that.

**B** Look, we both made mistakes then. I'm not blaming you. I'm over it. I know what I did was also wrong. But what you did hurt me. I'm sorry, but I don't think I will ever / forget it.

**A** And I have said I am sorry, many many times. I don't know what else I can do. So, let's put it in the past where it / belongs.

**B** I have tried to do that. I really have. I promise / you.

**A** Seriously? You say that, but yet you still keep bringing it up time / and time again.

**B** Yes, because it's a reminder that things can go wrong even between the best of friends / like us.

**A** We are older now, and much more experienced. We were children then. We know how to be more sensitive / and respectful now.

**B** I fear I'm frustrating you, but this is such a huge life change / for me.

**A** Look, it's a no-brainer. This job has prospects, you will make more money, and we will get to spend more time together. What's not to like?

**B** And I'll be able to live at your place?

**A** Yes. I've told you. There's a spare room. You can have / that.

**B** Ok!

**A** Really?

**B** Yes, really. I'm in. I'll do / it.

**A** It's the best, the only decision you could possibly make.

**B** I hope so.

**A** Amazing, fantastic, you won't regret it.

## Scene Two

*One Year Later*

**B** You wanted to see me?

*(Short pause.)*

**A** Yes, thanks for coming in. (*Short pause.)* Do take a seat.

**B** This sounds formal. *(Pause.)* By the way, do you want me to get some more milk for home? Have we run out? We seem to get through / a lot.

**A** Sorry, but this isn't the time or place to discuss milk. We're at work.

*(Pause.)*

**B** Just say what you need to say. This is getting a bit awkward.

*(Beat.)*

**A** Have you brought the files with you?

*(Beat.)*

**B** Files? *(Beat.)* Which files do / you mean?
**A** The files on the Cassidy case.

*(Pause.)*

**B** I'm still working on them, there's lots to do. I was only given them yesterday.

*(Beat.)*

**A** I need them back. *(Beat.)* Right now.

*(Short pause.)*

**B** Why? You know, I couldn't possibly have finished working on them already. We usually get them for at least a / week.
**A** They shouldn't have been given to you.

*(Beat.)*

**B** What do you mean? What's going on?

*(Pause.)*

**A** I'm sorry, but after what happened with the last case, those files should never have come into your possession. It was an error, a mistake.

*(Beat.)*

**B** I thought we had moved on from that. You said that my mistake didn't matter, that most people make the same mistake and that there was probably a glitch in the system. I can't believe you've brought this up. *(Pause.)* Ok, I'll bring them back if that's what you want. *(Beat.)* So, tell me, what can I be trusted to work on instead?

*(Long pause.)*

**A** Look, that's what I wanted to discuss with you.
**B** Sounds ominous. *(Pause.)* Go on then.

*(Long pause.)*

**A** This is very difficult to say.

*(Beat.)*

**B** Oh no, please don't tell me. I don't believe / this.
**A** I have to be professional / here.
**B** But my work is good. I've only made that one mistake in the whole time I've been here, and that wasn't actually my / fault.
**A** I'm afraid that it cost the company too much money. I wanted to ignore it, but unfortunately, the powers above / me …
**B** Don't give me nonsense about powers above you. You own the company. You said that it didn't matter and to forget about / it.
**A** I don't think those were my exact words, and the point is that it did matter and it does matter, and I'm not willing to discuss it further.

*(Pause.)*

**B** Well get on with it then. What's the disciplinary procedure? What do I have to do to prove myself again?

*(Long pause.)*

**A** I'm sorry, but I'm going to have to let you go.

*(Beat.)*

**B** Say that again.

*(Short pause.)*

**A** There's no longer a job for you here. I'm sorry.

*(Beat.)*

**B** You are joking? I can't / believe …
**A** Unfortunately, I am not joking. You will need to vacate the premises today. Obviously, I will continue to pay you until the end of the month, and I'll provide you with a fair reference for any future employment opportunities.

*(Pause.)*

**B** This has nothing to do with work, does it? At least be honest with me.

*(Beat.)*

A Of course, it's about work.

*(Beat.)*

**B** Don't lie. It's clearly about what happened last month. I knew you were holding a grudge.

*(Pause.)*

**A** It has nothing to do with that. This is only, and will only ever be, about what is best for my company, and for you.

*(Beat.)*

**B** You are unbelievable. You made me give up a perfectly good job, move away from my home, family and other friends. You have ruined my life.

*(Long pause.)*

**A** There's no point just standing there. At the end of the day, you decided to work here, so stop being so melodramatic.

*(Beat.)*

**B** You persuaded me.

*(Beat.)*

**A** As I said, it was your decision.

*(Beat.)*

**B** How are we ever going to manage sharing a home? *(Silence.)* Oh no, you're not kicking me out, are you?

*(Short pause.)*

**A** It's in your best interests if you look elsewhere.

*(Beat.)*

**B** Where? How? I no longer have a job. I can't believe this. I don't know you anymore, I really don't.

*(Pause.)*

**A** I'm genuinely sorry.

*(Short pause.)*

**B** Are you?

*(Beat.)*

**A** Of course, I wanted it to work out. I'm sorry it hasn't.

*(Pause.)*

**B** You are truly unbelievable!

## 2. The jacket

In this monologue, a young person addresses the audience about why they stole a jacket. Several different-length pauses are indicated in the script. This is a challenging activity, as students are required to elicit different responses from the audience towards the character. They can either work individually to create two performances of the monologue or work in pairs, with each student taking on responsibility for one of the interpretations. The two aims are:

1. To provoke sympathy and understanding from the audience towards the character.
2. To provoke disapproval and a lack of sympathy from the audience towards the character.

Spend time reading the monologue with the class, discussing ways in which they might use voice to achieve their intended impact. Design students could choose to work on the activity at the end of the monologue.

## The Jacket

**Alex** *has stolen a jacket from a store. In this monologue, Alex is telling the audience what happened. You are asked to perform this monologue to evoke one of two responses from your audience:*

1. *Your audience will sympathize and support Alex.*
   *or*
2. *Your audience will distrust and dislike Alex.*

*Think carefully about how you use your voice and what you do during the pauses to elicit the appropriate audience response.*

**Alex** I didn't plan on taking it. *(Short pause.)* I didn't actually plan to be in that shop. My phone was ringing in my pocket, and I stepped in to take the call. I didn't want to risk it on the street. You know how it is … too many people have their phones snatched nowadays. So I went into the shop, answered the call, which turned out to be nothing, so I shouldn't have ended up in that shop at all. *(Pause.)*

I'd never been in there before; the place didn't really hold any appeal to me. I'd walked by so many times but never been in. Anyhow, I looked round rather aimlessly, if I'm being honest, and that's when I spotted it … the jacket! *(Pause.)* It was incredible, striking and unusual, modern and unique. I could see myself in it. I could imagine how I would look to others and what they might say. *(Short pause.)* It soon became absolutely clear to me that I needed to have it. I needed to have that jacket. I had some cash on me; it had been my birthday a few weeks ago, and I'd been treated. I'd been told to spend it on something special. Well, this was it. This was my something special. This was what I wanted more than anything I had ever wanted. *(Short pause.)* And then I made my first fatal error. I tried it on before I looked at the price tag. And, of course, it was perfect, absolutely perfect. It fitted me like a dream; it was the right colour, the right style, and I looked better in this jacket than I had ever looked in anything in my whole life. It was obvious that I deserved to have it. It was made for me, and it was meant to be. *(Pause.)*

It was only then that I looked at the price tag and I realised why I had probably never been in this store before. It was so expensive, it was extortionate, it was out of my league! There was no way I could ever afford anything like this. I needed to put it back on the rail. Just put it back on the rail. *(Long pause.)* I looked at my reflection in the mirror, and the confident person who looked back at me seemed to be telling me what I should do next. I wasn't going to hurt anyone; I wasn't going to cause any trouble. But I was going to do something that I had never done before, and I would never ever do again. *(Pause.)* I was going to take that jacket. Now, I will always argue that fate meant this to be because, for some inexplicable reason, that jacket had no security tag. The others were tagged, but mine wasn't. Maybe if it had been, I wouldn't have taken it, but in my mind and my heart, at that moment, that jacket was destined to come home with me. *(Pause.)* It was easy. I slipped my large overcoat over it, completely concealing it. I then spent a few more minutes browsing through other items in the shop. I even asked an assistant if a shirt came in different colours. *(Short pause.)* And then I made for the door. I expected a hidden security tag to trigger the alarm to ring out, but there was absolutely nothing. *(Short pause.)* Silence! *(Pause.)*

I strolled down the street with my jacket safely on me. I didn't feel guilty. I actually felt very little. I had done something I thought I would never do in my life, but did it matter? *(Pause.)* I don't know. I just knew that at some point I would be seen in the jacket of my dreams, and I was convinced that I was going to feel so good, so special. *(Long pause.)* Do you understand?

### *Design activity*

This is an interesting monologue to challenge your students to consider how costume can impact an audience's attitude towards a character. Explain that when audiences watch a performance, they piece together all the various elements to create meaning. Students often relate to the idea of comparing the different elements of acting, costume, set, lights, props and sound to pieces of a jigsaw puzzle, which combine to make one picture. Explain that costume can help convey many things on stage, including a character's age, the period in which the play is set, the status of a character and their occupation. It can also be used to help suggest the personality of a character and steer the audience members to feel a particular way about a character. It is important to emphasize that in daily life, we should not judge people's personalities based on what they wear. On stage, however, the careful design of costumes combined with other performance elements can help guide the audience in their responses to a particular character.

With this in mind, students can work in pairs to design two costumes that help provoke different audience reactions to the character in *The Jacket*. One costume should help promote sympathy for Alex; the other should evoke a feeling of distrust. You might also want to consider how an actor works with a piece of costume to help portray a character. Ask your students to bring a long scarf to the lesson. Experiment with ways they might use the scarf to convey fear, anger and happiness.

To build on their earlier work on costume, remind students to consider the items of clothing and accessories, use of colour, type of fabric and condition of clothes when deciding what Alex might wear in the two interpretations.

### *Written activity*

For this task, students evaluate the work of another performer, focusing on the impact on the audience.

**Suggested title**: Discuss how another actor used pauses during their performance of *The Jacket* and how this impacted the way the audience responded to the character.

## Published script

### 1. *The Human Voice* by Jean Cocteau in a version by Daniel Raggett

The excerpt is taken from Daniel Raggett's version of Jean Cocteau's *The Human Voice,* first performed at the Comédie-Française, Paris, in 1930. Raggett's play premiered at the Gate Theatre, Camden, in 2018, resulting in two Off-West End awards, including best director. It is a one-sided telephone conversation in which a woman (although the gender is not relevant in this section) has a final call with her lover before their relationship comes to an end. This excerpt is from the beginning of the play, where crossed lines and poor audibility frustrate the woman. The whole play is more appropriate for older students, but the opening excerpt is an excellent piece for this age group to continue exploring how to apply pause.

Read the excerpt through, ensuring that students understand who the other people on the phone line could be. Link back to the 'telephone conversation' activity from the improvisation section. Students should consider how pause can be used to create the sense of other people speaking at the end of the line. For this exercise, students can start by working in pairs, taking turns to improvise what the other characters might be saying at the end of the phone line. They then continue working independently or in pairs to bring the monologue to life for performance. Individual design students can work with actors to establish a basic set and how it is used in performance.

## Context for students

This excerpt is from the 2018 version of a 1930s French one-person play called *The Human Voice.* This section features the central character attempting to arrange an important telephone call. At this point, other people are repeatedly phoning, and the call quality is poor. Originally, the play was performed using an old-fashioned cable phone, while the 2018 version used a mobile phone. Think carefully where and how you use pause to show your character responding to the problems on the line.



Hello, hello, hello
No, you've got the wrong number, hang up
Hello
You've got the wrong number
Oh!
hello!
No, put the phone down
Hello                    hello
Stop calling me
I can't cancel if you're on the phone
No, that isn't –
hello!
this is ridiculous
Why are you asking me? I don't know.

*She hangs up, keeps hold of the phone. It rings.*

Hello!
Well, what do you want me to do?
You're really rude
What? My fault
it's not at all
no way
Hello!
hello
Look, someone's trying to call me and I can't
speak to them because the whole universe is
trying to ring this number. And you can shut up
as well.

*She hangs up. It rings.*

Hello! Is that you?
are you there?

Yes
I can't hear you very well
you're far away, you sound – really far away
Hello!
this is painful
there's too much going on
Call me back. Hello! *Call. Me. Back.*
I said: *you* call *me* back

*She hangs up. Another call.*

No, stop calling me. I've told you I'm not –

*She hangs up. It rings.*

Hello!
Ah! finally
it's you
yeah
fine
hello!
yes
It was impossible trying to get hold of you with all that going on – the phone hasn't stopped
yes
yes

no
well, that's lucky
I got back ten minutes ago
Did you try and call before?
ah!
no, no
I went out for dinner
at Martha's
must be about quarter past eleven
Are you at home?
Just look at the clock
That's literally what I just said

## *Written activity*

The emphasis of this task is to develop students' ability to incorporate personal responses into their written work. In other subjects, students might be advised to avoid using the first-person singular; however, in exam drama responses, they are required to include their personal thoughts and reflections. After watching performances of the excerpt from *The Human Voice,* focus all questioning on drawing out your students' personal response to the way pauses and any other skills were employed to deliver the monologue. The type of responses you are aiming for include:

1. The long pause the performer used made me feel sorry for the character, as I could sense their frustration, and I could imagine what the other person was saying at the end of the line.
2. When the performer raised her voice, I felt annoyed towards the character.
3. I felt very sad for the character by the end of the piece, as the performer was tearful and used a very emotional tone of voice.
4. I found myself laughing as the character kept getting the wrong person on the end of the telephone line. The performer's exaggerated facial expressions during the pauses enhanced these comic moments.

Students must write about the skills a performer uses to elicit a response from them towards a character.

**Suggested title**: Based on any of the performances of *The Human Voice,* give four examples of how you personally responded to the skills used by another performer.

## 2. *The Effect* by Lucy Prebble

Lucy Prebble's *The Effect* was first performed in 2012 at the Cottesloe Theatre (now the Dorfman) at the National Theatre. It was revived at the National's Lyttelton Theatre in 2023. It focuses on the relationship between Tristan and Connie, who meet in a drug trial for a new antidepressant. They fall in love but find it impossible to tell if their feelings are real or connected to the effects of the drugs. For this exercise, the gender of the performers is not relevant.

Read the excerpt with students and discuss how pauses of different lengths can be used to help convey Tristan's confusion, magnify Connie's attempts to remain patient and support him, and convey the awkwardness between them. Clearly, a faster pace would be appropriate in places, allowing you to link to work students covered in Part Two, Chapter One.

### Context for students

This excerpt is taken from the end of the play *The Effect*, which features two characters, **Tristan** and **Connie**, who have been involved in a drug trial. At this point, **Tristan** has experienced an adverse reaction to the trial; he has been given a blood transfusion and is suffering from amnesia. In this excerpt, **Connie** is visiting him; the dialogue has a cyclical feel as **Tristan** fails to remember everything. After witnessing the connection between their characters and the development of their relationship, the audience needs to see that an awkwardness has developed between them.



*Now it is* **Tristan** *in a bed on a drip.*

**Connie** *enters, looks at him. Eventually, he sees her.*

**Tristan** I'm thirsty. Do you have water?

*Beat.*

*She sees there is water, or gets water from her bag.*

**Connie** Hello.

**Tristan** What day is it? You look scared. What happened? Is it me? What happened?

*He touches his face.*

**Connie** It's Friday.

**Tristan** I don't know anyone. Why am I here? You look frightened? What happened?

**Connie** You've had a blood transfusion. They told me you have something called transient global amnesia.

**Tristan** Have I? Yes. Why are you looking at me, am I still me?

**Connie** Yeah. You just have new blood. It's okay.

*He panics.*

**Tristan** Can I see?

**Connie** See what?

**Tristan** I need a mirror.

**Connie** Oh.

*She thinks, looks round, scrabbles in bag, opens up a bit of make up with a tiny mirror, hands it over.*

**Tristan** *looks at himself.*

**Tristan** What's happening? What day is it?

**Connie** It's Friday. It's your birthday.

**Tristan** How is that today? Show me a thing saying that's today.

**Connie** The date?

**Tristan** Yeah.

*She hunts, comes up with only her phone and shows it to him.*

You could have changed that.

**Connie** Why would I do that?

**Tristan** Have I been asleep then?

**Connie** You've got something called transient global amnesia.

**Tristan** Yes, I – transient, does that mean –

**Connie** It's going to pass. They don't know when or how long –

**Tristan** What was I doing before you got here?

**Connie** I don't know. I wasn't here.

**Tristan** What day is it?

**Connie** Friday. It's your birthday.

**Tristan** No. Is it? Something else.

**Connie** That it's my birthday too. You remember that?

**Tristan** No. Oh god oh god oh god.

**Connie** You don't know me, do you. You're not retaining any new memories. It's me. Do you know my name?

*No answer.*

**Connie** How do you feel?

**Tristan** I'm hungry.

**Connie** *finds a yogurt, gives it to him.*

**Connie** We were on a trial. Do you remember?

**Tristan** Something awful's happened, I don't know where I am!

**Connie** You're in the hospital. Do you know what day it is?

**Tristan** Yes.

**Connie** It's okay if you don't.

**Tristan** What day is it?

**Connie** Friday.

**Tristan** *looks at the yogurt in his hand. Meaning drains from it. He offers it to her.*

**Tristan** Is this yours?

**Connie** I'm going to find a spoon.

**Tristan** Okay.

**Connie** And then we'll go from there.

**Connie** *has flowers instead, she's bright and cheerful, busy, casual, taking care of things, livening up the room.*

**Tristan** I don't know anybody here. Why am I here?

**Connie** Shh, it's okay. I know. I was just here.

**Tristan** No, you don't understand, I just woke up!

**Connie** I know, you've got something called transient

global amnesia –

**Tristan** Transient, does that mean –

**Connie** Yes, it's going to pass.

**Tristan** What day is it?

**Connie** It's Tuesday.

**Tristan** Is that right?! Show me something, with the date on.

**Connie** *gives him a newspaper, practisedly.*

**Tristan** I need to see my face –

*She gets out a mirror, practisedly, he looks at himself.*

I have to go! I – why am I here?

**Connie** You're having trouble remembering, forming new memories.

**Tristan** I'm trying to think the last thing I remember.

**Connie** That's okay.

**Tristan** But I know you.

**Connie** That's right, Tris.

## *Design activity*

This is a good point to introduce this age group to some of the fundamental principles for applying stage make-up. Regardless of skin tone, all actors must wear make-up on stage as harsh stage lighting can dull complexion and definition. Outline these guidelines:

1. All performers should apply a base (foundation) on their faces, which should be one to two shades darker than their skin tone, to create a natural-looking complexion under stage lights.
2. To create the impression that a character is unwell, choose a base colour that is one to two shades lighter than the performer's natural complexion.
3. To create the impression that a character has been outdoors in the sunshine, choose a base colour that is three to four times darker than the performer's natural complexion.
4. Regardless of gender, brown eyeliner should be used on all performers to define their eyes.
5. Regardless of gender, a natural coloured lipliner should be used on all performers to define their lips.

There are many other areas students can explore if they continue with the subject. At this stage, they can work in pairs to determine the appropriate make-up for performers playing Connie and Tristan in the excerpt from *The Effect*.

# 2

# MOVEMENT – PHYSICAL THEATRE 'DYNAMITE'

**Photo 3-2-1** Physical theatre.

## Introduction

In this chapter, you will explore more sophisticated movement and physical theatre approaches, drawing connections to practitioners such as Merce Cunningham, Frantic Assembly, Kneehigh and Complicite.

Emphasis is placed on how movement can convey meaning, moods and emotions in performance. There are also opportunities to develop more abstract sequences, examining how actors utilize different elements of movement, such as action, levels, spatial pathways and dynamics to create exciting, original performance pieces. Original scripts have been developed to explore how actors can incorporate movement into their performances, allowing physical theatre techniques to merge with dialogue.

The games and warm-ups provide foundations for more complex exploration in the improvisation and script tasks. This age group respond well to these challenging activities, and the ideas and skills they develop can be used and applied by those who continue to study the subject at exam level. All students should gain practical experience of these approaches, but there is also scope for individuals to focus on designing sets and costumes during the scripted activities.

# Games

## 1. Plasticine play

Students sit or stand in a circle. Start by demonstrating how to mould a small piece of imaginary plasticine into a usable object, such as a toothbrush, tennis racquet, computer or bike. Model how students should aim for precision and detail when creating their object, and then demonstrate how to mime using the moulded object. Pass the object to the next student, explaining that they need to take what has been created before moulding it into a different object of a completely different size and shape. Challenge students if you find that their moulding and mimes are not detailed and accurate enough. This game can be played in smaller groups once the expectations have been established.

## 2. Mood statues

This is a more sophisticated version of the childhood game *Musical Statues.* To music, students walk around the space using movement and physicality to communicate a given attitude or mood. When the music stops, they convey that attitude and mood through an exciting freeze position. Avoid playing the game competitively to determine a winner, as students lose out on developing ideas and technique. Suggested titles for walking and freezing:

1. Carefree.
2. Late for an appointment.
3. Lost and confused.
4. Fearful.
5. Celebratory.
6. Excited.
7. Suspicious.
8. Angry.
9. Disappointed.
10. Intimidating.
11. Intimidated.
12. Cold.
13. Hot.
14. Delighted.

# Warm-up

## 1. Speed miming

In this exercise, students individually mime different situations. They must aim to be as clear, detailed and accurate as possible. At first, they should try to deliver the mime at real speed. On your command, they perform at a fast speed and then in slow motion. Stress that when working at a fast speed, the movement must retain accuracy and clarity. Mime topics:

1. Working on a computer.
2. Flying an aeroplane.
3. Sketching another person's portrait.
4. Working on a jigsaw puzzle.
5. Putting a cover on a duvet.
6. Making pancakes.

## 2. Dynamics

This is an important exercise designed to teach students how to apply dynamics to movement to evoke mood and atmosphere. Explain that dynamics are essentially the flavours we add to simple movements and actions to make them more interesting. To illustrate, teach the students this simple movement sequence:

> Raise both arms in the air as if to take something off a shelf, and then lower your arms. Move your right arm forward as if to shake another person's hand, and then lower it. Raise your left hand as if to ask a question in class, and then lower it. Take two steps forward.

Once the students have learnt the sequence of movement, they should perform it using different dynamics. You may want to add pieces of music to help them create the desired effect. The dynamics are:

1. Fast, sudden, strong, abrupt.
2. Soft, slow, floaty.
3. Sustained as if pushing through mud.
4. Alternate the dynamics. Use fast and strong for the first action, and then switch to soft and slow for the second, and so on.

Discuss with the students how these different dynamics evoke different moods, and what impact they might have on an audience.

To develop further, split the students into pairs to mime washing dishes and wiping up. They should consider how their characters are feeling when performing this task (they can think differently from one another). They should apply a mix of the most appropriate dynamics to their sequence to convey their chosen attitudes and feelings. Watch and evaluate some examples of the work. Discuss how this pedestrian activity becomes more engaging when it is performed with attitude and different dynamics.

## 3. Storytelling

Before teaching this exercise, take time to introduce your students to some of Steven Berkoff's ideas. I always start by discussing his training in mime in Paris, recalling my experience of seeing his revival of *One Man* at the Riverside Studios, Hammersmith, in 2011. In this performance, he demonstrated a remarkable ability to make his audience visualize objects and sets through the strength of his mime. It is perhaps an opportunity to discuss the power of the audience's imagination when watching theatre and how an actor can convey so much through their acting skills without the need for a complicated set, costume and lights.

In this exercise, students work independently to mime a story as you read it out. The objective of the exercise is to make the mime as detailed and convincing as possible. Remind the students to draw on their earlier work on miming and dynamics to help bring the story to life. They are required to use their imaginations as the story jumps from location to location. Depending on your teaching area, provide students with guidance on the amount of space they can use. The story can be mimed in a very contained area if required. Appropriate background music is a helpful addition. The story:

> You are standing in your bedroom, looking out of the window. You draw back the weighty, velvet curtains and look out at the glorious, sunny day. You start to walk down the old spiral staircase, taking great care not to make any noise, as you don't want to be heard. You come to the massive old wooden door. The key is in the lock, and you have to work hard to turn it. You press down on the handle and use your weight to push the heavy door open. As you look out, you feel the sun on your face, and you take a moment to enjoy the sensation. You step out, realizing that your feet are in mud, and it is with great difficulty that you manage to take a few steps forward. You become aware that you are surrounded by bushes and trees, and find you have to twist and turn to manoeuvre through and around them. Suddenly, in front of you is the most beautiful baby deer. You cautiously touch it, and then stroke it more confidently as you realise that it wants to befriend you. It starts to rain. As you watch the deer run away, you notice an umbrella on the ground. It's ancient and difficult to open, and you are forced to persevere to do so. The rain gets heavier and heavier, and you can feel the water growing deeper and rising up your legs. You tiptoe through the water, which is gradually growing colder and colder. Without warning, the rain stops, and you find yourself on warm sand. You close the umbrella and put it down carefully on the ground. The sand is getting hotter and hotter, and it is hard to keep your feet on it. A ladder appears in front of you, which you carefully climb up until you are at the top of the world. You look down at everything below you.

To develop their skills, students can construct their own imaginary sequences to perform in pairs or groups.

### *Design activity*

Individually or in pairs, students work on a proposal for how lights and sounds might enhance their performance of the 'storytelling' activity. They should decide the following:

1. The type of lanterns to be used. These were introduced in Part Two, Chapter Two, after *The Moon* script.
2. The colour and intensity of the lights.
3. The type of sound effects needed.
4. Imagining there are four speakers, the volume and the direction from which the sounds are to be played.

## 4. Grapevine

Consider how to organize the group in your space before attempting this exercise. Split the class into groups of four. Students label themselves **A, B, C** and **D**.

Organize the class in the space so that the **A**s and **B**s sit facing one another. **C**s and **D**s must not be able to see the **As** and **Bs** from their group or any other group. Once you are confident with the set-up, out of the earshot of your **B**s, **C**s and **D**s, describe this sequence of events to the **A**s only, and the activity can then begin:

> You are sitting watching a terrifying film on television. You use the remote control to switch channels and start watching a comedy which you find extremely funny. It ends, and you switch the television off. You go to the fridge and take out a can of drink. You open it and start drinking. At this moment, your cat arrives and starts rubbing around your legs. You put the can down and stroke the cat. You open the fridge, take out the milk and pour some into a bowl for the cat. The doorbell rings. You go to the door and open it. Someone is collecting for charity. You take a few coins out of your pocket and put them in the collection tin. You close the door. Your mobile phone rings, you take it out of your pocket and answer it. Your friend is shouting at you as you are late for a social occasion. You apologise, hang up, and run to the door to go out.

**A** has one chance to mime the story to **B,** aiming to be as accurate and detailed as possible. Once the mime is over, **A** taps their **C** on the shoulder. **B** sits in **A**'s chair, and **C** takes the other chair to observe. **A** can watch what happens next, but they are not allowed to say or do anything. **B** performs the mime exactly as **A** performed it for them. Once **B** has finished, they tap **D** on the shoulder. **C** takes the seat used for performance, and **D** observes. **B** is allowed to watch but not participate. **C** must perform exactly what **B** performed to them.

Once **C** has performed, **D** must wait until all other groups have finished their performances. To the whole class, each **D** describes the story they have just seen performed to them by **C**. Using the present tense, they must provide a clear description, inventing what they believe happened, even if they are unsure. Before revealing the original story, you can then go back along the line and ask **C**s and **B**s to describe what they thought they were doing. You will probably find that some mimes lacked clarity, and moments were omitted as the story travelled through the group. You can conclude by reading the story aloud, asking the whole class to perform it simultaneously.

# Improvisation

## 1. Mechanical movement

Start by demonstrating a simple eight-beat movement sequence. Your example should model simple actions, different levels and different facings. For example:

*(Start standing centre, facing front, arms by side.)*

**Beat one**: Lift your right arm in the air.
**Beat two**: Lift your left arm in the air.
**Beat three**: Turn forty-five degrees right.
**Beat four**: Drop both arms back to the sides.
**Beat five**: Touch the floor.
**Beat six**: Stand upright again.

**Beat seven**: Turn forty-five degrees right (to face the back), lifting both arms in the air.
**Beat eight**: Turn ninety degrees (to face the front), dropping arms back to sides.

Give students about four minutes to create an individual, simple eight-beat movement sequence. Emphasize that the movements must be uncomplicated so that others can easily learn and repeat accurately. Watch the whole class perform and advise if any sequences appear too intricate and challenging for others to copy. Students now perform to a piece of mechanical music with a regular 4/4 beat. Several examples are provided in the *Recommended Music* section. You can experiment with a slow beat and a fast beat.

Divide the students into groups of four to teach their sequences of movement to the other members of their group. Advise them to simplify the movement if they find that any member of the group is unable to perform the sequence accurately. Once the class appears confident, start experimenting with the different ways they can link the movement together. Examples of methods for groups of four (not exhaustive):

1. Perform all sequences together in unison.
2. All perform their own sequences at the same time (four different sequences are all performed simultaneously).
3. Three students perform in unison whilst the final student freezes or performs their own sequence over and over again.
4. Two students perform one sequence in unison; the other two perform a different sequence in unison.
5. One student performs, whilst the other three freeze.

Students now develop a more extended sequence of movement linking everything together. Allow about fifteen minutes for them to create as much as possible, advising that they work on a section at a time, repeat and perfect before moving on. Give them time to practise with the music. They can adopt an appropriate attitude to help apply interesting dynamics and facial expressions.

Watch and evaluate the work. Discuss how these sequences might be used in a longer piece of theatre to convey mood and atmosphere.

**Photo 3-2-2** Mechanical movement.

### *Written activity*

Working individually or in groups, students create a proposal for an original drama that includes a mechanical movement sequence.

## 2. Lyrical movement

This is a simple way to adapt the 'mechanical movement' technique to develop a piece of movement that is more lyrical, peaceful and calm. Individually, students create a sequence consisting of eight movements to be performed to a relaxed eight counts. For this exercise, the movements should be performed to a more atonal piece of background music to create a soft, free-flowing sequence. Model an example which could consist of the following:

- Start in a kneeling position on the floor, and slowly lift one arm in front.
- Lift the other arm so both arms are held high.
- Stand and slowly lower both arms down.
- Softly bend the knees, taking one arm out to the right side.
- Take the other arm out to the other side.
- Slowly turn, keeping the arms out to the sides.
- Slowly lower the arms down.
- Kneel to return to the starting position.

When demonstrating this sequence, ensure that you connect all the movements. There are no rigid counts, and the sequences can vary in length. Give students time to perfect their movements. Working in groups of four, students use the methods they employed when working on the mechanical sequences to connect their work. Because they are now performing with a slow and sustained dynamic, they will find it easier to follow one another. Watch examples of the work discussing how these sequences could be included in a longer piece of drama and what they might communicate to audiences.

### *Written activity*

Working individually or in groups, students create a proposal for an original drama that includes a lyrical, free-flowing movement sequence.

## 3. Much more than miming

This exercise is based on a technique Frantic Assembly used when developing the play *Pool (no Water)*. Actors were first asked to create a mime based on all the paraphernalia of going sunbathing. Once the sequences were fixed, the actors then isolated and reordered moments from that initial mime to create a new, exciting sequence. This is an ideal point to introduce the company to your students. Formed in 1994, Frantic Assembly mainly creates new, original material that draws on physicality to tell its stories. In the *Further Reading* section, two books are listed that you might wish to reference. Many of their techniques are more suitable for exploration when working with older students, but this particular exercise is an interesting starting point. Start by asking all students to practise miming this sequence of events:

> You have been to the supermarket and arrive back at your home with two heavy bags of shopping. You unlock the door, carry the bags in, and start to unload the goods, placing everything in the right place. Some items need to be stored in the fridge, some in the freezer, and some in separate cupboards. You have also purchased items of clothing that need to be kept in cupboards/wardrobes.

Once the students have worked on their individual mime, divide them into groups of two or three. They should now create a sequence of movement to be performed in unison, where they can select any elements, in any order, from their initial individual mimes. They can vary the speed of the mime, exaggerate any moment and apply different dynamics. Add music and share the work.

## 4. Abstract still images

Divide the class into groups of about four. Explain that you are revisiting still images, but instead of presenting characters and stories, the still images are to be designed to convey mood and atmosphere. Students should think of themselves as a gigantic lump of plasticine to be moulded into a shape. Showing pictures of abstract sculptures is helpful to illustrate what you mean. Revise the different elements which make an effective still image, such as absolute stillness, levels, connections and strong facial expressions. It is up to you to decide how long students have to create an image. You could use a ten-, twenty- or thirty-second countdown or give them a more extended period of time. To connect to this year's focus on in-the-round spaces, students should prepare their images to be performed with the audience in a circle around them. Titles of still images:

1. Anger.
2. Determination.
3. Kindness.
4. Fireworks.
5. Stormy seas.
6. Clouds.

Watch examples of the work.

## 5. Chance choreography

In setting up this exercise, introduce students to the American dance choreographer, Merce Cunningham, and his technique of experimenting with chance to create dance. Students are usually surprised to discover that Cunningham's dancers were sometimes only introduced to their music on opening night, having previously learned the movements without it. Stress that some of Cunningham's approaches can be helpful to performers in theatre. You can find materials in the *Further Reading* section.

Building on the previous exercise, divide students into groups of two to five to create an abstract still image, that will be used as the opening and ending moment of a more extended sequence.

The objective of this exercise is to create an exciting piece of movement that connects the starting and ending abstract positions. They need to consider four movement areas:

1. Direction in space.
2. Actions.
3. Levels.
4. Dynamics.

Each student creates their own thirty-two-beat movement sequence using the concept of chance choreography. The thirty-two beats should be broken down into four sets of eight counts. (Depending on your group, you can choose to reduce the sequence to sixteen beats.) Clarify that the starting position of the work is the group abstract still image. Each student begins by considering how they will use their first eight beats. At this stage, they must not discuss their ideas with other group members. Talk through the different decisions they need to make to determine what they will do during the eight beats:

1. **Direction in space**: Students should decide on the direction of their movement, considering where they will be travelling and the pathways they will take. Emphasize that they do not need to be travelling all the time and that pauses and stillness are allowed. They should consider whether they are moving in circular pathways, walking in straight lines or a mix of ways.
2. **Actions**: Once students have determined the pathways in their minds for the first eight counts, they should start selecting their actions. Suggest different ways of moving, such as walking, running, jumping, skipping and turning. They should imagine applying these actions as they travel on their chosen pathways.
3. **Levels**: Remind students of how different levels can make movement work more interesting and ask them to consider whether they can apply higher or lower levels to any of their ideas.
4. **Dynamics**: Stress that different dynamics help bring their movement to life and ask them to imagine adding a range of dynamics to the eight-beat sequence. They can consider using fast, sudden, slow, gentle and sustained dynamics in different places.

Talk through the four (or two) sets of eight-beat sections so that all individual students have imagined their complete sequence of thirty-two (sixteen) beats before they physically try it out. This process of putting the long sequence together for the first time usually generates much excitement.

Before the students perform, discuss what they think might go well and what could go wrong. They are usually quick to pick up the fact that they might collide. Take time to convey that it is likely that some unusual and exciting movements will emerge.

At this stage, the students undertake their first performance of the movement sequence. Starting from the still image position, count out the thirty-two beats for them using a slow pace. Remind them that by beat thirty-two, they should be back in their still image position. Emphasize that it does not matter if any of them are a bit early or late to that final position. Observe closely to see what works well and what doesn't. Often, students move outwards from their initial still image, leaving all of them outside a potential audience's field of vision. Clarify what has gone well and try to pick out those magical moments, such as lovely shapes, chance connections, different levels and dynamics and exciting actions.

Students now spend about ten to fifteen minutes perfecting their work. Emphasize that they should improve, develop and polish the sequence they have created by chance. Stress that their counting should be relaxed and quite loose, and they should begin to memorize the movement. Encourage them to embed more connections between performers. Add some background music which lacks a regular beat to help provide mood and atmosphere.

## 6. What's happening?

Start by showing students image 3-2-3.

**Image 3-2-3** Stimulus

Ask them to discuss what might be happening. Try to draw out as many examples as possible. Ideas might include:

1. An argument between friends or family members.
2. Friends rehearsing lines for a play.
3. Students discussing a difficult exam paper.

In pairs, students should recreate the image and improvise a short piece of dialogue to exemplify their interpretation. Watch some examples of the work. They should then repeat the exercise using a mixture of still images and mime to tell their story.

## 7. Telling a difficult story

This exercise is inspired by a powerful physical theatre scene from the 2010 production of Complicite's *A Disappearing Number* at the Novello Theatre, London.

The play presents the story of a Cambridge professor's collaboration with Srinivasa Ramanujan from Chennai, who, despite no formal training, made significant mathematical discoveries in the twentieth century. Interspersed with the story are scenes that explore the life of a modern-day mathematician, Ruth, and her husband. The play shifts between different times and locations, offering an exciting exploration of how different worlds and experiences connect. As a whole text, it is more accessible to older students, but it does provide some interesting and creative opportunities for practical work with this age group.

This is a valuable moment to introduce students to the theatre company Complicite and some of its key principles. The founders were inspired by Jacques Lecoq's (introduced in Part One, Chapter

Two) methods of developing and devising work through experimentation involving the entire company. Complicite also built on the idea of exploring physicality to understand how to communicate the essence of an idea on stage. You might also start examining how the company combine text, music, projection, dance, light and sound in their work in innovative and challenging ways. The *Further Reading* section references some useful material.

Scene 11 of *A Disappearing Number* features exchanges between the modern-day mathematician Ruth and her husband Al, unfolding to depict Ruth's realization that she is losing the baby she is carrying. In the early part of the 2010 performance of this scene, the style was naturalistic; as the tragic events developed, physical theatre was employed to depict the loss of the child. In the stage directions, it is stated that the two characters grab hold of one another and then roll over the bed. In this production, the moment was performed in slow motion, culminating in Ruth hugging a piece of fabric like a baby, which she gradually unravelled to represent the loss of the child.

It is up to you to decide whether you want to discuss all the particular details of this scene with students of this age; you know your students best. Kneehigh's 2008 version of the film *Brief Encounter* at the Birmingham Repertory Theatre offers alternative examples. The moment when the two central characters fall in love at first sight was depicted through a piece of physical theatre. Starting from a seated position, they both performed a short burst of jumps and turns before returning to their chairs to resume their conversation. Later in the performance, after drinking champagne, they were flown on wires high above the bar to show that they had literally been swept off their feet. When a new character entered, they were flown down and quickly brought back down to earth.

Whatever approach you take, stress how powerfully physical theatre conveys sensitive ideas on stage, including those that might be difficult, off-putting and triggering for audiences to view in a more naturalistic form.

Depending on your students and their experiences, choose one of the following situations:

1. Two characters have just been given news that a friend or family member has died.
2. Two characters have been told that they have been found guilty of a crime and are going to serve a jail sentence.
3. Two characters have been expelled from a country or school.

Students work in pairs to depict their sensitive situation using physical theatre only. Using a combination of techniques explored throughout this chapter, such as slow motion, mime, still image and chance choreography, they should aim to show how the two characters are feeling without using any words.

Watch the performances and evaluate.

## *Design activity*

Background music is a wonderful way to enhance a piece of performance work and help build students' confidence. At the end of the book, there are suggestions for different styles of music, which I have found particularly effective in supporting practical work. Based on their 'difficult story' improvisation, students select their own background music. You will need to guide them to appreciate that music with lyrics can often be a distraction in a scene with words. Music which is very well known and has other strong associations should also probably be avoided. Spend some time with your students analysing what works best.

### *Written activity*

This task requires students to evaluate the impact of another group's physical performance skills on the audience.

**Suggested title**: Discuss how effectively another group used physical theatre techniques to communicate their ideas to an audience.

# Original script

## 1. The gift

This monologue explores the wrapping of a present for an important friend, linking text and movement together. Read the script through, highlighting all the movement tasks. Students can work individually or in pairs.

### The Gift

**Billie** *is wrapping a present for a very important friend. The present must look perfect before taking it to the friend's party. The scene is set in* **Billie's** *bedroom.*

*(Start by creating a thirty to forty-five second sequence of mime, adding the finishing touches to the wrapping of the present. Make sure that your face reveals your determination to get it absolutely right. Every movement must show how much you care.)*

**Billie** That looks good. I think it's perfect … well, almost perfect. It won't be as remarkable as Jayden's offering, but then Jayden's sister will have wrapped it up, and Jayden's sister is at art school, so what chance do I have? Mine looks fine. I've done my best.

*(Pick up the present, stare at it disapprovingly. Hold this freeze for at least five seconds, then put the present down.)*

It's no good. It's dreadful, amateurish, laughable. I need this to stand out from the crowd. This is momentous. I'm depending on being noticed by Daz tonight. Daz holds the key to my future happiness. If Daz can see I am out of the ordinary, something special, a bit different, then I might get the coveted offer to go on holiday with Daz and family and stay in that fabulous luxury holiday villa. This gift is the catalyst for happy days, and this gift just isn't up to standard. Right, start again. Start again.

*(Mime ripping the paper off furiously. Create a mechanical eight-beat wrapping sequence that you should repeat several times, gradually increasing the speed. Finish with another five-second freeze, looking at the gift with a big smile on your face.)*

That's it, that's it. I have done it. Wonderful, glorious, a total success. Never mind art school … this is utter perfection. I might as well start packing my suitcase now, as I will be lounging by the pool in the fabulous luxury family villa with Daz at my beck and call.

*(Finish with another freeze, holding the gift like a trophy above your head with a massive smile on your face.)*

## 2. An unwelcome visitor

This monologue examines the impact of an unwelcome guest on a character's life and explores how movement can reveal attitudes and feelings. Read the script through, highlighting all the movement tasks. Students can work individually or in pairs.

### An Unwelcome Visitor

**Blake's** *embarrassing and often unkind aunt has unexpectedly arrived for a visit.* **Blake** *has been sent to the kitchen to prepare afternoon tea.*

*(During the opening part of the monologue, pace around the stage, use lots of circular directions to show* **Blake's** *annoyance, confusion and distress.)*

**Blake** What on earth is she doing here? Why wasn't I told? Why wasn't I warned? Mum obviously knew she was coming. It makes sense now, yes, those new lilies on the table. They were for her. Mum always wants to impress her. If I'd known, I could have gone out; I could have escaped; I could have been anywhere apart from here. She's already started by commenting on my new hairstyle with that slightly sneering, underhanded tone. And to rub salt into the wound, I've now been sent in here to prepare her *afternoon tea*. When do we ever have *afternoon tea*? I'm now expected to make tea in a pot and cut the *freshly baked* cake. Of course, that's why Mum baked a cake last night. She never bakes cakes! She knew Auntie Abominable was on her broomstick, winging her way here and decided to bake for her. It's unbelievable. It's unreal!

*(Tip-toe to the door to listen. Take at least ten seconds to show the audience that you don't like what you are hearing.)*

As I thought, she's in there criticizing me. She doesn't approve of my hair or clothes. She thinks I have a sneaky look about me! A sneaky look! How dare she? I'll show her. She wants *afternoon tea*, she will get *afternoon tea*! Right, let's start with the cake.

*(This section should be mimed in slow motion with exaggerated actions and sustained dynamics. Take the cake tin out of the cupboard, open it, and remove the cake. Make your movement as slow, sinister and exaggerated as possible. Take the top off the cake and start spreading some chilli sauce onto it.)*

An extra spread of chilli sauce to bring the jam to life.

*(Add a squirt of washing-up liquid.)*

Just a little, tiny-weeny squirt of washing-up liquid to cleanse her nasty insides.

*(Put the top back on the cake and pick up the salt and start sprinkling it on top of the cake.)*

Ahhhhhh … an extra sprinkling of salty sugar to provide a little more flavour and depth to the cake. That's more like it. I'm sure Auntie will relish a little extra bite to match her personality. Now for her cuppa.

*(Now create a fast-beat sequence showing the making of the tea. The aim is to do it quickly, conveying that you don't care about what you are making. Remember to make your actions clear and accurate, but the dynamics should be loose and sloppy to show your attitude towards the tea.)*

Perfect. An *afternoon tea* to remember and then never return. *(Calling out.)* Auntie, afternoon tea is served. I hope you are feeling peckish.

## 3. The meeting

This scene for two performers explores what happens when two teenagers **X** and **Y**, who met briefly on a family holiday the previous year, reunite one year later after keeping in touch via social media platforms. Movement and physical theatre techniques explored in this chapter are embedded to help convey the awkwardness between the two. Read through the script, discussing all the movement tasks.

### The Meeting

**X** *and* **Y** *first met very briefly on the last day of their family holiday about a year ago. They hit it off and have kept in touch through various social media platforms. One year later, they meet again as their families decide to holiday in the same resort. The scene is set during their first evening on holiday in a café bar where they have arranged to meet.*

*For the opening of the scene, use the 'mechanical movement' technique. Both of you should develop an eight-beat movement sequence, based on operating the mobile phone. You can exaggerate your movements, remembering to use different levels and facings. Once you have created both individual sequences, teach them to one another. Now, combine the sequences. Remember to consider the different options you have learnt for connecting your ideas:*

1. *Performing movement in unison.*
2. *Performing different movements at the same time.*
3. *Using some stillness/freezes.*

*The purpose of this movement section is to capture how the relationship between* **X** *and* **Y** *has been conducted via social media over the past year, and to convey the fact that they now feel somewhat awkward about meeting again in person. Once you have performed your sequence,* **X** *will cut in with the opening line.*

**X** Well hello.

**Y** Hello.

**X** It's good to see you again.

**Y** Yes.

**X** Are you pleased to be back?

**Y** Yes, I think so. *(Pause.)* Are you?

**X** Of course, I've been looking forward to meeting up with you again, but we always come here, so in some ways, I'd prefer to do something different. Anyhow, as I say … it's good to …

*(***X** *is cut off by the bleeping of* **Y***'s phone.* **Y** *looks at the phone and starts laughing loudly.* **Y** *types quite a lengthy reply.* **X** *waits.)*

**Y** Sorry … sorry … that was my friend from school. Up to no good as usual …

**X** Oh yes? What have they done?

**Y** It's a bit hard to explain. You sort of need to have been there … if you know what I mean.

**X** Oh ok.

**Y** Sorry.

**X** No worries! *(Long pause.)*

**Y** What are you doing tomorrow?

**X** Well, as it's the first day, I thought it might be fun to spend some time on the beach and swim in the sea. Do you want to come?

**Y** I can't swim, actually.

**X** Oh really, I didn't know that.

**Y** I guess it didn't come up.

**X** No, I suppose not.

**Y** I probably hide the fact. It's a bit embarrassing.

**X** I could help you learn.

**Y** No, I've tried so many times, I can't do it. I've decided that I'll just have to live without being able to swim.

**X** What about some sort of float?

**Y** Oh no, that looks ridiculous!

**X** They have some fun-looking ones now. My mum prefers to use one even though she can swim.

**Y** No, I don't want to have a float.

**X** Ok … I just thought …

**Y** *(sounding impatient)* Well, please don't think … I feel stupid enough without you going … *(**Y** is cut off as **X's** phone rings.)*

**X** Sorry, I need to take this. *(As **X** speaks on the phone. **Y** starts texting.)* Hi … Yes, we've arrived … look, I'm sorry but I can't speak now. I've just met up with my friend … yes, the one I met last year … we're in a café … no, we've only just met. Look, can I call you back? Yes, I'll call tonight. Is there something wrong? You're making me feel a bit anxious. Ok, ok, we'll speak later. Take care. Bye.

*(**X** notices that **Y** is still texting, so they also start texting. Now create four still images showing **X** and **Y** texting. Draw on your abstract still image work to create four interesting and exciting shapes. Hold each still image for at least five seconds. Consider whether you can develop any interesting connecting movement sequences between the still images. You aim to show that **X** and **Y** are finding it difficult to connect and that their outside lives and their phones are preventing them from developing their friendship.)*

**Y** I'm sorry.

**X** It's fine.

**Y** I don't mind coming to the beach, though, if you would like to go. There's more to the beach than just swimming.

**X** We could go to an art gallery. My teacher said that there's an amazing one here.

**Y** Oh not for me, I've probably been to them all. It's why we didn't meet until we were about to leave last year. I'd been trudging around boring galleries all week. My parents are obsessed.

**X** Ok, it was just a thought. *(Long pause.)* Do you want to get a drink?

**Y** Yeah, we could do. What do you fancy?

**X** I'm not sure. I'll have a look at the menu.

*(**Y**'s phone bleeps. The scene ends with **X** looking at the menu and **Y** sending texts.)*

## *Design activity*

Focusing on colour and intensity, ask students to consider how lighting could enhance the awkwardness between the two characters in *The Meeting.*

## *Written activity*

This task enables students to continue evaluating how physical theatre conveys meaning to an audience.

**Suggested title**: Discuss some of the movement and physical techniques you used to convey the awkwardness between the two characters in *The Meeting*. Discuss how you wanted the audience to feel.

# 3

# SPACE – IN THE ROUND

# 'ROUND AND ROUND WE GO'

**Photo 3-3-1** In the round.

## Introduction

This age group thrives on rising to challenges, and we should look forward to stretching them. Exploring in-the-round staging is an exciting area of study, enabling our students to work creatively and develop more sophisticated skills. Begin by discussing some notable in-the-round productions and spaces. Alan Ayckbourn's work at the Stephen Joseph Theatre, Scarborough, is an interesting starting point. There are also spaces such as the Crucible Theatre in Sheffield, the Octagon in Bolton, The Royal Exchange in Manchester, @sohoplace in London, Arena Stage in Washington DC, Circle in the Square Theatre in New York and flexible spaces such as the Dorfman, Bridge Theatre and the Young Vic in London, which can be configured for in-the-round productions. There are several notable plays which worked wonderfully in the in-the-round setting, and you might want to draw attention to Mike Bartlett's *Bull*, Alan Ayckbourn's *Confusions* and the musical *The Little Big Things*, which premiered at @sohoplace in London.

# Warm-up

## 1. Teacher demonstration

Seat the students in an in-the-round formation in your space. Establish four separate banks of audience and explain that the four aisles between them would be used for the audience to access their seats and for the actors' entrances and exits. Highlight that audience members view the actors from different angles in this formation. Read out a poem, story or newspaper article, demonstrating how the space can be used so that no audience members feel excluded. Consider moving around the space in the following ways:

1. Start between two banks of audience at the bottom of one of the aisles.
2. Cross the space to stand between two other banks of audience at the bottom of the aisle.
3. Move to a chair in the middle of the space.
4. Walk slowly around the chair.
5. Sit on the chair, twisting to demonstrate how it is easy to open up and connect with audience members on different sides.
6. Walk around the edge of the space almost directly in front of the audience.
7. Walk across the space using a criss-cross pathway and turning 360 degrees at some point.

Give students a poem to read aloud, planning how to move around the space to deliver it. Watch about four students rehearsing simultaneously.

## 2. Why am I doing this?

One of the challenges students face when working in the round is ensuring that movement around the space is driven by the character's (not the actor's) situation. A performance can become very stilted if an actor only moves because they need to face a different direction. Movement must be motivated by what the character is experiencing and feeling. To explore this, ask the students to work independently on a mime involving preparing a room for an important occasion. They must ensure they make full use of the space and connect with the entire audience, considering why they would be moving around. Suggest that the character might have tasks to perform in various parts of the space, prompting them to face in different directions. Watch some of the performances and evaluate.

## 3. An in-the-round conversation

Divide the students into pairs to improvise a conversation between two characters, applying what they have learnt so far about working in the round. Remind them to consider their positioning in the space and how and why they move to make their performance accessible to the audience in this configuration. Sometimes it helps for students to make notes on positioning. Stress that they must always consider the reasons why a character is moving at any given point. Suggested conversations:

1. A friend is telling their best friend that they are moving away suddenly and unexpectedly.
2. A fourteen-year-old is telling their famous artist parent that they do not want to study Art as a GCSE option.
3. A sibling is begging their older sibling to let them copy an essay they wrote several years ago for an important assessment.

Spend time discussing ideas on how students could develop these conversations in interesting ways. Encourage more nuance and originality at this stage of the course.

Watch and evaluate the scenes, focusing on how effectively they have been staged for an audience in the round.

# Original script

In the following sections, both original and published extracts are used to enable students to perform in an in-the-round setting. One of the published excerpts is taken from Brecht's *The Resistible Rise of Arturo Ui,* which also provided the stimulus for the original text *The Hidden Threat*. The longer *Sun Rises, Sun Sets* is an original non-sequential piece of text set in different time periods and can also be explored in the light of Brechtian theories.

## Exercises based on the theories of Brecht to use before staging *The Hidden Threat, Sun Rises, Sun Sets* and Brecht's *The Resistible Rise of Arturo Ui*

Before working on these excerpts, spend time introducing students to some of Brecht's theories. At this stage, communicate Brecht's desire to inform and educate the audience, avoiding pure emotional investment, and breaking down the barriers between actors and audience. Discuss the word *Verfremdungseffekt,* explaining that it is a difficult word to translate into English to convey Brecht's meaning accurately. The frequently used translation of alienation and distancing can sound rather unfriendly and cold, and does not reflect Brecht's intention to entertain an audience. It is worth introducing the students to the word *spass*, which means fun. Brecht always aimed for his work to be enjoyable.

Explore the idea that Brecht taught his actors to consciously select the acting skills they would employ when playing a character. This approach helped prevent both the actors and the audience from becoming too emotionally invested in the performance, encouraging critical reflection on political, social and moral ideas. Several books are listed in the *Further Reading* section that you may want to reference.

There follows a list of exercises you can explore with students after introducing them to the context and principles of his work:

## Breaking the fourth wall

In pairs, students improvise a simple scene between a physical education teacher and a drama teacher. They are discussing/arguing about a clash between a vital cup final and the school production dress rehearsal, which both require the same students to attend. Once your students have improvised the scene, introduce the concept of direct address to the audience, explaining that this breaks down the barrier between audience and actors, allowing characters to reveal insights into their inner thoughts and feelings. Instruct students to revise their scene, each incorporating two moments of direct address to the audience. Watch the scenes and evaluate.

## Narration

Introduce the concept of using narration as a way of furthering a drama. Explain that an actor can take on the role of a narrator to share information and explain ideas to the audience. Students often find

**Photo 3-3-2** Exploring Narration.

narration challenging and can fall into the trap of using a rather lacklustre and apologetic tone of voice, so it is worth spending some time developing skills. Start by giving the students a list of information about a new play:

- It is 2142.
- The central character is Pip.
- Pip is 141 years old.
- Pip has been programmed to be a sprinter.
- Pip's personal-best time for 100 metres is 8.21 seconds.
- Pip always wanted to paint pictures, but all art was banned in 2129.

Students work individually or in pairs, compiling the information into a narration script to be delivered to an audience in an in-the-round setting. Remind them that when narrating, they are still performing and need to connect with and entertain their audience. They must think carefully about their use of voice and movement when delivering their speech. Watch some of the work and evaluate.

## Non-sequential

In pairs, students improvise a scene which follows a clear sequential pathway. The scene depicts a parent/guardian informing their teenage son/daughter that they are moving to a new part of the country. The drama includes the following four stages:

1. The parent/guardian tells the child about the move.
2. The child tries to persuade the parent/guardian not to go ahead with the move.
3. The final moment in the old house before the move.
4. The first moments in the new house.

Once the students have improvised the scene, introduce the concept of non-sequential drama. Explain that in an attempt to keep audiences thinking and reflecting, Brecht would sometimes present scenes out of order. This is also an appropriate point to discuss the concept of episodic drama and how plays can be composed of scenes, which function as separate units and can be arranged in different orders. Students should revise their scene, performing the four stages in reverse order. Watch and evaluate.

## Multi-roling

Introduce the concept that actors can play multiple roles in a production. As an example, cite the original production of Caryl Churchill's *Love and Information,* where sixteen actors played over one hundred characters. Explain that multi-roling encourages audience members to become more attuned to how actors use voice and movement to play a range of characters. This next improvisation presents an opportunity to explore how actors can portray characters of significantly different ages than their own.

Divide the students into pairs to work on a two-scene improvisation, in which they play different characters in the two scenes.

**Scene One**: Students take on the roles of parents/guardians discussing their two eight-year-old children. Both parents/guardians are highly competitive and believe that their child is more successful than any other. They both offer a range of additional activities to allow their children to shine. Both want to convince the other that their child is the best.

**Scene Two**: Students now play the roles of the two eight-year-old children. They are both complaining about their parents/guardians and the demands placed on them to do extra activities, which they don't enjoy. They are both convinced that they are having the worst experience.

Watch some of the work evaluating how the students use voice and movement in different ways to create the two contrasting roles.

### *Written activity*

**Suggested title***:* Give four examples of how you used voice and movement to differentiate between playing the parent/guardian and the eight-year-old child.

## Switching roles

Building on the multi-roling exercise, introduce the technique of actors switching roles midway through a scene. In pairs, students improvise a conversation between an elderly person who is seeking help from a teenager to set up their new mobile phone. The elderly person is a complete beginner; the teenager is very advanced and can't believe how little the elderly person knows. Remind students to think carefully about how they employ voice and movement to depict the two characters. Halfway through the improvisation, the students switch roles. The switch must be seamless, using voice and movement carefully, so there is no confusion for the audience.

## Placards

Introduce the concept of using placards to convey key information, such as the title of a scene or an important message about that scene or moment. Explain that placards can be carried by actors or placed or flown in on stage; in contemporary productions, the information can be projected on screens. Divide the students into groups of four or five to create a still image communicating a moment of their own choice. Explain how Brecht used still image (tableau) as a way of emphasizing a key moment in a scene. Students decide on the title of their scene and a key message to be communicated on placards to enhance their performance.

## 1. The hidden threat

Students work in pairs, taking turns to direct one another in performing the monologue, *The Hidden Threat*, in the in-the-round configuration. The monologue is from the perspective of an employer addressing a group of sales staff in a top sports store regarding expectations and sales targets. On the surface, the employer appears charming and flattering, but beneath this exterior lies a menacing and threatening tone. This monologue mirrors the excerpt used from Brecht's *The Resistible Rise of Arturo Ui* later on in this chapter. Design students could choose to create a costume for the character.

### The Hidden Threat

**Avery Abbott** *is the manager of the flagship branch of High Energy Sports Shop. In this speech,* **Avery** *addresses the sales team about what is expected of them and how much money they should be making. On the surface,* **Avery** *is very charming but actually cares very little for the staff and is only really interested in profit and success.*

*You should work in pairs, taking turns to help your partner stage the extract in the round. Remember that your audience is on all sides. Direct the speech to them, imagining they are the sales team, and ensure that you move around the space, considering the reasons why* **Avery** *might be moving.*

**AVERY ABBOTT** Good morning. I hope you have all had a splendid Sunday and are returning fully energised and excited for another week here at High Energy Sports Shop. It's a lovely day; the sun is out and you all look absolutely splendid. However, I should remind you that just because it's warming up, our standards do not slip. We have a dress code, so I do not expect to see your different interpretations of summer sportswear on my shop floor. The regulation high-energy summer sports kit must be worn with pride. I know you realise how privileged you are to work here. I know you recognise how many others out there are just desperate to be in your position. They are virtually banging down the doors to step into your shoes. You can't imagine how many enquiries I deal with every day from people who want to be part of this exceptional team. I assume you all appreciate just how lucky you are to be working here.

Now, I want to start by thanking you. We did well last week. We met our targets. We achieved our goals. But is that enough, I hear you ask? Is it enough to merely meet our goals? I know what you are all thinking. Yes, I can read your minds. You want to do better. You want to do more. And that's what I want too. Actually, it's what I demand. I am demanding it of you because, as I look out there at your lovely faces, I can see that I have the best team in the world. Yes, you are the best, the very best. So, we are not going only to meet our targets, we are going to double them. This week, we will make twice as much money as we did last week. I have complete confidence that you can all aspire to this because you have the talent, the experience, the drive, the determination and the will to succeed.

But, of course, for those who are not so sure, for those who feel they can't double up on what they did last week ... well ... I'm here to help you, to guide you, to support you, to motivate you, to push you.

And if there are any such people out there, I say, never forget, never forget for a moment that if you can't do it, there are plenty more who can and are ready to take your place. Now, get to work.

### *Written activity*

**Suggested title**: Give five examples of how another performer moved around the stage space. Discuss the reasons they found for moving and how effective this was for the audience.

## 2. Sun rises, sun sets

This script has been written to provide further opportunities to explore Brechtian principles and to challenge students to stage a longer piece of work in the round. The scenes are set in different years, allowing you to lay the foundations for the type of textual exploration required at examination level by exploring the various social, cultural and historical contexts.

*Sun Rises, Sun Sets* is an episodic play exploring the theme of expectations and how people are categorized into specific roles. The title derives from the idea that the characters encounter similar experiences across different periods. Students can perform the scenes in any order with the **Narrator**'s epilogue at the very end. There are six roles in total, but through multi-roling, two or four students can perform the whole script. There are some gender-specific roles, but as the play is being explored in the context of Brecht, you can be flexible. Individual design students can work on the activity described at the end of the text. Start by reading through the script with your class.

### Sun Rises, Sun Sets

### *Scene One – 1922- Central Station, New York*

**Edith Clarke** My name is Edith Clarke. In 1919, I was the first woman to be awarded an electrical engineering degree. Now, in 1922, I have become the first professional female electrical engineer in the United States, working in the Central Station engineering department. I can't sum up the pride and delight I feel. Don't think for a minute that it's been easy. It came with a vast amount of determination and resilience to buck a system which didn't believe that women could succeed in this field. For years, I was told that it wasn't my place to be here. Of course, I never listened to any of that. I always knew what was right, and I kept moving forward. I am now where I always wanted to be. I have made it at last.

### *Scene Two – 1978 – A school office*

(**Mr Newton**, *careers advisor, is scribbling notes whilst* **Suzanne**, *a fifteen-year-old pupil, waits nervously.)*

**Mr Newton** *(eventually speaks)* Sit down girl, you're making me nervous standing there.

**Suzanne** Thank you, Mr Newton.

**Mr Newton** So Susan …

**Suzanne** It's Suzanne!

**Mr Newton** Sorry?

**Suzanne** My name is Suzanne, not Susan.

**Mr Newton** Same difference isn't it? Susan, Suzanne, Susie, Suzette, Suzannah … it's really the same name. Of course, we can debate this if you want. But it's not why I'm here. You do know why I'm here, don't you?

**Suzanne** Yes, Mr Newsome.

**Mr Newton** Newton not Newsome dear! Oh, I see what you did there! Cheeky little thing, aren't you? Your teachers said you were smart. Well, be careful not to be too smart, it's not very appealing.

**Suzanne** Sorry!

**Mr Newton** Apology accepted. Now, I suggest we crack on. I have your last school report. It's glowing. Your folks must be pleased with you. I see you are particularly good at Maths. That's quite unusual, isn't it? Who do you get that from? Does your dad or your brother help you with your homework?

**Suzanne** My brother hates Maths, and my dad works away, so he's not around much.

**Mr Newton** So who helps you?

**Suzanne** *(to the audience)* I can't believe he's asking me this. He's supposed to be supporting me. *(To Mr Newton.)* I work it out for myself, Mr Newton. I like working it out.

**Mr Newton** *(to the audience)* She's obviously not admitting the truth. Very unwise. *(To Suzanne.)* Well, that's very nice, Susie, it really is, but it's not going to be much use to you in the future, is it? Maybe it will help you calculate how much you have to spend on the weekly shop, but you probably should make a bit more effort to improve your grades in your sewing and cooking classes as well. Those reports are a little disappointing.

**Suzanne** I'm sorry, but I don't like sewing, Mr Newton. And I don't want to be a cook.

**Mr Newton** Even so, I suggest you try a bit harder. Now let's not waste any more time. As I said, you are obviously a bright girl. Do you have any idea about what you might like to do when you get a bit older? If you don't, don't worry. That's what I'm here for … to advise, to point you in the right direction, so to speak.

**Suzanne** No, I know what I want to do.

**Mr Newton** Go on, dear.

**Suzanne** Engineering.

**Mr Newton** (*to the audience*) Oh dear, we have one of those. The deluded teenager! I hope she's joking. *(To Suzanne.)* I'm sorry?

**Suzanne** I want to be an engineer. As you said, I'm good at maths, so it seems logical.

**Mr Newton** Logical, eh? I see. Well, that's just not going to be possible, I'm afraid.

**Suzanne** Why?

**Mr Newton** It's a particularly difficult field to get into.

**Suzanne** What do you mean?

**Mr Newton** Engineering, it's more of a man's world, that sort of thing. I think you would end up feeling very disheartened.

**Suzanne** (*to the audience*) I can't believe he would say such a thing. I mean, this is 1978! *(To Mr Newton.)* So, you are saying it's not open to girls?

**Mr Newton** It's just very difficult, probably impossible.

**Suzanne** What about Rachel Parsons?

**Mr Newton** Who's she when she's at home?

**Suzanne** She studied mechanical sciences at Cambridge and established the first all-female engineering company in 1920. That was over fifty years ago.

**Mr Newton** Yes well, obviously, there will be a few exceptions.

**Suzanne** There are many others. You must have heard of Edith Clarke, the first professional female electrical engineer in the United States?

**Mr Newton** Um, well yes, er, of course. Look, I'm sorry Susan, Suzanne. You really do need to be a bit more realistic. Why don't you consider something like nursing? I'm sure your maths will come in handy. Or what about retail work? Your interest in calculations will be perfect for that type of job, and there would be lots of wonderful opportunities for a bright girl like you. I'm sure you could become a manager if you put your mind to it.

**Suzanne** But, I have an ambition, a dream, and that's not what I want to do.

**Mr Newton** Look, we don't always get to do what we want. Life is full of compromises. The best advice I can give you is to buckle down and get your head out of the clouds.

## *Scene Three – present day- A school office*

**Ari** Good morning Ms/Mr Morgan.

**Blake** Call me Blake, Ari. I am not one of your teachers. I'm a PFGS, a professional future guidance specialist.

**Ari** Ok, thank you, Blake.

**Blake** Firstly, let me thank *you* for filling in the online deep dive questions so thoroughly. How long did that take you, Ari?

**Ari** About two hours, I think.

**Blake** That's impressive, and because you dedicated this time, it has given us a report of 99.8% accuracy, so I am totally confident that I have found the most appropriate future professional pathway for you.

**Ari** I do know what I want to do, Blake.

**Blake** (*to the audience*) I see, we have another one of these young people who always thinks they know best. (*To Ari.*) Well, let's find out what the experts believe.

**Ari** But who are the experts, Blake?

**Blake** I think you are aware Ari, that your responses have been evaluated by an exceptionally sophisticated and sensitive system which produces very nuanced and highly individualised reports.

**Ari** So AI?

**Blake** Artificial intelligence is one component of the system, but human reflections and interactions are also key.

**Ari** And that's you? (*To the audience.*) The PFGS who still hasn't actually asked me what I want to do.

**Blake** Yes, that's me. Right, well, let's see what we have for you, and I think you are going to be delighted. I am thrilled to confirm that you have the capabilities to excel in a highly professional capacity. With your academic ability, organizational skills, logic and reasoning, it is absolutely clear that you should become a doctor, or at the very least, a teacher or academic in a scientific field.

**Ari** Yes, I have thought about that.

**Blake** That's super. We're on the same page, then.

**Ari** No, we are not on the same page, because it's not what I intend to do.

**Blake** Ok, and what do you *intend* to do?

**Ari** I am not entirely sure of my final specialist area, but I will become an artist.

**Blake** But that's totally alien to what the system has determined for you. I have seen many profiles in my time, and it is undeniable that you should be a doctor or an academic.

**Ari** Logically, I can see that, and I have thought about it carefully; however, I will succeed as an artist.

**Blake** The system, and I, of course, would not recommend this. There is nothing in your profile to suggest this would be an appropriate alternative for you.

**Ari** That's because I have never been asked to share my feelings or ambitions.

**Blake** You would be turning your back on a profession that would be the most financially lucrative for you. You would be taking a considerable risk.

**Ari** But it's a risk I long to take.

**Blake** I can assure you that you will have security and success if you follow my guidance.

**Ari** The machine's guidance.

**Blake** Designed to provide the best outcomes for you.

**Ari** But not designed to ask me what I actually want. Blake, I would be truly grateful if you could provide me with some guidance on the best art courses. I'm looking to explore different styles, mediums and materials. Please.

**Blake** I feel very uneasy about this.

**Ari** If you can't help me, I'll ask elsewhere.

**Blake** (*reluctantly*) Ok, ok, bear with me. I'll need to log on.

## Epilogue – Anytime

**Narrator** Open your eyes, your minds, your hearts. Don't get boxed in by restrictions and restraints, by constrictions and constraints. Question, query, interrogate, deliberate. Be inspired and empowered. Live in a world where there are floors and no ceilings. Champion yourself, champion others around you. Be your absolute best, and trust and believe. Be bold, be brave, be strong.

### *Design activity*

*Sun Rises, Sun Sets* can be used to extend this age group's understanding of how stage sets help establish locations in different periods for the in-the-round space. There are four locations:

1. Central Station, New York, 1922
2. A school office in 1978
3. A school office, present day
4. Anytime for the epilogue.

Start by discussing some of the different options, including:

1. **Projections**: Four screens behind the banks of audience members provide a simple way of projecting appropriate images to establish the different locations.
2. **Trucks**: Students can consider moving scenery on wheeled platforms or using the stage crew or cast to move items.
3. **Flying**: In the context of the in-the-round setting, they can consider flying down signs above the acting space or banks of audience to help establish the various periods and locations.

Stress that any set items students might want to include in a scene need to be carefully positioned so that they do not block the view of any audience members.

In groups of four, students take on the role of set designers, preparing ideas for a forthcoming production of *Sun Rises, Sun Sets.* They can present their ideas to an audience seated in the round.

# Published script

## 1. *The Resistible Rise of Arturo Ui* by Bertolt Brecht

Brecht's 1941 play *The Resistible Rise of Arturo Ui* uses a small-time gangster's journey to assume control of the green grocery trade in Cicero and Chicago to illustrate Hitler's rise to power in Germany. It is a powerful speech to study in the light of Brecht's theories, and for students to attempt to stage in the round.

Start by discussing the speech, exploring the rhythm and the building menace. At this stage of the course, there are various ways you could ask them to bring it to life in performance. They can work on it individually or in pairs, experimenting with ways it might be delivered in the in-the-round setting. Alternatively, students can work in groups using choral techniques to depict the threatening nature of UI's words.

### Context for students

This excerpt is from Scene Fifteen near the end of Brecht's *The Resistible Rise of Arturo Ui.* The play is allegorical; **Arturo Ui** represents Hitler, and his rise to power mirrors events in Nazi Germany. In this speech, **Arturo Ui** demands that the people of Chicago and Cicero vote to indicate their support for his leadership of the greengrocery trade. It is a speech full of menace and underlying threat delivered by **Arturo Ui** at the height of his power.



**Ui** Friends, countrymen!
Chicagoans and Ciceronians! When
A year ago old Dogsborough, God rest
His honest soul, with tearful eyes
Appealed to me to protect Chicago's green –
Goods trade, though moved, I doubted whether
My powers would be able to justify
His smiling confidence. Now Dogsborough
Is dead. He left a will which you're all free
To read. In simple words therein he calls me
His son. And thanks me fervently for all
I've done since I responded to his appeal.
Today the trade and vegetables –
Be they Kohlrabi, onions, carrots or what
Have you – is amply protected in Chicago.
Thanks, I make bold to say, to resolute
Action on my part. When another civic
Leader, Ignatius Dullfeet, to my surprise
Approached me with the same request, this time
Concerning Cicero, I consented
To take that city under my protection.
But one condition I stipulated, namely:
The dealers had to want me. I would come
Only pursuant to their free decision
Freely arrived at. Cicero, I told
My men, in no uncertain terms, must not be
Subjected to coercion or constraint.
The city has to elect me in full freedom.
I want no grudging 'Why not?', no teeth gnashing
'We might as well'. Half-hearted acquiescence
Is poison in my books. What I demand
Is one unanimous and joyful 'Yes'
Succinct and, men of Cicero, expressive.
And since I want this and everything else I want
To be complete, I turn again to you
Men of Chicago, who, because you know
Me better, hold me, I have reason to believe
In true esteem, and ask you: Who is for me?

And just in passing, let me add: if anyone's
Not for me he's against me and has only
Himself to blame for anything that happens.
Now you may vote.

### *Design activity*

In 1991, Antony Sher played Arturo Ui in a National Theatre production. Costume was used most creatively to convey Ui's state of mind in different parts of the play. In earlier scenes, when he bemoans his lack of power and status, Sher wore a tight, ill-fitting jacket which was buttoned incorrectly. This made him look physically small and insignificant. In later scenes, when Ui assumed control, he was dressed in a full-length coat with a huge fur collar and large shoulder pads to accentuate his physique. This larger-than-life, exaggerated version of a coat powerfully conveyed the figure he had become. These descriptions often inspire students to create their own original costumes for the Scene Fifteen excerpt.

Students can also explore how to use placards to enhance a performance of Ui's speech. Working in pairs, students decide what might be written or drawn on placards to be displayed during this scene.

## 2. *Retrograde* by Ryan Calais Cameron

Ryan Calais Cameron's *Retrograde* was first performed at the Kiln Theatre, London, in 2023. The play fictionalizes a real-life situation that actor Sidney Poitier suggested occurred in 1955. In a meeting to secure his professional future, Poitier faced pressure to denounce the actor, singer, athlete and civil rights advocate, Paul Robeson. The play is a brilliant exploration of the tensions of the period where McCarthyism, right-wing racism and the civil rights movement merged and clashed.

This is a challenging excerpt to stage in the round, as the style is naturalistic and Poitier's speech is directed towards two other characters. It can be helpful for students to work in groups of three so that they familiarize themselves with the positioning of the silent characters and Poitier's motivations for moving around the stage space. Design students can work on creating the set for this excerpt.

### Context for students

This excerpt is taken from towards the end of the play *Retrograde* and is set in 1955. To secure his position in the entertainment industry, the Black actor **Sidney Poitier** is being pressured to denounce his beliefs. In this excerpt, he recalls something his mother told him when he was young, helping him stay true to his own beliefs during this difficult meeting.



**Sidney** I was born two months early, and everyone had given up on me, but my mother insisted on my life. She passed a fortune-teller's stall, and she sat with this lady. The woman said, 'Don't worry about your son. He will not be a sickly child. He will walk with kings. He will step on pillars of gold. And he will carry your name to many places.' Believe that with or without this contract I'm still going to be somebody, not just an anybody, but my mother's son! Now look at me, look at me there's a job to be done, and I don't need a single second longer to think about it. There's something incredibly remarkable about to happen, something that this country, maybe even this world has never ever seen, and I don't want to miss that, I don't want to live a life regretting that I missed that moment.

### *Design activity*

In pairs, students create a 1950s-style office environment for an in-the-round stage.

### *Written activity*

**Suggested title**: Evaluate another performer's staging of Sidney's speech from *Retrograde,* discussing the impact on you as a member of the audience.

## 3. *Josephine and I* by Cush Jumbo

Written and performed by Cush Jumbo, *Josephine and I* was first staged at the Bush Theatre, London, in 2013, leading to an Olivier nomination for Jumbo. In it, she plays a young performer presenting the life and experiences of the entertainer Josephine Baker. Taking on the two roles, Jumbo merges and entwines the lives of the two women, revealing common and shared experiences. It was a remarkable piece of theatre, showcasing Jumbo's exceptional talent, and it is an exciting piece for students to explore staging in the round. You can also continue to explore Brecht's theories on breaking down the fourth wall and the technique of actors assuming different roles in a play.

Begin by providing students with a more detailed insight into the life of Josephine Baker. Read and discuss the excerpt, exploring ways they might perform the piece in the round. Given the length, it is an interesting extract for students to work on in pairs, splitting the performance into two parts.

### Context for students

This excerpt is taken from the beginning of the play *Josephine and I*. A young performer, **Girl**, arrives flustered and late for her own show. She starts building a relationship with the audience, speaking directly to them and introducing her initial connection with **Josephine Baker**, a famous performer who first appeared on stage in the 1920s.



**Girl** I'm *so* sorry for keeping you all waiting. I've come straight from my agent's office. I had a TV audition. I was walking Henry and suddenly my agent calls and he's like, 'Drop everything and get here now,' so I did. It's for this massive American series and I had to put it on tape and it took much longer than it should have and anyway, sorry, I'm waffling.

*She looks around. She is frazzled and has no idea what she should be doing.*

Right, so thank you for coming ...

Are there any actors here?

Right, well you'll know how I'm feeling!

And if you're not then, well just imagine your worst nightmare.

Complete and utter lack of control.

*The* **Girl** *begins getting herself together.*

*She wheels over a small table with shelves from the side of the stage. It is stacked with Josephine Baker collectables – DVDs, books, programmes, a piano score, a tape player, a scrapbook, tapes, CDs, a chain of Josephine cut-outs, a zoetrope.*

**Girl** And now what we're all here for.

*She reaches under the table to one of the shelves and produces a converted Tiny Tears* **Doll***. She holds it up for the audience to see.*

**Girl** This is Josephine.

Say hello to all these lovely people, Josephine –

*The* **Doll** *shakes her head.*

**Girl** What's wrong?

*The* **Doll** *looks at the* **Girl***.*

**Girl** Oh – you don't think you're looking your best?

*The* **Doll** *shakes her head.*

*The* **Girl** *fiddles with the* **Doll***'s outfit.*

**Girl** Yeah, well, you're probably right. I mean, I'm just being honest.

You are looking a tad bit rough these days.

*The* **Doll** *looks at the* **Girl***.*

**Girl** It's not your fault, you're practically vintage! I mean, when did I give you this Josephine Baker makeover? 1992?

*The* **Doll** *nods.*

**Girl** I mean that's … ages ago. Although I will say, when I first gave you that makeover you were stunning.

*The* **Doll** *flicks its head proudly.*

**Girl** Yes you were! But actually, even in your original form, before the makeover, you were an incredibly pretty doll.

*The* **Doll** *nods. The* **Girl** *puts the* **Doll** *down.*

**Girl** She was originally called Tiny Tears. Do you know what I mean by Tiny Tears? Right, well, I'd begged my parents for a Tiny Tears. I'd been staring at her wistfully in the Argos catalogue for months because … there was something about her face … I thought she looked like Ginger Rogers. You know, like a classic old movie star? It was her nose, or maybe her mouth … She looked like Jean Harlow, or Marilyn Monroe or something. You may find it strange that an eight-year-old girl born in the eighties *knew* the names of those actresses, but I was fascinated by them. I just wanted to sit inside by myself on Sunday afternoons and watch old movie stars. They were the most beautiful, glamorous, sassy, well-dressed, soft-haired, porcelain white things I'd ever seen. Untouchable glittering *stars*. And I decided that I wanted to be a star too. So, when the film was over I used to put a sweater on, take my arms out of it, pull it back over my head like it was blonde silken hair and prance around the front room. Taking bows, blowing kisses, ordering imaginary men about, pretending that I was beautiful, and glamorous, and sassy, and well-dressed, and soft-haired, and porcelain white … except I wasn't. Then. This one Sunday afternoon for the *first time ever* I see an old movie star that looks just like me, I mean really like me and I'm like, 'What?!' I see Josephine Baker.

*She picks up the DVD of the movie* Zou-Zou.

Josephine Baker stars in *Zou Zou*! It was this French movie. And there was this woman looking just like me, singing and dancing and looking just like me, and wearing dazzling dresses and looking just like me, surrounded by a cast of completely white people who didn't seem to notice at all. *And*, she wasn't the maid. She was the *star*. And it suddenly became apparent that Tiny Tears was in need of an *extreme* makeover.

# 4
# APPLYING SKILLS EXPLORED IN CHAPTERS ONE TO THREE
## 'FUSION'

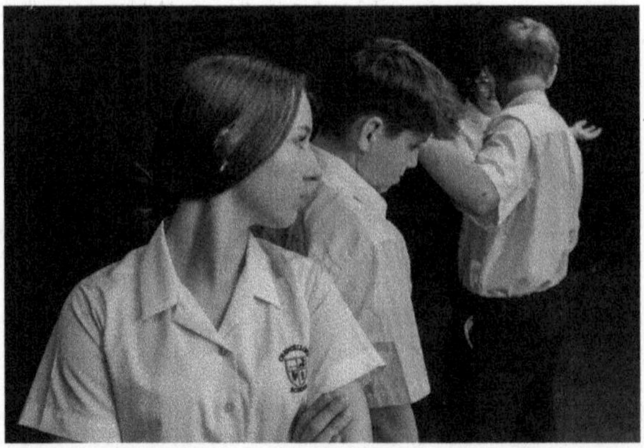

**Photo 3-4-1** Students applying skills.

## Introduction

In this chapter, the activities have been designed to enable students to integrate the various skills they have developed over the year. They are asked to explore how they might combine dialogue, with a particular emphasis on pause, with physical theatre for performance in an in-the-round space. They should also be reminded to apply the vocal and movement skills they explored in the first two parts. The chapter consists of an improvisation task, four excerpts from published texts and concludes with a devising project. Given the challenges of creating original material, it is advised that you leave the devising activity to the end of the year. Opportunities for students wishing to specialize in performance design are suggested throughout.

# Improvisation

## 1. Status improvisation

This is an enjoyable activity that will challenge students to consider how to develop multidimensional characters, drawing on the vocal and physical theatre skills they have studied over the year.

Begin by introducing the concept of creating new characters based on a status number. In this context, a number from one to ten is applied to determine a character's personality. A number one character is selfish, unkind, egocentric and mean-spirited; a number ten character is kind, unselfish, generous and warm; a number five character is changeable, consisting of contrasting traits. Without telling the students, select a status number of either three or seven. Instruct them to ask several 'what if?' style questions to determine your character's personality status number. For example:

- What if you found £5 on the ground and saw an old lady anxiously looking through her pockets?

Example answer for a number three character:

- 'I would feel a bit sorry for her, but then I don't really know what she might be looking for. She might be searching for a sweet. I could probably use an extra £5 – it's always good to have a bit of cash, so I think I'd take the money. I would feel a little bit guilty, but people need to be careful with their possessions.'

Example answer for a number seven character:

- 'Well, I would be slightly tempted to keep it. I always like to carry some cash on me, but I'd worry that it belonged to the old lady, so I'd ask her if she'd lost it. If she had, I'd give it back, although I would feel a tiny bit disappointed. If not, I'd probably keep it, although I would feel a bit guilty.'

Other sample questions:

1. What if you are going to your best friend's party and you suddenly receive an incredibly tempting and exciting alternative offer?
2. What if you are waiting for a bus and are not in a hurry; a pregnant lady is standing behind you in the queue; the bus arrives, and there is only one place?
3. What if you are due to sit an important school exam and your teacher leaves you alone at their desk, and you notice the exam paper and answers?

Ask the students to pose their 'what if' questions to determine your character's status number. Once you are confident that they are asking strong questions, invite them to guess your number.

Divide the students into pairs, labelling themselves **A** and **B.** Instruct them to choose their own status number (without sharing it with their partner). **A** should be given approximately three minutes to pose questions to determine **B**'s number. Stress that **A** can only guess **B**'s number when you instruct them to do so. Students then discuss the work and the character's behaviour before switching roles, allowing **B** to question **A**.

At this stage, introduce the idea that people change and do not always behave and react in the same way. For this reason, it is impossible to assign one number to an individual. Students now work in pairs to develop a more complex improvisation titled *Manipulation*. Read out the background to the scene:

**A** and **B** are seventeen years old and have recently taken on holiday jobs to earn extra cash. **A** is trying to persuade **B** to use the money to buy a car to share. **A** needs the vehicle for work purposes, so it is in their best interests to get **B** to agree. **B** wants to persuade **A** to use all the money to go on a holiday together. Both characters are absolutely determined to get their way and use a range of persuasive and manipulative methods to win the argument.

For the improvisation, students use the status numbers to structure their arguments. They can select the same or different numbers to employ at various points in the scene. They can change their numbers as many times as they want. They should incorporate pauses of varying lengths throughout their scene and be reminded to consider volume, tone of voice, gestures, levels, and pace. Emphasize that they are creating their work for an in-the-round theatre space.

To develop their work, students can also create a physical theatre sequence to be performed at the beginning of their improvisation. It should consist of four abstract still images which capture the mood of four contrasting moments from their dialogue.

During the rehearsal process, students will benefit from sharing moments from their work to illustrate how they are interpreting the status numbers in this context.

# Published script

## The director

Before exploring the four published excerpts, this is a good point in the course to continue introducing students to different directorial techniques. For this age group, I recommend further discussion of Steven Berkoff's approaches and an introduction to the work of Joan Littlewood.

In Chapter Two, students learnt about Berkoff's skilful use of mime and physical theatre to communicate ideas. Despite being renowned as a physical actor, Berkoff actually fuses many theatrical elements, including physical theatre, text, music, sound, costume, props and lights, in his performances and plays. His version of Kafka's *Metamorphosis* is an interesting example of how he put his theories into practice to produce what is known as total theatre. Students are often surprised by the idea of a person transforming into a beetle, but having experienced physical theatre techniques, they quickly accept that this is an exciting way to convey the pain and pressure an individual might experience. When staging any of the published excerpts, ask students to consider how they might attempt to combine different theatrical elements as Berkoff intended. You might also choose to discuss how Berkoff, the playwright, included extensive detail in his plays about how to bring the text to life on stage. This can lead to further discussions about the relationship between playwrights, directors and actors, and who has responsibility for bringing a text to life.

Joan Littlewood is an interesting practitioner to introduce to students. To discuss her approaches, reference Theatre Workshop's 1963 production *Oh What a Lovely War*. It is well chronicled that the piece was developed through a collaborative method where Littlewood tasked the actors to research and develop scenes through improvisation. This can generate some interesting discussion with students about the advantages and disadvantages of such an approach. There are several books listed in the *Further Reading* section if you wish to explore her work in more depth.

You might find it useful to compare these practitioners' methods by assigning students different directorial tasks. To reflect Berkoff, assign individuals to take total control of directing the group rehearsal of the fourth extract, *Musical Differences*. In contrast, other groups can be instructed to work collaboratively without a director. It is always interesting to share students' experiences.

## 1. *The Comedy of Errors* by William Shakespeare

When exploring traverse staging last year, students studied an excerpt from Shakespeare's *The Comedy of Errors*. This final exchange from the very end of Act Five, between Dromio of Ephesus and Dromio of Syracuse, is a lovely piece for students to apply the skills they have developed over the year. Read the extract through, discussing how pauses can be employed to communicate the astonishment the twins feel standing in front of one another. Students can also explore creating a physical theatre sequence using mirroring techniques and mime to convey their similarities. Individual students can focus on designing costumes and lighting for the extract.

### Context for students

This exchange between **Dromio of Ephesus** and **Dromio of Syracuse** takes place at the very end of Shakespeare's *The Comedy of Errors*. Having been separated at a very young age, the two twins are finally reunited, standing face to face for the first time. They are amazed at how alike they are and want to find out who is the oldest. Stage this short extract for an in-the-round performance, thinking carefully about how to use pauses to bring out their amazement. At the end of the dialogue, develop a piece of physical theatre to be performed before the characters exit the stage space.

Extract taken from The Arden Shakespeare edition (third series).

DROMIO OF SYRACUSE
There is a fat friend at your master's house,
That kitchened me for you today at dinner;
She now shall be my sister, not my wife.
DROMIO OF EPHESUS
Methinks you are my glass and not my brother:
I see by you I am a sweet-faced youth.
Will you walk in to see their gossiping?
DROMIO OF SYRACUSE Not I, sir; you are my elder.
DROMIO OF EPHESUS That's a question; how shall we
try it?
DROMIO OF SYRACUSE We'll draw cuts for the senior;
till then, lead thou first.
DROMIO OF EPHESUS
Nay then, thus: *[embracing him]* we came into the
world like brother and brother;
And now let's go hand in hand, not one before
another. *Exeunt*

## 2. *Sancho: An Act of Remembrance* by Paterson Joseph

This excerpt is taken from the beginning of Act Two of the 2018 revised edition of Paterson Joseph's *Sancho: An Act of Remembrance*. It is a solo show, originally performed by the playwright, presenting the life of the real-life character Charles Ignatius Sancho. He is an interesting individual who could be studied in more depth with this age group. Two books are listed in the *Further Reading* section.

Given its complexity, students may benefit from working in small groups, taking on the role of Sancho at different points. Joseph indicates pauses (beats), and students should draw on their skills to convey meaning through those pauses. They can also apply their physical theatre skills to depict a character who has grown old and uses a cane. Remind them to draw on the skills they developed over the previous two years of the course, and to present their work in the round. Design students can explore how to create an appropriate set and/or lighting design for the extract.

## Context for students

**Charles Ignatius Sancho** was born on a slave ship in 1729 and went on to lead a remarkably rich and varied life. He was a writer, actor, singer and dancer who expressed his political beliefs, becoming the first Black man of African origin to vote. In this excerpt, **Sancho** is directing his thoughts to the audience. He establishes that he is now married with young children, working as a shopkeeper and creating a variety of different materials, including books and plays.



**SANCHO:** (*Friendly, but distracted.*) Well, you took y'time.
Why, it's been twelve years since I invited you to London.
Where the devil have you been – Never mind. No time for that
now. I'm in the middle of a most desperate search. Most.
Desperate.

But, rest assured, you're not the only ones running late today.
*(Indicates above, backstage right, mildly peeved.*) Mrs Sancho
… (*Calls.*) My Hen! Sanchonettas! Descendez!
No time to waste, no time at all.

*He rummages about, desperate to find something. Taking a pile of papers and placing them on the 'counter'. Breath increasingly short.*

(*Mildly irritated but determined.)* It waxes increasingly
difficult to lay hold of any thing in this nest of chaos! I find
raisins where I look for figs and cabbage when I seek carrots
… (*Looks to us.*) Yes, Madam, I am a shopkeeper here – in
Westminster – and yet I write – I write to the ringing of the
shop doorbell – I write books, letters, sonnets, music, plays –
betwixt serving – gossiping – and lying down … (*A glimpse of
Act One Sancho.*) Alas! What cramps to poor genius! And in
case you wondered I'm fresh out of turnips –

*Goes upstage to fetch his cane. Feels a twinge in his back.*

Gone are the great parties and frolics of my hey-day – the
royal banquets I attended with my dear Montagus – gone, gone
… gone … (*Snapping out of his darkening mood.*) Come,
come, no time for melancholy, Sancho. (*Anne.) 'Idle hands,*

*the Devil's friend.'* As you-know-who often says (*Indicates off stage right. Conspiratorial.)*

*He notices the wilting vegetables.*

Truth be told – Trade is duller than I ever knew it – and money scarcer – (*Bitterly.)* In England nowadays, foppery runs higher and vanity stronger … (*Dreamily.*) I had thought that when this war with America passes, we'd go try our fortunes there … But we stay in Old England and talk about it. No time to talk now, however – I must find those papers …

*Wry smile. He grabs yet more papers and rifles through them, frustration growing.*

My Little Sanchonettas … I sometimes believe that children are sent of the Lord to try us. Do they hide things in hopes of having 'em as an inheritance once we've shuffled off? (*Stops. Guiltily addressing us.)* Oh no, now, mistake not Sancho – I say the more children the more blessing …

*A profoundly sad beat. Then he covers it with more bustle. Sounds of a crowd gathering creep in at the end of this next speech.*

… but by the Seven Stars, it wastes one's breath utterly, this infernal searching – *Tempus Fugit!* – Times a-flyin'! *'Time? Time? Why, it's seventeen-hundred and eighty!' (Laugh turns into a worried beat.)* And I cannot be late today – No, no – that would never do … For the crowds are gathering … *A beat of anxiety.*

Where are those blasted papers … For without them? I cannot …

*He finds something in his pocket! Letters, pretty scrunched up. Disappointed, he shoves them back in his pocket.*

Letters … Letters, you should know, have become something of a hobby of mine since leaving the service of my dear Montagus … (*Weak laugh.*) Leaving, ha. No, alas … dismissed … That awful morning – summoned into the drawing room – at Montagu House – for what would prove to be my final interview with my employer.

## 3. *10 Nights* by Shahid Iqbal Khan

*10 Nights* by Shahid Iqbal Khan is a one-actor play which was first performed at the Bush Theatre, London, in 2021. Chronicling Yasser's Itikaf, the actor speaks directly to the audience and also brings to life the other characters surrounding him. These include his Uncle Hakim, his father, Salah, an Itikaf expert, and his childhood rival, the opinionated Usman. This excerpt from Scene Three presents an interesting challenge to physically and vocally portray the different characters.

Students can work on an individual performance of the excerpt, bringing all the different characters to life. Alternatively, one student could play Yasser, and others could take on the additional roles. It is a challenging piece, so it is helpful to spend some time exploring ways of vocally and physically realizing the characters. Begin by reading the text, ensuring that students understand the various people in Yasser's life and the way the text is presented. When Yasser speaks directly to the audience, this is indicated by non-bold, unbracketed text. His conversations with other characters are in speech marks and are recorded in bold text in brackets.

## Context for students

This excerpt is taken from a one-person show called *10 Nights*, which centres on the character of **Yasser**. He has reluctantly agreed to undertake the spiritual practice of Itikaf over a ten-day period during Ramadan, which involves seclusion, fasting and prayer. This excerpt is taken from Scene Three at the start of **Yasser**'s Itikaf. In the original production, the actor playing **Yasser** acted out all the other characters. The non-bold text is delivered to the audience. The bold, bracketed text indicates the conversations between **Yasser** and other characters.



(**Hakim**) **'Is that comfortable?'**

(**Yasser**) **'Yes, very. Only £6.99 at Primark. Jeans were 15 quid at H & M.'**

(**Hakim**) **'Jeans are not right for praying in. There's no security. When you kneel down to pray, your jeans slide down and show your bum to the whole world.'**

(**Dad**) **'He's brought clothes with him. He will change. Don't worry!'**

(**Yasser**) **'It's very nice of you to be concerned about my bottom but I can assure you, I have no intention of letting anyone see it.'**

He eyes my bag. He takes it and has a quick glance through. It's like I'm being held in security at the airport of religion.

**Yasser** *gets his phone out to update his social media status.*

'Checking into Khizra Mosque –'

**Dad** *snatches the phone from* **Yasser**.

(**Yasser**) **'What you doing Dad!? Give me my phone back! … What if I need it for emergencies? What if there's a fire? I'm not gonna use it for social media. I get it, itikaf is complete isolation. But you can't take a phone away, that is like complete deprivation and abuse. It's a necessity.**

**HOW WILL YOU KNOW IF I'M DEAD?'**

Ugh.

(**Yasser**) **'Promise me you will look after it.'**

**Usman** *comes from upstairs.* **Yasser** *sees him and pauses.*

Usman. He sees us and stops dead in his tracks.

(**Usman**) **'Yasser bhai. Assalaam-o-alaikum, thank you for coming last night. Ramadan mubarak.'**

It's a bit late for Ramadan mubarak, it started about 20 days ago. Pretentious twat.

(**Yasser**) **'Ramadan mubarak to you too bro.'**

**Yasser** *watches* **Usman** *leave.*

Hakim Uncle and Dad lead me to the prayer hall.

They take me to a corner of the room. It's curtained off. Hakim Uncle opens the curtains.

(**Hakim**) **'This is your area.'**

There is a mat and a book-holder for the Quran. It's a great little hovel. No window view I'm afraid. That wouldn't go down well on tripadvisor.

*Closes curtains.*

I'll sit here and think about God. Thinking.

Thinking.

Hmm yes. God. Hmm.

What did Zaakir say? Resolutions? I will read the Quran twice. One in Arabic and one in English. Pray for everyone. Keep all the fasts and pray five times a day. What else is there? Oh yes, Allah has 99 names. I will try to learn all of them.

**Yasser** *picks up the book-holder and is about to go to the shelf to find a Quran. His hands begin to shake. He puts the book-holder back down. He holds up his hands to observe his hand tremors.*

*He sits down. His breathing fluctuates. Sound effect of footsteps.*

*Curtains open.*

Hakim Uncle and Dad have brought another man with him. He is tall, about 35-ish, with a long salt-and-pepper beard.

(**Dad**) **'This is Salah. He is also doing itikaf. He has done itikaf every year. How many years?'**

(**Salah**) **'9.'**

(**Dad**) **'He can show you the ropes.'**

They're leaving me with an itikaf expert. Great!

Even when I want complete isolation, I have to be shown how to do it.

## 4. *Musical Differences* by Robin French

*Musical Differences* is a fabulously flexible play written by Robin French as part of the National Theatre's 2017 Connections programme. It was developed collaboratively with this age group at a school in Hackney and at French's old school in the Midlands. French has created a text which can be staged in different ways, allowing groups to adapt the piece to play to their strengths. In his introduction, for example, he raises the possibilities of using musicians or dancers to bring the text to life.

The excerpt is particularly effective to leave until the end of the course, allowing students to experiment with and combine the many skills they have developed so far. Group sizes can vary, and it is an exciting section to stage in the round. There are opportunities to use choral techniques, and students can practise applying pauses of varying lengths, also revisiting some of their work on pace from Part Two. They can apply physical theatre techniques explored in Chapter Two, such as using connecting still images to capture the essence of the text and mechanical movement sequences to convey the repetitive nature of revision. Design students can focus on the activity described at the end of the excerpt.

Start by sitting your students in a circle to read one line each from the text before discussing the many possibilities for bringing it to life.

### Context for students

This excerpt is from the play *Musical Differences*, which was written for and with the help of young people. It follows the fortunes of a group of students from the ages of fourteen to eighteen. This section examines the pressures and anxieties they experience during the exam season.



It's summer. The weather is beautiful
But we are revising.
Exams terrify us.
We talk about how we don't care.
We talk about how little we revised.
How we never listened in lessons.
But even Darren Northcote's beautiful eyes show fear.
We talk about the last horrifying hours before we hand in our coursework.
How shit it is.
Very very shit.
Oh my God!
We text each other.
Text back straight away.

No way!
We dream of escape.
But the trap was set years ago.
From the first day we ever went to school.
There is no way out.
Some of us have worked hard for years.
Some of us have basically done nothing.
Some of us say that we've done nothing when really we have worked hard for years.
Our parents are *obsessed* with our revision.
Why don't they get a life of their own?
They watch us from the minute we get in.
It is like a police state.
Stasi.
They take away our phones and our laptops and our TVs.
Stop us going out.
Even on Saturdays.
We make detailed revision timetables.
This is prison.
We encounter whole subjects for the first time.
Chemistry. History. Geography.
We read our textbooks for the first time, thinking …
Oh, so *this* is what this is about! That makes so much more sense.
And sometimes we actually *like* reading our textbooks.
And we think wow, I'd really like to do a course in this subject someday.
Like study it.
We stare into space.
We stare at clocks.
And walls.
We stare at pets.
We stare at carpets.
And duvet covers.
We stare into mirrors.
For the first time ever, we're jealous of younger siblings.
And older siblings.
Jealous of anybody not our age.
Which is the worst age anybody could possibly be.
Because of our exams.
Summer is poison.
If we are good at school
If we are rubbish at school
It doesn't matter who you are.
Exams come for everyone.

Society *will* put its stamp on you. There's nothing you can do to avoid it.
The headmistress takes a sudden interest in us.
Calls us by first names in the corridor.
Everybody talks about how much these exams matter.
For our futures.
For the school.
So why aren't we working?
We can't work.
Because we think about why we don't work.
Instead of working.
Time is running out.
Our parents get us sandwiches and biscuits and cups of tea.
They promise Augusts beyond our wildest imaginations.
If we get 'A's.
Everybody else is working. But we're not working.
We're staring
At clocks.
And walls.
And pets.
At carpets.
And duvet covers.
We're staring into mirrors.

### *Design activity*

Use *Musical Differences* (or any of the four published extracts if you prefer) for an extended design task. Working in pairs or small groups, students produce set, lighting, costume and sound designs, drawing from everything they have learnt over the course.

## Devising project

Devising original theatre is a key component of all exam courses, and students of this age benefit from the experience of creating their own work. Provide clear guidance on how they might utilize and combine all the skills they have developed over the course to enable them to construct an effective piece.

In the future, students may need to create original work connected to the work of a specific practitioner. At this stage, focus on teaching them how to merge different ideas stemming from the range of practitioners and ideas they have encountered.

To begin, decide whether to provide a single stimulus or a range of options. Think carefully about what suits your students and try to find starting points which allow them to use their imaginations to develop different ideas and interpretations. Stimuli could include photos, news stories, poems, short stories, play excerpts, paintings and pieces of music. Working in groups of three or four will enable students to creatively experiment with a range of techniques in a structured manner. For individuals wishing to specialize in design elements, they could be assigned to work with a group to design sets, costumes, lights, or sound. Share the following guidance:

1. Your task is to create a piece of original drama lasting approximately ten minutes.
2. You should all have an equal role in the piece. You can play more than one role and can share a larger role among different performers.
3. Your work should combine many of the techniques you have explored over the year (or whole course).
4. You are creating one piece of work, so all scenes must be connected.
5. You are performing in an in-the-round setting. (You might decide to choose a different stage space.)

To support students in creating successful exam-level work, provide them with a guide on what to include in their pieces. Students can produce outstanding work when focusing on a particular skill, but can easily forget to draw on what they have learnt when asked to build a longer, original piece. At this stage, they will have the best experience of devising if you provide a clear structure. Possible models:

## Model one

Your drama will consist of five sections. It is up to you to decide on the order of the different sections. Remember to connect everything. The sections are:

1. A scene for two characters using pauses of different lengths.
2. A mechanical and/or slow motion movement sequence.
3. Four short monologues which can be performed at different times or connected to form one scene.
4. Group still images connected using the chance choreography method.
5. Another scene for two characters using fast pace.

## Model two

Your drama will consist of five sections. It is up to you to decide on the order of the different sections. Remember to connect everything. The sections are:

1. A mime to music using a variety of levels and speeds.
2. A scene for two characters using fast pace and overlapping dialogue.
3. A choral piece (linked to work completed on the text *Musical Differences*).
4. Three or four mini monologues combined in one scene, which include pauses of varying lengths.
5. A sequence based on the Frantic Assembly 'much more than miming' activity (explored in Chapter Two).

Designers should keep a log documenting their ideas. It is essential to be clear on exactly what they should achieve, for example:

- **Set:** Plan and establish the set for all sections of the drama, working with the actors on transitions.
- **Costume:** Plan, create and make or find costumes for all performers.

- **Lights:** Plan and operate the lights, including at least six different changes.
- **Sound:** Plan, create and find eight pieces of music and/or sound effects.

It is up to you to judge how much support a particular class might need. Sometimes it is appropriate to guide them through one section at a time and then allow them to order their different scenes as they wish. Other groups will cope with more freedom to develop their own work.

When students create performances consisting of different scenes, it is always advisable to stop and evaluate during the process to ensure that they are applying the skills they have developed over the course. Keep reminding them of previous activities and how they link to what they are now doing. To allow time for students to explore ideas but not lose focus and enthusiasm, allocate about four or five (50 to 70-minute) lessons for this project. This is an important activity to watch in full and evaluate.

At an appropriate point during rehearsals, teach your students creative ways to connect their work.

## Examples of ideas to teach students how to connect scenes in devised drama

When devising longer pieces of work, students can fall into the trap of creating several short scenes that do not connect, resulting in a fragmented piece of work. If they have access to stage lights, they can often focus on ending scenes in blackout and dealing with any changes during that blackout. As devised work is relatively short, they should learn to connect their different scenes and sections to create a whole, complete piece. Encourage students to be imaginative and creative when connecting sections. Discuss and explore some of the following techniques:

## Example of a way to transition between the end of a scene involving a group of three, four or five performers to a scene with just one performer

Ask the students to imagine that they have just finished a scene involving a group of performers. The next scene features just one performer on stage delivering a monologue. Suggest that the group hold a still image for five counts at the end of the scene. The performers then exit the space one at a time using different speeds, including running and walking. They exit in different directions, and as they do, they should look at the person who is left in the space for the monologue.

## Example of a way to transition between the end of a scene involving one performer to a scene involving a group

Ask students to imagine that one performer has performed a monologue on stage. The next section of the drama consists of a group scene, so they need to consider how the other performers enter the stage space. Suggest that the individual on stage perform a mime in slow motion linked to their previous monologue. All other members of the group move into the space from different points, performing the same mime as they travel. As soon as they are in position, they snap into the start of the next scene.

## Example of a way to transition between the end of one pair scene and the start of another pair scene

Suggest that the two performers who have finished their scene face each other and slowly start mirroring one another, moving together in unison. The other two performers enter from different directions and join in with the mirroring. The two performers who are due to exit can either run off or walk off slowly. An alternative approach is for the first pair to repeat the final two lines of their scene continually. When the other two performers enter, they join in with these repeated lines. It would be particularly impressive if the lines could somehow link to the context of the second pair's scene. Once the second pair are in position, they begin their scene as the first pair exits.

## Example of how to move chairs out of the stage space

All performers sit on chairs in the space, imagining that it is the end of a scene. Since the next scene does not require chairs, they should find a neat and creative way to remove them. Suggest that the students all stand at the same time, walk around their chair in the same direction for two and a half turns, so that they are now standing behind their chair. In unison, they pick up their chairs and exit the stage space in different directions.

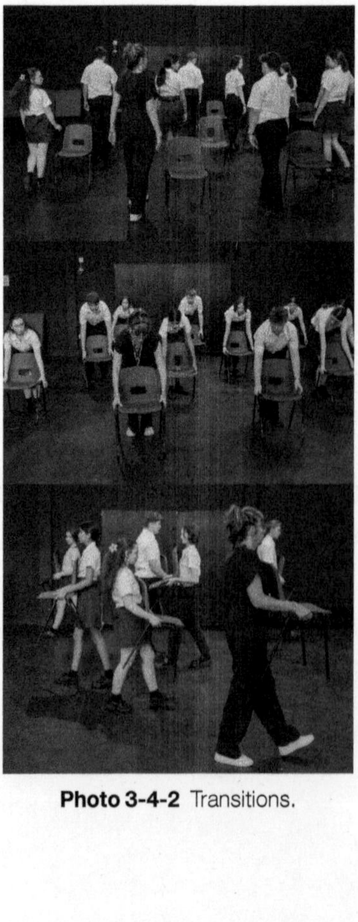

**Photo 3-4-2** Transitions.

## Example of how to move chairs into the stage space

All performers enter the space from different directions at different times, carrying a chair. They should place their chairs onto the floor using different dynamics, ranging from slamming the chair down to putting it gently into position. They then take a different position on the chair, such as sitting on it while facing different directions, sitting astride it or standing on it.

Once you have explored these particular transitions, divide the class into groups of three to five. Give them different challenges to work on, encouraging them to think creatively about how they move from one moment to the next, and manage moving any props or set items.

### *Design activity*

Ask students to consider how they might use music and sound effects in transitions.

### *Written activity*

This extended essay task can be applied to any of the performance work undertaken in this final chapter. It can also be adapted to produce reviews of live or recorded professional work seen. The task requires students to connect the different written elements explored over the course. It should be divided into several separate class or homework activities, and is excellent preparation for those students who go on to study the subject further.

**Suggested title***:* Discuss and evaluate how one performer used voice, movement and stage space in two different moments to create an interesting character for the audience. Incorporate examples of your personal reactions to their performance.

Your answer should reference some of the areas you have explored over the course, such as:

1. **Voice**: for example, volume, pace, pause and tone of voice.
2. **Movement**: for example, gestures, levels, body language, facial expressions and physical theatre techniques.
3. **Stage space**: for example, movement around the stage space (end-on, traverse, in the round).

Once you confirm exactly what the students will be reviewing, begin by defining what is meant by 'one moment' in the question. Students often try to discuss too much, so their answer ends up lacking focus. You might decide to specify which moments students focus on in their writing. This could include the opening or ending of a performance or scene, a monologue, a short exchange between two characters or a movement sequence. Clarify that they can discuss their chosen performer's interactions with other performers. Explore some of the many reasons they might give for finding an actor's performance to be interesting.

Similar to the final written activity in Part Two, students should begin by recording their observations about specific moments in a performance in a structured manner.

Once the students have compiled notes on moments from the performance, guide them step by step to develop their complete response. Suggested structure:

1. **Introduction**: Students include the name of the production, as well as the location and date they saw it. They state the name of the performer they are evaluating and the name(s) of the

**Table 3-4-1** Performance record sheet for evaluative writing.

| **RECORD OF MOMENTS FROM A PERFORMANCE** | |
|---|---|
| NAME OF PRODUCTION | |
| VENUE | DATE OF PERFORMANCE |
| NAME OF CHARACTER | NAME OF PERFORMER |
| VOICE- e.g. volume, pace, pause and tone | IMPACT ON AUDIENCE |
| MOVEMENT- e.g. gesture, levels, body language and facial expressions | IMPACT ON AUDIENCE |
| STAGE SPACE- e.g. movement around the stage space (end-on, thrust, traverse, in the round) | IMPACT ON AUDIENCE |
| WHAT COULD HAVE BEEN DONE BETTER/ DIFFERENTLY? | PERSONAL RESPONSE |

character(s) played. They should attempt to make a general comment about what was interesting about the actor's performance.

2. **Moment one:** Students start by giving a brief outline of the context for the first moment to be discussed. They continue by analysing how the performer employed voice, movement and stage space, and what this communicated to the audience. Remind your students to combine their discussion of the different skills and to try to use the keyword 'interesting' at some point. At the end of this section, students include their own personal response and suggest how this moment could have been performed differently and/or developed and improved.
3. **Moment two**: Students use the same structure as outlined for moment one.
4. **Conclusion**: In this final short section, students include a final personal response to the performance. Again, they should try to embed the word 'interesting'.

# FURTHER READING

## Voice

Berry, Cicely. (2000), *Voice and the Actor*, London: Virgin Books.
Berry, Cicely. (2000), *Your Voice and How to Use It: The Classic Guide to Speaking with Confidence*, London: Virgin Books.
Churcher, Mel. (2023), *The Elemental Actor: How to Release Your Hidden Powers*, London: Nick Hern Books.
Gillett, John and Gutekunst, Christina. (2021), *Voice into Acting: Integrating Voice and the Stanislavski Approach*, London: Methuen Drama.
McCallion, Michael. (1998), *The Voice Book*, London: Faber & Faber.
Morrison, Annie. (2021), *The Moment of Speech: Creative Articulation for Actors (RADA Guides)*, London: Methuen Drama.
Nelson, Jeannette. (2025), *Centre Stage: Lessons from Actors on the Art of Charisma*, London: Penguin.
Palmer, Chris. (2019), *Voice and Speech for Musical Theatre: A Practical Guide and Video*, London: Methuen Drama.
Rodenburg, Patsy. (2022), *The Right to Speak: Working with the Voice*, London: Bloomsbury Academic.
Rodenburg, Patsy. (2023), *The Actor Speaks: Voice and the Performer*, London: Bloomsbury Academic.
Rodenburg, Patsy. (2023), *The Need for Words: Voice and the Text*, London: Bloomsbury Academic.
Rodenburg, Patsy. (2023), *The Woman's Voice*, London: Methuen Drama.
Turner, J. Clifford. (2007), *Voice and Speech in the Theatre*, London: Methuen Drama.

## Movement

Callery, Dymphna. (2015), *The Active Text: Unlocking Plays through Physical Theatre*, London: Nick Hern Books.
Conroy, Colette. (2009), *Theatre and the Body*, London: Red Globe Press.
Pisk, Litz. (2017), *The Actor and His Body*, London: Methuen Drama.
Raitt, David. (2023), *The Improv Illusionist: Using Object Work, Environment, and Physicality in Performance*, London: Methuen Drama.
Snow, Jackie. (2012), *Movement Training for Actors (RADA Guides)*, London: Methuen Drama.

## Space

Elsam, Paul. (2014), *Stephen Joseph: Theatre Pioneer and Provocateur*, London: Methuen Drama.
Joseph, Stephen. (1967), *Theatre in the Round*, London: Barrie & Jenkins.
Mackintosh, Iain. (2023), *Theatre Spaces 1920–2020: Finding the Fun in Functionalism*, London: Methuen Drama.
McMillan, Joyce. (1988), *The Traverse Theatre Story 1963–88*, London: Methuen Publishing.

Schiele, Jinnie. (2005), *Off-centre Stages: Fringe Theatre at the Open Space and the Round House, 1968–1983*, Hatfield: University of Hertfordshire Press.

## Directing

Meckler, Nancy. (2023), *Notes from the Rehearsal Room: A Director's Process*, London: Methuen Drama.
Shevtsova, Maria and Innes, Christopher. (2009), *Directors/Directing: Conversations on Theatre*, Cambridge: Cambridge University Press.
Waugh, Rosemary. (2023), *Running the Room: Conversations with Women Theatre Directors*, London: Nick Hern Books.

## Actor-Managers

Poser, Norman S. (2018), *The Birth of Modern Theatre: Rivalry, Riots, and Romance in the Age of Garrick*, Abingdon-on-Thames: Routledge.
Ritchie, Leslie. (2021), *David Garrick and the Mediation of Celebrity*, Cambridge: Cambridge University Press.

## Ira Aldridge

Bourne, Stephen. (2025), *Trailblazers of Black British Theatre: From Ira Aldridge to Cleo Laine*, Cheltenham: The History Press.
Hoyles, Martin. (2008), *Ira Aldridge: Celebrated 19th Century Actor*, Stevenage: Hansib Publications.

## Alan Ayckbourn

Allen, Paul. (2002), *Grinning at the Edge*, London: Methuen Drama.
Ayckbourn, Alan. (2004), *The Crafty Art of Playmaking*, London: Faber & Faber.

## Steven Berkoff

Berkoff, Steven. (1993), *The Theatre of Steven Berkoff*, London: Methuen Drama.
Berkoff, Steven. (2019), *A World Elsewhere*, Abingdon-on-Thames: Routledge.
Cross, Robert. (2004), *Steven Berkoff and the Theatre of Self-Performance*, Manchester: Manchester University Press.

## Brecht

Barnett, David (ed). (2024), *The Great European Stage Directors Volume 2: Meyerhold, Piscator, Brecht*, London: Methuen Drama.
Brecht, Bertolt (author), Silberman, Marc, Giles, Steve and Kuhn, Tom (eds). (2018), *Brecht on Theatre*, London: Bloomsbury Academic.

Unwin, Stephen. (2014), *The Complete Brecht Toolkit*, London: Nick Hern Books.
Zoob, David. (2018), *Brecht: A Practical Handbook*, London: Nick Hern Books.

## Complicite

Warren-Fisher, Russell (designer) and Ainslie, Sarah (photographer). (2010), *Complicite Rehearsal Notes*, London: Complicite.

## Merce Cunningham

Meade, Fionn and Rothfuss, Joan. (2017), *Merce Cunningham: Common Time*, New York: Distributed Art Publishers.
Starr, Frances and Cunningham, Merce. (2019), *Merce Cunningham: Changes: Notes on Choreography*, New York: The Song Cave.

## Frantic Assembly

Evans, Mark and Smith, Mark. (2021), *Frantic Assembly*, Abingdon-on-Thames: Routledge.
Graham, Scott and Hoggett, Steven. (2014), *The Frantic Assembly Book of Devising Theatre*, Abingdon-on-Thames: Routledge.

## Greek Theatre

Dugdale, Eric. (2008), *Greek Theatre in Context*, Cambridge: Cambridge University Press.
Ley, Graham. (2007), *A Short Introduction to the Ancient Greek Theater*, Chicago: University of Chicago Press.
McLeish, Kenneth. (2003), *Guide to Greek Theatre and Drama*, London: Methuen Drama.
Wiles, David. (2000), *Greek Theatre Performance: An Introduction*, Cambridge: Cambridge University Press.

## Kneehigh

Grose, Carl and Murphy, Anna Maria. (2022), *Kneehigh Anthology: Volume 1: Tristan & Yseult; The Bacchae; The Wooden Frock; The Red* Shoes, London: Oberon Books.
Tomlin, Liz. (2015), *British Theatre Companies: 1995–*2014, London: Methuen Drama.

## Jacques Lecoq

Lecoq, Jacques. (2020), *The Moving Body (Le Corps Poétique): Teaching Creative Theatre*, London: Methuen Drama.
Woodall, Ed and Rokison-Woodall, Abigail. (2024), *Shakespeare and Jacques Lecoq: A Practical Guide for Actors, Directors, Students and Teachers*, London: The Arden Shakespeare.

## Joan Littlewood

Finburgh Delijani, Clare and Boenisch, Peter M. (2021), *The Great European Stage Directors Volume 6: Littlewood, Strehler, Planchon*, London: Methuen Drama.
Holdsworth, Nadine. (2015), *Joan Littlewood's Theatre*, Cambridge: Cambridge University Press.
Leach, Robert Dr. (2006), *Theatre Workshop: Joan Littlewood and the Making of Modern British Theatre*, Exeter: Exeter University Press.
Rankin, Peter. (2014), *Joan Littlewood: Dreams and Realities: The Official Biography*, London: Oberon Books.

## Medieval Theatre

Beadle, Richard and Fletcher, Alan J (eds). (2008), *The Cambridge Companion to Medieval English Theatre*, Cambridge: Cambridge University Press.
Van Pelt, Nadia Thérèse. (2019), *Drama in Medieval and Early Modern Europe: Playmakers and Their Strategies*, Abingdon-on-Thames: Routledge.

## Katie Mitchell

Mitchell, Katie (adaptor). (2008), *Waves*, London: Oberon Books.
Mitchell, Katie. (2009), *The Director's Craft: A Handbook for the Theatre*, Abingdon-on-Thames: Routledge.

## Charles Ignatius Sancho

Sancho, Ignatius. (2022), *Letters of the Late Ignatious Sancho*, USA: Legare Street Press.
Webb, Simon. (2022), *The Life and Times of Ignatius Sancho: An African in Eighteenth Century London*, Durham: The Langley Press.

## Shakespeare

Alexander, Bill. (2023), *Exploring Shakespeare: A Director's Notes from the Rehearsal Room*, London: Nick Hern Books.
Rodenburg, Patsy. (2023), *Speaking Shakespeare*, London: Methuen Drama.

## Stanislavski

Barrouk, David. (2024), *Stanislavski and the Method for the 21st Century Actor: A Practical Guide*, London: Methuen Drama.
Merlin, Bella. (2014), *The Complete Stanislavsky Toolkit*, London: Nick Hern Books.
Stanislavski, Constantin. ([1936] 2013), *An Actor Prepares*, London: Bloomsbury Academic.
Stanislavski, Constantin. ([1946] 2013), *Building a Character*, London: Bloomsbury Academic.
Stanislavski, Constantin. ([1957] 2013), *Creating a Role*, London: Bloomsbury Academic.

Tait, Peta (ed). (2024), *The Great European Stage Directors Volume 1: Antoine, Stanislavski, Saint-Denis*, London: Methuen Drama.

## Design

Association of British Theatre Technicians and Shewring, Margaret (eds). (2024), *Theatre Buildings: A Design Guide*, Abingdon-on-Thames: Routledge.
Casey, Helen. (2023), *Wigs, Hair and Make-Up: A Backstage Guide*, London: Methuen Drama.
Deiorio, Victoria. (2018), *The Art of Theatrical Sound Design: A Practical Guide*, London: Methuen Drama.
Fraser, Neil. (2018), *Stage Lighting Design: Second Edition*, Marlborough: Crowood.
National Theatre. (2017), *National Theatre: All about Theatre*, London: Walker Books.
Pilbrow, Richard. (2008), *Stage Lighting Design: The Art, the Craft, the Life*, London: Nick Hern Books.
Poe Durbin, Holly. (2022), *The Costume Designer's Toolkit: The Process of Creating Effective Design*, Abingdon-on-Thames: Routledge.
Winslow, Colin. (2006), *Handbook of Set Design*, Marlborough: The Crowood Press.

## Other referenced plays

Ayckbourn, Alan. (2015), *Confusions*, London: Methuen Drama.
Bartlett, Mike. (2015), *Bull*, London: Nick Hern Books.
Berkoff, Steven. (1988), *The Trial, Metamorphosis, in the Penal Colony. Three Theatre Adaptations from Franz Kafka*, London: Amber Lane Press.
Complicite. (2008), *A Disappearing Number*, London: Oberon Modern Plays.
Coward, Noël and Rice, Emma (adaptor). (2018), *Brief Encounter*, London: Methuen Drama.
Euripides (author), Cole, Emma (ed). and Taylor, Don (translator). (2024), *The Women of Troy*, London: Methuen Drama.
Levy, Andrea and Edmundson, Helen (adaptor). (2019), *Small Island*, London: Nick Hern Books.
Lorca, Federico Garcia and Edwards, Glynne (translator & ed). ([1933] 2020), *Blood Wedding* London: Methuen Drama.
Martel, Yann and Chakrabarti, Lolita (adaptor). (2022), *Life of Pi*, London: Methuen Drama.
Orwell, George and Wooldridge, Ian (adaptor). (2004), *Animal Farm*, London: Nick Hern Books.
Ravenhill, Mark. (2008), *Ravenhill Plays: 2* (including *Pool (No Water)*), London: Methuen Drama.
Shakespeare, William. (2021), *Romeo and Juliet*, London: The Arden Shakespeare.
Theatre Workshop. (1967), *Oh What a Lovely War*, London: Methuen Drama.

# RECOMMENDED MUSIC

## Music with a regular 4/4 beat (works for mechanical movement exercises)

- Drum and Bass (Instrumental)- Thomas Crane- 2017- 658813 Records DK
- Dusting for Smoke (Edit)- Daniel Avery- 2020- Phantasy Sound
- Oliver Twist (Remixes)- EP- D'banj- 2011- Mercury Records
- You Talk about Yourself (Instrumental Mix)- Damien J Carter- 2009 Cr Records Ltd.

From the album *60 Electronic Masters- Best of Top Dance Club Anthems 2013*–2013- EDM Records.

- High Attack- Vaktun and Nobu Kamata
- Loco-motiv' (feat. Cristo Disto & Hich')- Polypheme

From the album *Atmospheric: Music for Film*- 2016- Shepherd Audio.

- Underworld

From *Rolling Blues* EP- Makai- 2011- Progrezo Records.

- Census
- Rolling Blues

From *Slumdog Millionaire (Music from the Motion Picture)*- Various Artists- 2008- Celador Films Ltd./ Channel Four Television Corporation.

- Jai Ho- A.R. Rahman

## Tense, suspenseful background music

From the album *Atmospheric Music for Film*- 2016- Shepard Audio.

- Shutting Down the World

From the album *Decision Time: Tension and Suspense*- Various Artists- 2013- Purple Fox Limited.

- Deep Drone- Tom Howe and Mike Reed
- Drama Drone- Tom and Mike Reed
- Frozen Ropes- Vasco
- One Door Is Closing- Vasco

From the album *Firewatch (Original Score)*- Chris Remo- 2016- Chris Remo.

- Exfiltration
- Something's Wrong

From the album *Gladiator (Soundtrack from the Motion Picture)*- Hans Zimmer- 2000- Universal Classics Group, a division of UMG Recordings Inc.

- Progeny
- The Wheat

From *Slumdog Millionaire (Music from the Motion Picture)*- Various Artists- 2008- Celador Films Ltd./ Channel Four Television Corporation.

- Riots- A.R. Rahman

From the album *Stranger Things, Vol. 1 (A Netflix Original Series Soundtrack)*- Kyle Dixon and Michael Stein- 2016- Lakeshore Records.

- One Blink for Yes
- Stranger Things
- Walking Through the Upside Down

From the album *Stranger Things, Vol. 2 (A Netflix Original Series Soundtrack)*- Kyle Dixon and Michael Stein- 2015- Lakeshore Records.

- Hopper Sneaks In
- In Pursuit
- Spiked Bat
- Walking Down the Tracks
- Where's Barb

# Lyrical, emotional and uplifting background music

From the album *Atmospheric Music for Film*- 2016- Shepard Audio.

- Lost in Thought
- Something to Believe In

From the album *Gladiator (Soundtrack from the Motion Picture)*- Hans Zimmer- 2000- Universal Classics Group, a division of UMG Recordings Inc.

- Earth
- Sorrow

From the album *Islands- Essential Einaudi*- Ludovico Einaudi- 2002- Decca, a division of Universal Music Operations Limited.

- I giorni

From the album *Light Songs*- Dennis Korn- 2021- Klangdorf Music.

- Follow the Light
- Good Morning
- Peace

From the album *Plaisirs d'amour*- René Aubry- 1998- Hopi Mesa.

- Salento
- Le vent

From the album *Rudderless (Original Motion Picture Soundtrack)*- Various Artists- 2014- Lakeshore Records.

- The Gig Is Off- Eef Barzelay

From *Slumdog Millionaire (Music from the Motion Picture)*- Various Artists- 2008- Celador Films Ltd./ Channel Four Television Corporation.

- Latika's Theme- A.R. Rahman

From the album *Stardust (Music from the Motion Picture)*- Andy Brown, Ilan Eshkeri and London Metropolitan Orchestra- 2007- Paramount Pictures, under exclusive licence to Polydor Ltd (UK).

- Snowdrop
- The Mouse

From the album *The Kite Runner (Original Motion Picture Soundtrack)*- Various Artists- 2007- Deutsche Grammophon GmbH, Berlin.

- Hassan Theme- The Hollywood Studio Symphony & Michael Nowak
- The Truth- The Hollywood Studio Symphony & Michael Nowak

## Music for slow motion work

From the album *Film Noir*- Various Artists- 2005- Milan Music.

- The Elephant Man- John Morris

From *La Revancha del Tango* (Bonus Track Version)- Gotan Project- 2001- XL Recordings Ltd.

- Época
- Santa Maria (del Buen Ayre)

## Comedy tracks (appropriate for fast movement work)

From the album *Slapstick Stories (From Buster Keaton up until Today)*- Antonio Coppola- 2008- Primrose Music.

- Buster Boy
- Buster-go-round
- Buster Start
- Circus Promenade
- Fast Opening

From the album *The Ultimate Pink Panther*- Henry Mancini- 2004- BMG Music.

- Shades of Sennett

## Faster, upbeat and dramatic background music

From the album *Big Night (Original Motion Picture Soundtrack)*- Various Artists- 1996- TVT Soundtrax.

- Il Pescivendolo- Matteo Salvatore
- Stornelli Amorosi- Claudio Villa

From the album *Invités sur la terre*- René Aubry- 2001- Hopi Mesa.

- Frénésie

From the album *La La Land (Original Motion Picture Soundtrack)*- Justin Hurwitz, Benj Pasek, Justin Noble Paul, Emma Stone & Ryan Gosling- 2016- Interscope Records.

- City of Stars (Humming) (feat. Emma Stone)- Justin Hurwitz
- Herman's Habit- Justin Hurwitz
- Summer Montage/Madeline- Justin Hurwitz

From the album *Nigeria Rock Special: Psychedelic Afro-Rock & Fuzz Funk in 1970s Nigeria* Various Artists- 1971- Soundway Records.

- In the Jungle (Instrumental)- The Hygrades

From the album *Plaisirs d'amour*- René Aubry- 1998- Hopi Mesa.

- La grande cascade
- Prima donna

From the album *Prison Break: Seasons 3 & 4 (Original Television Soundtrack)*- Ramin Djawadi- 2009- Twentieth Century Fox Film under exclusive license to Varese Sarabande Records, Inc.

- Breaking and Entering
- Revenge

# INDEX